Chicken Soup
for the Soul.

Just for Teenagers

Chicken Soup for the Soul: Just for Teenagers
101 Stories of Inspiration and Support for Teens
Jack Canfield, Mark Victor Hansen, Amy Newmark

Published by Chicken Soup for the Soul Publishing, LLC   www.chickensoup.com
Copyright © 2011 by Chicken Soup for the Soul Publishing, LLC. All Rights Reserved.
No part of this publication may be reproduced, stored in a retrieval system or transmitted in any form or by any means, electronic, mechanical, photocopying, recording or otherwise, without the written permission of the publisher.

CSS, Chicken Soup for the Soul, and its Logo and Marks are trademarks of Chicken Soup for the Soul Publishing LLC.

The publisher gratefully acknowledges the many publishers and individuals who granted Chicken Soup for the Soul permission to reprint the cited material.

Front cover photos courtesy of iStockphoto.com/RoyalFive (© Jared DeCinque), and Getty Images/Digital Vision. Back cover photo courtesy of Photos.com. Front cover and interior illustration courtesy of iStockphoto.com/amathers (© Alex Mathers).

Cover and Interior Design & Layout by Pneuma Books, LLC
For more info on Pneuma Books, visit www.pneumabooks.com

Distributed to the booktrade by Simon & Schuster. SAN: 200-2442

Publisher's Cataloging-in-Publication Data
(Prepared by The Donohue Group)

Chicken soup for the soul : just for teenagers : 101 stories of inspiration and
  support for teens / [compiled by] Jack Canfield, Mark Victor Hansen, [and]
  Amy Newmark.

      p. ; cm.

  Summary: A collection of 101 true personal stories from teenagers and adults about
  their teenage years, recalling issues with friends, embarrassing moments, bullies, family, sports, self-confidence, crushes, life lessons, and learning to do the right thing.
  Interest age group: 012-017.
  ISBN: 978-1-935096-72-6

  1. Teenagers--Conduct of life--Literary collections. 2. Teenagers--Conduct of life--
Anecdotes. I. Canfield, Jack, 1944- II. Hansen, Mark Victor. III. Newmark, Amy. IV.
Title: Just for teenagers

PN6071.T34 C483 2011
810.8/02/09283   2011906217

                    PRINTED IN THE UNITED STATES OF AMERICA
                           on acid∞free paper
     20 19 18 17 16 15   06 07 08 09 10

Chicken Soup for the Soul.

Just for Teenagers

101 Stories of Inspiration and Support for Teens

Jack Canfield
Mark Victor Hansen
Amy Newmark

Chicken Soup for the Soul Publishing, LLC
Cos Cob, CT

Chicken Soup

www.chickensoup.com

for the Soul

Contents

❸

~Liking Yourself~

❹

~Love and Relationships~

5

~Family Ties~

6

~Tough Times~

7

~Taking a Stand~

❽

~Giving and Getting Kindness~

❾

~Funny Moments~

❿

~Setting and Reaching Your Goals~

Bonus Stories from
Chicken Soup for the Soup: Teens Talk High School

Introduction

When I was a kid, I used to think everything changed on your thirteenth birthday. I remember going to sleep and thinking that when I woke up, I'd be a totally different person. A teenager! Suddenly, I was going to be like every cool character in the books I read and movies I watched. The difference between twelve and thirteen seemed huge.

Of course, when I woke up the morning of my thirteenth birthday, I wasn't any different. You learn quickly that just being one of them—a teenager—doesn't change everything. But seven years later, on the morning of your twentieth birthday, you're bound to look back, realize how much you changed, and wonder when it happened.

Why did we call this book *Chicken Soup for the Soul: Just for Teenagers*? Simple. Teenagers really do need a book that's just for them while so much is happening. Chicken Soup for the Soul has always provided support to teens over the years, but that doesn't mean that being a teenager gets any easier. The challenges are different now (I mean, is it really okay to break up with someone in a text message?) but the basic struggles of teenagers stay the same. Who are my real friends? Where do I belong? Why am I so short or tall or big or small or... different? And the age-old question: why doesn't my skin seem to understand that it's Homecoming and I really can't have a pimple?

That's where this book comes in. These are stories from real teenagers who are making their way through the obstacle course right now. They're having their first kisses and getting their hearts broken. They're learning to be kind to others and to themselves. They're finding their place in life, the things they're passionate about, and discovering just how much they love their family, their pets, and their friends.

Within these pages you won't find out how to be popular, or how to get good grades, or even how to please your parents. What you will learn is how other teenagers felt about the good and bad times they had. Maybe you'll feel the same, or maybe you'll feel different—but you definitely won't feel alone.

I hope you enjoy these stories and, as always, thank you for reading. Who knows? Maybe some day you'll be in these pages, giving comfort to teenagers around the world.

~Madeline Clapps, Editor, Chicken Soup for the Soul

Friendship

The language of friendship is not words but meanings.

~Henry David Thoreau

A Cheer for Friendship

It is amazing how much you can accomplish
when it doesn't matter who gets the credit.
~Author Unknown

Tallying the votes took about five minutes, but from where I sat in the bleachers it seemed like an hour and a half. At last, after three long years, the "HCS" letters on my uniform sweater would soon be trimmed in gold cording, identifying me as the all important Captain of the Holy Cross School cheerleaders. At least that's what I was counting on. Captain of the cheerleaders is quite an accomplishment when you're an eighth grader preparing to close out your grade school days in a blaze of glory.

As Coach Maguire emerged from her office, the chatter subsided and all eyes zeroed in on her. Just as she raised her clipboard and prepared to make the announcement, I inched to the edge of my seat ready to spring to my feet as soon as she said my name.

I lived for cheerleading. Nothing came between me and practice—ever. Putting on that red and white uniform on Saturdays and marching onto the field instilled in me a pride and confidence that carried over to every other class and activity that came my way.

"Girls," she began, "it is my pleasure to announce that Terry Shaw has been elected Captain of the Holy Cross School cheerleading team." A resounding cheer was heard throughout the gym, but it was all I could do to contain my hysteria. I didn't know if I was going to throw up or pass out.

How could this be? I hadn't missed a practice, a game, or a single pep rally in three years. Terry couldn't claim this flawless record. Was everyone blind? Didn't they realize I had my heart set on this?

Everyone gathered around Terry with hoots and hollers, but I was glued to the bleacher seat that only moments before was the springboard to my throne. I didn't take one single step in her direction. She had stolen my thunder and swept my dream right out from under me.

After a few minutes, I walked over to Terry on shaky legs and managed a flimsy "Good luck, Terry," in a whisper that barely masked my urge to cry. Terry hugged me close and said, "I wasn't expecting this, Annie. What a shock." I didn't lash out at her but in my heart I wanted to do just that.

Who was she to claim the title I had worked three years to earn? All the way home, I sobbed. There was no way I was going to stay on a team so blind they couldn't see the one most deserving of being named captain. I slammed the front door, stomped up the steps and threw myself onto my bed in a dramatic display of sobs and sighs that eventually gave way to sleep. Mom didn't even wake me for dinner.

The next morning I marched over to my closet and took out my uniform. Once it was in my hands and I held it close to me, I knew I couldn't quit. As heartbroken as I was, my true love was cheering with my teammates.

How very hard it was to go to that first practice after Terry had been named captain. When I arrived, right away Coach Maguire asked me to take three of the new girls and work with them on our basic drills. Terry was assigned three new girls as well.

Just then Terry asked me if we could pool all the girls and work with them together. I reluctantly agreed. She could tell I wasn't thrilled about the idea but at least it broke the ice between us.

About halfway through the practice she asked me if I had any ideas on how to improve our routines and invited me to stop for a soda on the way home and talk about how we could make the team better. We? Was she kidding? I just wanted to hate her and she kept making it harder and harder for me to do that. It wasn't just that she showed interest in me—her interest was warm and genuine.

After a while, practices once again became routine. In a few weeks I was out on the field again "bringing up the rear," a joke everyone made because I was tall and always last in the line-up.

Terry always made sure to include me when discussing changes in our routine with the coach and eventually I got over myself and we grew to be very close friends. Every time Terry led us onto the field, she called back to me at the end of the line and said, "Whenever you're ready, Annie," and I would call back, "Move out!"

At the end of the year, the annual Sports Award Banquet was organized and the cheerleaders decorated the hall as usual. Terry and I twirled roll after roll of red and white crepe paper, and wound it around the stage and every banquet table, giggling and reminiscing the entire time about all the good times we had shared during our last year together. It was a bittersweet moment as we finished decorating the hall for the banquet. We knew that a very special time in our lives was coming to an end. I can still see her waving goodbye and grinning at me as she hopped in her mom's car and they drove away. I just wanted to freeze that moment in time.

Later in the evening we arrived with our parents and listened as the various trophies were awarded to the most valuable player of each sports team. Of course the team captains all received trophies too. With great enthusiasm I cheered as Coach Maguire handed Terry her captain's trophy.

Just as Terry walked off the stage Coach Maguire stepped up to the microphone again and announced that there was one final trophy to be awarded. The cheerleading "Spirit Award" would now be presented to the girl who showed the most dedicated effort.

When I heard my name announced I imagine I was as shocked as Terry was the day she was voted captain. As I stood up and headed toward the stage, Terry was coming down the aisle toward me. When we were face to face we threw our arms around each other, and Terry whispered in a tone that barely masked her tears, "Nobody deserves this more than you."

Terry never knew that quitting was all I had on my mind the day she was named captain. She read the disappointment in my shallow words of congratulations and embraced me in spite of myself, planting tiny seeds of kindness and respect. From her effort grew a friendship that, to this day, I hold close to my heart.

~Annmarie B. Tait

What Is Wrong with You?

The antidote for fifty enemies is one friend.
~Aristotle

"Isn't your cross supposed to be upside down?" The freshman boy looked at me with eyebrows raised too innocently, while his friends behind him snickered and did a poor job of hiding their laughter. I gripped my lunch tightly, helplessly aware that there were no more places to sit, no holes to squeeze myself into and just disappear... forever.

"Why would my cross be upside down?" I asked, rolling my eyes. I was tired of this and finally starting to get angry.

Delighted in the attention he was getting from his inquiry, he gestured to me, "Aren't you Gothic?"

I couldn't answer. My tongue was classically stuck to the roof of my mouth.

"Um, hello... what is wrong with you?"

I coughed out a quick, "Yeah, right," and walked away.

It's already difficult being a freshman. It's impossible being a Goth freshman at a Christian school. All the teachers know your name. You're at the top of an intervention list. I didn't make much noise but I could silence a room instantly and clear a lunch table in less than thirty seconds. Routinely I was sent to the principal's office: Was I struggling in my spiritual life? Had I ever dabbled in witchcraft? Why did I want to look like that? Was someone hurting me? Was I hurting someone?

However, the reason I wore black was actually very boring: I liked black and I liked old-fashioned dresses. Today we call it "steampunk" and it has a more positive, trendy association, but to everyone at my school it was considered nothing short of walking with the Devil. I hadn't really wanted to fit in or be popular, but I had wanted to be accepted and somewhat liked. Before long, I realized that only the beautiful people made the grade, figuratively and literally. There seemed to be an entirely different set of rules for the prettiest, most athletic girls. Honestly, I didn't mind them doing their thing—why couldn't they just let me do mine?

I dreaded going to bed at night, because going to bed at night meant waking up in the morning and going to school. As we pulled into the parking lot every morning, my chest would tighten painfully and my pulse would start to race. Walking through the gate, I would cringe and ignore the urge to cry. With each disapproving stare from teachers and sneer from "good students," I tried not to cover my face and run from the building. It wasn't long before I started asking myself: What is wrong with me?

Then, when it seemed like things were already too hurtful to bear, a growing pain in my lower abdomen began matching my emotional pain. I often left class for the restroom, where I lay on the cool floor and cried from a deep, lacerating clawing in the middle of my body.

One night, I was carried into the emergency room with crippling pain. Over the next few weeks, I was given a series of tests, hormone therapy, and medication. The doctors diagnosed me with endometriosis and a broken cyst. I probably wouldn't be able to have kids, and in the future a hysterectomy might be necessary. There was no cure.

Back in school, I was limited to walking the track during P.E., and I was actually thankful for the seclusion. However, like bloodhounds, high school girls smell fear and pain. The popular girls jumped on another girl while I was separated from them.

"So, what's wrong with you?" they asked her.

She was slender and delicate, blond with fair skin and pretty hazel eyes. I disliked her on principle because she looked like a Disney princess. She wore pinks and pastels, short skirts and girly sandals, and her make-up always seemed perfect. In junior high, she struggled with her weight. Now she was trim, elegant, a content resident of the popular table. Her name was Missy, and as far as I was concerned, she was one of them.

While I laced up my shoes, I heard Missy explain to the other girls that she had been absent due to a flair-up of lupus. Two of the girls jumped back immediately, thinking lupus was contagious. The other two went on about how lucky she was to get to walk instead of play sports.

Lucky? I mean, really? Disgusted, I turned around and started walking. Instead of the seclusion I had hoped for, quiet little Miss Cinderella joined me around the track.

I watched her cautiously from the corner of my eye. The safe thing would be to say as little as possible. Gradually, however, Missy and I began to chat. I was surprised when I didn't have to explain words like "endometriosis" and "broken cyst" to her. She understood the havoc hormone therapy was having on my emotional life and she didn't respond with false cheerfulness or the other extreme: horror. In a strange twist of fate, Missy and I found ourselves comforting and understanding each other. I knew how we looked together, me with my combat boots, occasional trench coat, corset, and long skirts, and Missy with her summery blouses and trendy slippers. We just did not belong. I was knocked off balance to realize that, princess though she seemed, she was hurting the same way I was.

As I got to know Missy, I realized people were talking about her almost as much as they were talking about me. Her popularity had come with a high price, one she didn't choose to pay. When her doctor switched her medicines between eighth and ninth grade, she lost her childhood baby fat and got her elegant adult figure, because she was constantly sick to her stomach.

Once Missy and I became visible friends, a sharp line was drawn between her and her old friends. Sure enough, she started hanging out with me less and less, and for a short time not at all. But then she did come back, arriving late to lunch, looking like she'd been hassled.

Missy and I became best friends, and years later, we're still best friends. In fact, under the protection of our friendship, I've been known to wear pink lace and she's been known to wear black boots. It was some time later I learned why Missy had come to lunch late, looking exhausted and uncomfortable. In a style that would have made the Spanish Inquisition proud, Missy had been set upon by her old "friends" and interrogated... about me.

Is she a witch?

Is she demon possessed?

Is she insane?

Does she worship Satan?

It had been a perfect chance for Missy to secure her position at the top of the ninth grade social food chain. Instead, she cast her lot with me—social suicide. She just told those girls that I liked black and there was nothing wrong with me.

~Faith Northmen

Burial Grounds

No love, no friendship, can cross the path of our destiny
without leaving some mark on it forever.
~François Mauriac

As kindergarten buddies, we shared juice boxes. As young girls, we shared crushes on the cutest boys in the school. As sixth graders, we shared a neighborhood; only one hill stood between us. We will never know how many times we rolled down that hill, made snow angels on it, or stormed off as angrily as possible just to make it known that we were currently "not speaking," but what we do know is that buried at the very top of that hill, in our secret place, are our childhood tokens.

As one beautiful spring day came to a close, one of our trio made a suggestion. "Let's bury some of our favorite things. That way we can come back some day and dig them up," Kelsey said.

With a doubtful look, Bailee replied, "Like those time capsule things we made in Girl Scouts?"

"Yeah! Just like those, but our own," said Kelsey.

"Well, what are we going to bury?" I inquired.

Kelsey had apparently been anticipating our hesitation, and she already knew the answers to our questions. "Lip gloss and Beanie Babies... and stuff that we used to love but now we don't really use anymore."

Scrambling around our houses that night, we dug up tiny tokens of ourselves. I found things like my favorite little doll, a scrunchie I wore in my hair practically every day of the third grade, and other little things. The next day, we carefully placed our items in plastic sandwich bags, ready to find the perfect place to bury them.

Our first option was just beyond the fence at the top of the hill. It was perfectly shaded, and we were the only ones who walked there. As we waved goodbye to our things, the sudden reality of actually digging the hole set in. We needed a shovel. After an hour-long search for a shovel that we could actually reach in the garage, we began to dig. Three hours later, we decided to find a new spot. Sweaty and aggravated, we moved to a location with looser dirt. Well, this would have to work. We dug a hole just deep enough to fit our things into, and deposited them. Feeling reminiscent and quite grown up, we waved goodbye to childhood. Middle school was upon us and it was time to get serious about this "growing up" concept. Patting down the freshly turned soil, it was time to become strong, serious women.

Years quickly passed, and our trio drifted apart as we made other friends. Different activities and changing personalities separated us. All the while, we remembered that bond, the unbroken one. Our neighborhood no longer set the scene for our lavish adventures. Instead we moved away, leaving behind that part of town forever frozen in our minds as if under a glass case.

Four years later, a reunion was in order. A few phone calls later, we were standing at the top of the hill, all together again. It was almost a flashback in time: a snapshot of years past. Once again, we found ourselves searching for a shovel. The motions were strangely familiar. We walked to the garage and found the same shovel we had used before. At the top of the hill again, we argued over the exact location of our treasure. We had not made a map; we simply had the memories of wandering around trying to find a suitable place for our hole. After a few failed digging attempts, the shovel pierced something just below the earth's surface.

"Found it!" yelled Kelsey.

"Don't break open the bags, just be careful!" scolded Bailee.

We carefully unearthed the wrinkled plastic bags. Rapidly, the vivid, glorious pictures in our minds were wiped away. What we had once seen as objects of affection were now gone. Only disintegrating, malodorous, bug-eaten bits of fabric and dirty plastic remained. As insects crawled out of the once soft fur of my Beanie Baby, I could not help laughing. "These things," I screamed. "These nasty old things! We looked forward to this?" Slightly disgusted, we laughed until we could laugh no longer.

Kelsey asked the question we had all been wondering. "What should we do with this stuff now?"

"Let's bury it for a second time, then we never have to see it again!" replied Bailee. That's what we had all been thinking. With fresh, stronger plastic bags we carefully placed our treasures into the ground once more. Never to be seen again, we said goodbye.

I believe that on that day, we buried more than just our putrid junk that we had once cherished. As high school began, our friendships ended. There is no resentment today, just good memories. I look back at my younger years and see nothing but good times. In a symbolic way, we had unearthed treasures that were better left behind. Our friendships were wonderful while they lasted, but eventually it was time to move on to bigger and better things. Sometimes the best memories are those left buried far underground, undisturbed.

~Sami Smith

Fast Friends

Unselfish and noble actions are the most radiant pages
in the biography of souls.
~David Thomas

It was my first year teaching in a special needs classroom, and I wasn't sure what to expect at our annual Special Olympics track meet. My students had a range of challenges, from mild learning disabilities to severe cerebral palsy.

Mark was one with the latter. Confined to a motorized wheelchair, he had to fight his spasms just to control his movements. Nevertheless, he always had a positive attitude and greeted everyone each morning with a huge smile.

His classmates loved him and always took the time to make sure he was included in group activities, especially Mike, Andy and Lucas, three boys who excelled at sports. In his heart I knew Mark wanted to be like them, unrestricted by the limitations of his body, and watching the grace with which they moved on the playing field seemed to fill him with wonder.

When track and field day came, Mike, Andy and Lucas placed well in their heats, and gave the normally placid crowd something to cheer about. Mark sat on the sidelines, cheering them on, placing last in his own heat because his wheelchair wouldn't go fast enough.

The final event of the day was the 400-meter race. Everyone was invited to either walk or run, according to their ability, around the entire length of the track. We watched as the sprinters took off—Mike, Andy and Lucas determined to prove who the better athlete was.

But when the exhausted trio reached the finish line they paused and turned to look behind them. At the back of the crowd, determined not to be left behind, was Mark. His classmates had passed him by and even the slowest walkers were outdistancing him. He was alone on the track with over half the distance left to cover.

Mike, Andy and Lucas looked at each other, and a silent thought passed between them. Slowly, they jogged back towards their friend, where they slowly enfolded Mark in a tight circle and kept pace, cheering him on as he had done for them moments before.

The progress was slow, but in the end the three star sprinters and Mark crossed the finish line together to the enthusiastic cries of their teachers and classmates. Seeing the look on Mark's face as he crossed the finish line, hands upraised and laughing, I came to understand what makes the Special Olympics, and the determined athletes who compete, so extraordinary.

Years later, I'm still cheering them on.

~Laura Miller

From Hare to Tortoise

Success is blocked by concentrating on it and planning for it.... Success is
shy — it won't come out while you're watching.
~Tennessee Williams

I entered my freshman year of high school with a definite philosophy: work hard and stick to whatever I could succeed at. In this way, I reasoned, I'd be able to skate through high school and out the other side with a 4.0 and some impressive accomplishments. I wouldn't waste my time in areas where I didn't excel.

And this philosophy served me well. I worked hard in my classes and on cello practice and got the results I wanted, usually in the shape of grades, successful recitals, and other materialistic rewards. My academic standards were high, because my dreams for the future were ambitious. An A- would've been the end of the world. My friends would tease me about my all-or-nothing attitude, but in my eyes, it was the only sure path to success.

At the beginning of sophomore year, I fully intended to keep that same attitude. Then I joined the cross-country running team, a year after I'd watched cross-country races and said, "I could never do that!" I joined mainly because my brother was on the team; he was entering his senior year, and I wanted to spend as much time with him as possible before he left for college. Also, most of my friends were on the team, and they'd been trying to cajole me into running for months. When I came to the first practice, I was filled with optimism and grandiose dreams of making the varsity team.

But as the distance we ran each practice gradually increased from three, to four, to six miles, I realized with surprise that no matter how hard I tried, I wasn't physically capable of running as fast as my friends. I wouldn't be on varsity; in fact, I was one of the slowest on the team. This concept eroded my dream of running prowess. And the muscular strain of cross-country was often unbearable, especially on the last scorching and humid days of summer. With every step I ran, my mind reined me in with an endless string of complaints. Not only did I suck at running, but I was having no fun! What was the point of putting myself through so much pain? I'd never make points for U-32 in a race; I'd just be letting down my team. After the first few weeks, I wanted to quit.

Then we had our first cross-country meet. When we got off the bus at Lamoille High School, decked out in our blue uniforms with our team name emblazoned on the jerseys, the sight of the other teams warming up made me cringe. I wasn't the only one; our whole team was wired with nervous anticipation. We jogged to the start-ing line and went through our warm-ups silently. When we started the race, I felt the enormous pressure of expectations sink onto my shoulders. I watched the churning tide of runners begin to surge past me and was overwhelmed with frustration. It was a brutal course, comprised of a series of short, steep hills that looped around twice, and after a while I stopped running and struggled to walk up the last mammoth hill.

But then I heard my coaches yelling my name from the top of the hill, their cries of encouragement mingling with those of my team-mates. I felt confused and embarrassed; why were they cheering for me? I was running terribly!

As I broke into a weary jog up the last stretch of hill, I realized that my coaches didn't care how fast I ran. Neither did my teammates. During the rest of the season, they were always on the sidelines of every race, cheering for me just as loudly as they'd cheered for the frontrunner. Those expectations that had weighed on me so heav-ily at the beginning of the race were simply my own. And once I realized that, I decided to cast them away. I began to put my effort into supporting my teammates instead of obsessing about my own performance. In that way, I celebrated my teammates' victories as if they were my own; I felt their pain and exhaustion as if they were my own. After a while, it didn't matter if the runners struggling up the hill were on my team or not—I rooted for them anyway. And they would always return the favor whenever I needed it most, because we were linked by the understanding of having been in the same position.

The relationships forged within our cross-country team are ones that will carry on past our running days and into old age. The comradeship of sharing the intense emotions which sprung out of a grueling sport made the bonds between my teammates and me surpass friendship. And often, the emotions we shared were frustration, pain, disappointment, and sheer exhaustion. But together, as a team, we were able to push through those moments together and come out as champions—not as champions of ribbons or trophies, but as champions of perseverance. The memories that stand out most clearly aren't the bitter ones; they're the moments when a teammate loses his shoes in the bog, keeps running barefoot, and laughs about it at the finish line. They're the expressions of pride on my coaches' faces when I tell them I didn't walk once during a whole race. They're the subconscious grins that spread over the runners' faces when they hear us yelling ridiculous things from the sidelines, and the frenzied jumping-up-and-down finish line moments when a teammate breaks his previous best time by two minutes.

To be honest? I don't remember the exact grade I got on my U.S. History summer assignment. When I got my first A- at the end of sophomore year, the world managed to keep turning. Cross-country running made me realize that I don't need to be the best to be successful in life. It taught me to value my relationships with people more than my relationship with my ego. It taught me to cheer for others even if I never learn their first names. High school doesn't last forever. But maybe someday, way down the road, an old high school friend will call me out of the blue. We'll gradually ease back into the familiar with summer memories we shared and jokes we used to laugh at. Maybe we'll stretch our memories all the way back to the days when we were limber enough to run three miles, and she'll say with a laugh, "Do you remember that State Championships meet when there was that downpour and Zac lost his shoes in the bog...?"

And I will.

~Juliette Rose Wunrow

Here for You

*A friend is one of the nicest things you can have,
and one of the best things you can be.*
~Douglas Pagels

As I sit and ponder,
Ways to make you smile,
You're crying on my shoulder,
And we've been here for a while.

I try to make you think about,
The laughs of yesterday.
And how we've been through all of it,
But it all turned out okay.

Nothing makes you smile at me,
You look so small and sad.
So I try to remind you,
I've been with you, good or bad.

And I'll be here tomorrow,
The next day I'll be here too.
So friend you needn't worry,
I am always here for you.

~Ashley Démoré

Encountering Grace

The world is hugged by the faithful arms of volunteers.
~Terri Guillemets

Her eyes glowed the day I walked into room 571. She was not your typical nine-year-old, surviving an intense liver transplant just a few days earlier. Typically, volunteers are not provided with this information beforehand; it is at the discretion of the patient to tell us. Grace openly told me about her illness the day we met. She was eager to be a normal kid again, but her body was not cooperating. Her stringy blond hair, bloated belly, raspy voice, and blue eyes rimmed by extremely thick glasses made it evident her illness had taken over. Grace was confined to her small hospital room on contact isolation, and desperately needed someone with whom to play.

After dressing myself in the dreaded plastic smock and putting on the turquoise nitrile gloves, I gave a slight knock on the door and walked in. Her room was different from any hospital room I had ever seen since becoming a teenage volunteer at Children's Medical Center. The walls were papered with her artwork. Disney Princess coloring book pictures were the décor of choice. The windows were adorned with purple curtains, and she was surrounded by a menagerie of stuffed animals. *Monopoly*, *Life*, *Guess Who?*, and a variety of other board games were stacked high in her closet and were accompanied by her bountiful movie selection. She had converted a grim room into her very own palace. The elaborate array of colors made the rest of the hospital look bare in contrast.

Even more striking, Grace's hospitality was well beyond her years. The minute I walked in, she asked me if I was hungry. Despite my "No, thanks," she called downstairs and ordered two bags of Lay's barbecue chips. "What do you want to do?" she asked, and then she suggested that we color more Disney Princess pictures, specifically Ariel the mermaid. When her appetite for coloring was satiated, we watched *The Princess Diaries* until she fell asleep. Every Friday after that, Grace would call the volunteer depot to see if I had arrived yet to come play with her. As soon as I checked in at four, I would immediately be deployed to room 571. Grace quickly took over my job of providing entertainment to her, and would always have a plan for what we were going to do.

As time passed, Grace and I became good friends. We would play together for the duration of my shift every Friday. She would ask me about life outside the hospital, a life she dreamed about knowing. We talked about boys, dances, school, birthday parties, and friends, none of which she had experienced. My heart broke to see such a sweet and innocent girl fighting a sickness that she had no way of controlling.

Although her parents had not told her, Grace's days were numbered. In just the little time she had left, Grace was teaching me how to pay attention to the little joys of life. The troubles in my life no longer appeared as significant, as I always remembered frail Grace confined to her hospital room day after day.

On October 11th, five months from the day we met, I arrived early for my shift. I checked in at the depot and immediately began my routine trek to Grace's room. When I entered room 571, I was shocked to discover that the walls, so recently covered with artwork, were barren. The bed was pristinely made with starched white linens. The walls were void of the color they once knew and the curtains had vanished.

Grace's mom, who usually used the time I came to decompress and escape the anxiety of being in a hospital room, startled me as she sat in a rocking chair by the empty bed. Teardrops trickled down her face. Before she opened her mouth, I knew. Grace was gone. The cruel disease had defeated her body. A lump formed in my throat. I could not fathom the reality that she had died. Her mom had been waiting for me to arrive, and invited me to sit down. I learned that Grace had not been responding to the medication or the new liver, and apparently there was nothing that could be done to stop the disease. Her expression of gratitude moved me to tears, especially when she shared with me how much my Friday night dates with Grace inspired her to keep battling.

When I think about grace, I think of a divinely given blessing, and that's what Grace was to me. Although her disease was not a blessing, the impact she had on my life was. Her simple elegance and high regard for others despite her tribulations was a testament of her unfailing love. Her bright smile is imprinted on my mind and inspires me to live life to the fullest. Even though I was flattered by the idea that I helped Grace, the truth of the matter is that Grace will never know how much she touched me. In room 571, a fragile girl showed me how to find and disseminate joy. Her legacy glows even today.

~Avery Atkins

Just for
Teenagers

101 Stories of Inspiration
and Support for Teens

Chapter
2

Life Lessons

You learn something every day if you pay attention.

~Ray LeBlond

The Driver's License

You have enemies? Good.
That means you've stood up for something, sometime in your life.
~Winston Churchill

On a cold day in February, I was sitting in class, staring out the window, and fantasizing about escaping the miserable cold. My French teacher mentioned something about "summer," catching my attention. I woke from my reverie to see her holding a poster with smiling teens standing on a university campus. She explained that the program was for English-speaking students interested in learning French by staying at a campus in Québec during the summer. The program appealed to me, so I decided to apply.

Around this time, my life began changing. I was a straight-A student, a member of many school clubs, and a recipient of a couple of awards. I had been subjected to peer pressure, but I had always refused to do anything rash. Unfortunately, the pressure became so strong that I eventually caved in. Wanting to be "cool," I started going to parties and drinking. I would come home late, drunk beyond recognition. My life took a turn for the worse.

In June, I landed my dream job. I was exposed to a variety of different people through my workplace, and some people were better role models than others. One co-worker, Clemens, offered me his driver's license. "Take this," he said. "We practically look identical, and you can pretend to be twenty-one years old. Have fun in Québec!" I pocketed the license. I'd seen friends walk into liquor stores with fake licenses and come out carrying a twelve-pack of beer, beaming proudly. I knew that I would be away from my parents for the entire summer. I worried about the consequences of getting caught, but I thought that I could outsmart all the adults.

At Trois-Rivières, Québec, there were over 300 students from across Canada on campus. We were a group of strangers. It was interesting to see how quickly the student body formed into cliques. My new circle of friends was very different from my circle back at school.

A monitor led me to my residence and I started to unpack. I noticed the fake license at the bottom of my luggage. I heedlessly slipped the license into my wallet. I promised myself that I wouldn't use the license until the last week of my stay, but I easily got carried away.

On the first night, my new acquaintances and I roamed around the town. We came across a Petro Canada store. Kai asked, "Does anyone have a fake license?" Everyone shook his head. I cleared my throat and said, "I do." Everyone looked at me with admiration. Kai gave me twenty dollars and instructed me to buy a twelve-pack. Without thinking, I boldly agreed to take on the task. I walked into the store and looked at the selection of alcoholic drinks. I wasn't sure about what kind of beverage Kai wanted, so I grabbed a case of beer. I walked up to the cashier and dropped the case on the counter. I noticed the suspicious look in his eyes. Not knowing what to expect, I pulled out my wallet and offered to pay. "Not so fast, young man. Let me see your ID," he said in French. Fair enough, I thought, as I pulled out the license. The cashier glanced at the photo, looked at me suspiciously, then looked back at the photo. "You are from British Columbia? That's a nice province." I sighed with relief as he accepted my cash and gave me my receipt.

I grabbed the case and bolted out the door with a bounce in my step. Suddenly, out of the corner of my eye, I noticed one of the monitors. Afraid that she would recognize me, I turned my face and shielded the case with my body. In an awkward manner, I staggered in the opposite direction. I clenched the box in fear when the monitor began following me. Luckily, Arielle and Keeley saw my dilemma and intercepted the monitor by striking up a conversation. I safely arrived at my residence. I changed my shirt so that the monitor wouldn't recognize me.

When I found the boys waiting for me and the drinks, they cheered and gave me pats on the back. "You're the man," someone said to me. The compliment boosted my self-confidence.

The next two weeks passed by quickly. I outright ignored my resolution to save the partying for the last week. I don't remember what happened, but I knew that I had fun, looking at the pictures afterwards. What I do remember, however, is the night when the fun ended.

It was a Friday, and there was a dance in the evening. A few of my friends insisted that we drink before the dance. They pestered me, the "ID man," to buy alcohol. I knew something could go wrong, but I trusted everyone to be responsible. I took the cash and bought what they wanted.

Later that night, at the dance, I was enjoying myself. Suddenly, Ethan tapped me on the shoulder and solemnly said, "Cristian isn't okay." Worried for my friend, I went to assess the situation. I saw a huge figure stumbling on the dance floor, which I recognized as a drunk Cristian. A towering football player, Cristian was the last person I expected to be overly drunk. I sat him down and gave him a bottle of water. One of the monitors, however, noticed that something wasn't right. He called the ambulance and Cristian lost consciousness.

I vividly remember seeing the paramedics pulling Cristian into the ambulance that night, his unconscious face drooping over the white sheets. I had never seen a situation like this before and I was concerned. After midnight, when I was asleep in my bed, the campus security officer busted the door in and shined a flashlight in my face. "Did you buy the alcohol?" he asked. I knew that there was no point in denying the truth, so I admitted, "Yes, I did." Like a caught criminal, I was overcome with shame.

In the interrogation room, I admitted everything that happened. I learned that Cristian's condition was serious. I was lucky that he didn't suffer any permanent damage. Moreover, I was lucky that the monitors decided to have mercy and not report the incident to the police or my teachers. My punishment was much less than what I deserved: I was merely expelled from the program.

As I sat in my room back at home, with the rest of my summer ruined, I thought about the stupid mistake that I had made. The reason was obvious: peer pressure. I learned you should never do something you believe is wrong just because someone else is telling you to. Don't sacrifice anyone's wellbeing to gain the approval of others. Be confident about yourself, despite what others say about you. I shredded the fake driver's license and threw it away.

~Joseph Chan

The Girl Behind Me

*You don't have to be a "person of influence" to be influential.
In fact, the most influential people in my life
are probably not even aware of the things they've taught me.*
~Scott Adams

I was really nervous about English class this year because I was an eleventh grader taking a twelfth grade class. I knew that I wouldn't know anyone in the class, and that scared me a little. But since I didn't know anyone, I had the chance to do something I love almost as much as socializing—people watching.

One of the most interesting girls in the class sat directly behind me. She was always laughing and talking, and she just seemed so genuinely happy. She was friendly, too—she was one of the very few people in the class who made any attempt to acknowledge me. She was one of those people you just liked, even if you didn't really know her.

At the end of the year, we were assigned a big project. It was a very open-ended project, where the instructions were basically to read something, then read or watch something else that related to it, and then come up with a class presentation based on what you learned. The presentations were spread out over the last month of school, and because everyone had chosen such different topics and different ways to present those topics, we had some of the most interesting and varied presentations I've ever watched.

The Girl Behind Me presented on one of the very last days. She got up in front of the class, and told everyone how she had read about eating disorders, because she herself had struggled with one. Since it would have been too difficult for her to talk to us about it directly, she and a friend (who had also suffered from an eating disorder) had made a movie, where they interviewed each other about their eating disorders, how they had felt while they were struggling with them, and how they had overcome them. By the end of the presentation, almost everyone was in tears. Several people put up their hands to comment on how brave she was to stand up and talk about it, and how strong she was to have overcome the disorder.

The most shocking thing about the whole presentation was how surprising it was. I never expected that she would have had a problem like that. She always seemed so happy and confident; it was hard to picture her counting calories because she thought she wasn't good enough.

The main thing that I took away from her presentation was how difficult it is to judge people. You never know just by looking, or even from observing them for a semester, what type of person someone is.

You also never know what kind of impact you have had on people's lives. The Girl Behind Me may never see me again. She may not even really know who I am now. But she isn't someone I'm going to forget any time soon. Her courage to stand up in front of thirty people and talk about something so personal, and her strength to ask for help and overcome her problems have inspired me. That's why I dedicate this story to The Girl Behind Me, and I hope someday she sees this and knows that she has touched the lives of people she hardly even knew.

~Haley Whiteway

One Friday Night

Better a thousand times careful than once dead.

~Proverb

My sister Megan always felt a little creepy babysitting at the Quinns' house. It was set back from the road by a long, winding driveway, and the yard was filled with so many pine trees that she couldn't see any of the neighbors' lights. On this particular night, the snow was coming down in swirls, and large flakes clung to the bushes outside the front window.

The girls begged her to read them their favorite story, and afterward they each wanted a drink of water, but then they fell asleep. Megan settled on the sofa to watch an old movie on television.

Around ten o'clock, she heard wheels on the gravel driveway. Thinking that Mrs. Quinn had returned early, she clicked off the television and walked to the front door. Her hand was on the deadbolt, just about to turn it, when a loud knock startled her.

Megan's hand froze. She spied through the peephole and saw a middle-aged man standing in the entryway. He was wearing a black knit cap.

"Who is it?" she asked.

"Ben."

"Ben who?"

"Your brother Ben."

Megan realized the man had mistaken her for his sister. She replied, "Mrs. Quinn can't come to the door right now."

"Ask if Ben can come in."

Our mother had always warned us: Never open the door for a stranger while you're babysitting.

"Go over to the window," Megan said. She moved to the living room and slid up the window, a blast of cold air chilling her bare arms. The man stepped forward between the bushes. He was tall and fat and had a big nose. Megan thought that he looked a little like Mrs. Quinn.

"The truth is I'm babysitting," she said through the screen. The words were out of her mouth before she remembered her mother's second warning: Don't advertise that you're alone. Megan quickly added, "Mrs. Quinn will be home soon."

The man inhaled from a glowing cigarette stub and then threw it in the snow. His breath came out as a white cloud. He bent down in front of the window and rubbed his palms together. "It's awfully cold out here. Can I wait inside?"

Megan hesitated. "Couldn't you come back in a little while?" she asked.

"I drove all the way from Newport. I don't have anywhere else to go." The man smiled. "Please let me in. I promise I won't bother you."

It bothered Megan just to hear him promise that. She didn't want to spend the rest of her night here with a stranger. How could she be sure he was telling the truth? "Mrs. Quinn didn't say anything about you dropping by tonight."

"That's because she didn't know I was coming. I was planning to surprise her on her birthday."

Her birthday? Could that be why Mrs. Quinn went out? But Megan hadn't seen any birthday cards lying around, or wrapping paper and bows. Her heart raced. What should she do? She remembered the telephone number stuck to the refrigerator with magnets. "Mrs. Quinn left a number for me to contact her," she said. "I'll call her and see what she says."

The smile vanished from the man's face. "You're going to leave me outside to freeze to death in the meantime?"

"It'll just take a minute," Megan said.

"Wait until she finds out you wouldn't let me in!" he yelled. "You'll be in so much trouble!"

Megan trembled. Maybe it was true. Maybe she would get in trouble. All that mattered was that she was feeling more and more uncomfortable with this man. After that outburst from him, she wasn't going to let him in the house now, even if Mrs. Quinn gave her permission.

"I'm not letting you in, sir," she said. "You'll have to come back later." She quickly shut the window and locked it. The man stared at her, his eyes piercing. He turned, stormed to his car and sped down the driveway.

Megan closed the drapes, sat on the living room couch and hugged a pillow. What if Mrs. Quinn asked her why she didn't let her brother in? How could Megan explain that he was downright rude, and that he scared Megan so much that she shook? Would Mrs. Quinn think she was not mature enough to babysit? Maybe she'd never call her again.

A little after eleven, a key turned in the knob. Megan got up from the couch and went to the foyer, where Mrs. Quinn was rummaging through her purse. She pulled out her wallet and asked, "How did everything go?"

Megan bit her lip. "I didn't have any problems with the girls. But later, when they were asleep, your brother came to the door. He kept insisting that he should wait inside for you, but I was afraid to let him in. When I told him I wasn't going to open the door, he got really mad at me and left. I'm sorry."

Mrs. Quinn frowned. "My brother? I don't have a brother!"

Megan was proud of herself for following her instincts. She had kept Mrs. Quinn's kids—and herself—safe that night. Later she realized she also should have called the emergency number Mrs. Quinn left her and perhaps the police as well. It was a valuable lesson for my sister and for me.

~Mary Elizabeth Laufer

Pictures Don't Lie

Don't handicap your children by making their lives easy.
~Robert A. Heinlein

T he first time I ever got drunk my parents took pictures of me throwing up and passed out on my bed. When they gave me one of those pictures the next day, I was furious. I just grabbed it and slammed my way out of the kitchen. I did not want to talk about it and I ripped that picture to shreds. I didn't know there were several more even worse than that one.

For the next few mornings, there was a different picture next to my plate. "When you're ready to talk about it, we're ready to listen," my mom said. By the time the last picture showed up, I was ready to talk about it.

This all started when Mike Emery invited me to his birthday party. I was so excited. He was turning fourteen and had worked out a theme to have fourteen people, seven girls and seven boys. I could not wait to get on my cell and find out if Gayle, my best friend, had also gotten an invitation. Gayle and I have been best friends since third grade and our birthdays are only three days apart. She and her brother Steve had lived with their mom since her parents' divorce, and Gayle's mom had already let her go to a couple of parties before this one.

My mom and dad are pretty strict, especially my dad. They finally agreed to let me go, mostly because Mike's parents would be around during the party. Mom and Dad laid down some rules about when I had to be home. Really lame rules, in my opinion, but I was ready to agree to anything.

Gayle and I must have changed our minds a hundred times about what to wear. We were going to go in jeans until Mike texted us to "look pretty." I decided to wear my favorite yellow dress that made my tan really look good. Dad bought the dress for me a few months before for my cousin's wedding. It was definitely the most expensive dress I had ever owned.

You should have seen their expressions when I got dressed and walked into the living room with my hair piled up on my head in a way I had never done before. I used a lot of hairspray and some gold sparkles and, frankly, I had never looked so hot. My parents just stared at me and, finally, Mom said, "Honey, you are so beautiful!" Dad stared at me a few minutes; then he went for the camera, insisting on taking pictures.

Gayle's mom dropped us off at the party and her brother, Steve, agreed to pick us up at 11:30 and drop us off at home. Steve is eighteen and loves any excuse to drive his mom's Mustang.

As soon as we got to Mike's house, I started feeling really nervous. I'm not sure why. I knew most of the people there, but I just wasn't used to being all dressed up and wished I felt as good as they said I looked. The dining room table had a big bowl on it full of pink punch, with sliced peaches floating on top. There was plenty of food on the table, but nobody was eating any of it. I was kind of surprised that I hadn't seen Mike's parents around after the party got started, but someone said they were in the den watching TV. Mike put on some good music, but nobody was dancing. In fact, the girls hung out at one end of the room and the guys at the other, just kind of pushing each other around and acting like jerks. I kept flashing looks at Gayle, but she didn't catch on to how uncomfortable I was feeling.

That's when I saw Mike pour a bottle of vodka into the punch. I heard him say to nobody in particular, "We've gotta get this show on the road." Another boy said, "Yeah Mike, this party really sucks. Do it."

I remember going to the table with an empty glass in my hand and asking Mike to fill it up. Then I drank it fast, all at once, and asked for more. I remember my eyes doing strange things and the room going around and around. That's about all I remember. I have no clue how I got home.

When I saw that first picture, I felt sick all over again. There I was, hurling all over my dress, with my hair all stringy and matted. The ones of me passed out on my bed made me look dead. It scared me to look at those photos. After ripping up that first one, I did not even want to touch the others.

Of course, my parents were totally upset and they called Mike's mom and dad the day after the party. They came right over, with Mike, and did a lot of apologizing. I had to stand there and it was so embarrassing. All I could say was, "It's not Mike's fault." What I really wanted to do was just go to bed and be left alone.

For that whole weekend, my head ached, my eyes hurt, and I did not want to talk to anyone, including Gayle. My mom kept looking at me with this sad expression on her face. And my dad was definitely very angry. Mostly what they kept saying was, "When you want to talk about it, let us know."

I'm not sure when I decided it was time to talk about it. I think it was the last day of pictures when they put the "before" ones down next to the "after" ones. You would not believe it was the same person. I couldn't believe it. My parents did not have to tell me how ugly I looked, bombed out of my mind. I could see for myself.

Maybe if my dad had not taken all those pictures, I would never have known what I looked like when I got drunk... and maybe I never would have talked to them about it. Not that I had much to say. What I did tell them was this: "I lost a couple of hours of my life last weekend. I swear it won't happen again."

And it hasn't.

~Becca Johnson

Fortunes

Choices are the hinges of destiny.
~Pythagoras

I peered into the cavern of my fortune cookie through an unsealed opening. I could see a thin slip of paper inside that was waiting for me to crack it free. I broke open the shell, carefully pulled out the paper so as not to tear it, and my excitement mounted. My future was held in the very ink of this Chinese fortune. I directed my focus to the miniscule Times New Roman lettering.

It read: "Write your own fortune" followed by a line of fine print: "Visit us at www.wontoncookies.com!"

After staring at the delicate strip of paper for a good amount of time, somewhat disappointed by its lack of philosophical weight, I concluded that this must have been a prank cookie, and looked in the paper bag to see if the restaurant had given us an extra. No luck; my fortune was a dud. Apparently the Chinese Gods considered me completely unworthy of receiving a proper fortune. I glanced over at my sister's cream-colored slip, which read: "Now is the time to ask for a raise."

If only I had not so unfortunately reached for the cookie that was cracked open on my plate, if only I had known that there was a raise at stake!

My sister didn't even have a job. She didn't actually need to work either, unlike me; the things I spent all my money on—primarily clothes and make-up—she had no need for. Why would she buy her own sixty-dollar skirt, when she could just stretch, stain, and rip mine?

But enough complaining. Although I could unquestionably write an entire novel about my havoc-wreaking sister, this is not the time.

A few days after throwing my useless fortune in the trashcan, a special day came along. August twelfth, my six-month anniversary with Jon. I had been hinting at everything, from jewelry to chocolate. He was two years my senior, and worked full time at a construction company that dished out reasonable paychecks. Every time I brought up my birthday he would respond, "Don't worry, I got you something awesome."

Reassuring.

When the day finally rolled around, I woke up to my phone buzzing next to my bed. I answered in a groggy voice, and was greeted by an unusually perky boyfriend.

"Morning! Get dressed and come outside. I have a surprise!"

First thought that entered my mind was: "Good Lord, he's up at 10 a.m.!"

Second thought: "Wow, I've been seeing the same guy for six months!"

And lastly: "A surprise! Maybe he bought me roses, and a necklace!"

I threw off my covers and rushed to get ready. After quickly tossing on jeans and a stretched-out sweater (thank you, sister), I wove my wild hair into a neat French braid. Hardly able to contain myself, I flew out the front door.

Now, this is the part that will surprise you, and quite honestly surprised me too. Once I had managed to get out of my house somewhat decent looking, I laid eyes on my boyfriend. My gaze then trailed down to what he was holding. No, not flowers, or a stuffed animal. It was a helmet. This may seem extremely anticlimactic, but this helmet was not just any helmet—I knew very well what this helmet was for. It was a helmet crafted for riding the most dangerous machines on earth, a helmet that I had hoped would never touch my head, a helmet for people who were gutsy, courageous, brave... all the things that I was not.

"Never in a million years will you get me on the back of that thing," I had once said to Jon. "Never in my life will I ride a motorcycle."

I suppose I am either horrible at making promises to myself, or horrible at keeping them, because I did end up riding that giant, black and yellow two-wheeled monster.

Once I got past the terrifying death rates, I learned to enjoy biking. Racing the wind and being blinded by the passion of speed was somewhat satisfying. I learned that trying new things, however scary or completely ludicrous they might sound, isn't nearly as bad as never trying them at all. If I had never pulled that helmet over my head, where would I be today? Most likely still a frightened sixteen-year-old girl who would never drive anything but her father's Toyota.

I wrote my own fortune that day by seizing an opportunity that may never have come again. And you know what? I don't regret it. Perhaps my fortune should have read: "You will ride a motorcycle, and love it," but somehow I don't think I would've listened. I realize now that I had been given a meaningful fortune cookie after all. The choices we make define our lives, and give us the power to write our own fortunes.

~Vickie Vainionpaa

What Nobody Tells You about High School

Today is the tomorrow we worried about yesterday.
~Author Unknown

I walked into school the first day and my eyes widened in fear,
I took a deep breath and carefully walked by my peers.
I frantically searched for a familiar face in the group,
But found nobody, leaving me feeling so out of the loop.
As I failed to open my locker I groaned and I thought,
"Why doesn't anyone tell you what you really need to be
      taught?"

Like where to sit on the bus on the way to school,
Or why one group of students is considered "cool."
Or what table to sit down and eat lunch at,
Or who to turn to when you need to chat.
It'd be nice to know which friends you should make,
So you can avoid all the other ones who are fake.

I turned back to my locker and tried to open it,
After several failed attempts I decided to quit.
I began to walk to my first class of the day,
But soon I realized I was going the wrong way!

As I turned back around, I grumbled and I thought,
"Why doesn't anyone tell you what you really need to be
     taught?"

~Lauren Lesser

14

The Lucky One

The happiest moments of my life have been the few which I have passed at home in the bosom of my family.
~Thomas Jefferson

Megan Williams. The most popular girl at Northlake High. She was head cheerleader, Prom Queen, Student Body President and a straight-A student. She was so perfect that it made me want to dislike her, but I couldn't. Because the truth was that Megan was a really nice person.

When I passed her in the hallway at school, she always smiled at me but rarely stopped to talk. Megan was friendly with everyone, but her true friends were all in the popular crowd. And I wasn't exactly hanging with them.

But when I saw Megan at the drugstore one Saturday morning, she was chatty and all smiles. "Hi, Diane," she said. "How are you?"

I smiled back. "I'm doing great. How about you?"

"I'm good, but kinda tired. I had to cheer last night."

"Oh, yeah, I forgot about the game. Did our team win?"

She nodded. "You weren't there?"

I shrugged. "I don't go to a lot of school stuff."

"Oh, you should. It's really fun."

I shrugged again and said nothing. But in my head, I thought, "Well, sure, everything is fun if you're Megan Williams."

I glanced at Megan's cart and spotted several bottles of hair conditioner. Megan's hair was gorgeous and I instantly decided to switch brands.

"Well, I guess I'll see you later," Megan said, starting to push her cart down the aisle. "Have a fun weekend."

"Yeah, you too," I said, already knowing that she would.

I grabbed a bottle of Megan's brand of conditioner and the other things I needed and then went through the checkout line. Megan got behind me in line.

I waved awkwardly and said, "Hi again."

She smiled and waved back.

I paid for my stuff and went out to my car, an old hatchback. It was my brother's car, which was passed down to me when he went away to college. It was a real junker, but it was mine.

I put my stuff in the back and was climbing into the car when I heard someone calling my name. It was Megan. "Diane, your car — it's so cute!"

"You think my car is cute?"

"Well, not the car itself, but the windows. That's really sweet."

I nodded and glanced at my car windows. I'd forgotten about the car's homemade decorations. On one window were the words, "I love you," written in wipe-off marker. Another window said, "You are beautiful," and a third read, "I believe in you."

"That's so nice," Megan said, "but I didn't know you had a boyfriend."

"Oh, I don't," I said, suddenly ashamed of my cute car windows.

"Then who wrote on your car?"

"Well, um, my dad did," I answered quietly.

"Your dad did that? Your dad took the time to write on your car windows, just to, you know, make you feel good?"

I nodded, wishing like crazy I'd thought quickly enough to make up an imaginary boyfriend from another school. But I'd told the truth, which was beyond embarrassing.

I looked at Megan and realized she had tears in her eyes. "My dad would never do that for me," she muttered. "You are so lucky."

My mouth dropped open. Megan Williams thought I was lucky?

"I bet your mom's great too, right?"

I nodded. "Yeah, I guess. She stays at home with my little brother and sister. She bakes cookies and helps me with my homework and stuff."

Megan sighed. "I'd give anything to have a family like that."

"But you have everything," I said. "A perfect life."

She shook her head. "Not really. Not in the ways that matter."

After that, Megan always stopped to talk with me in the hallway. We even started hanging out outside of school. I'd offer to meet her at McDonald's or Subway, but she always wanted to come to my house. She seemed to love talking with my parents over a homemade dinner and playing board games with my family.

It was totally uncool, but it was what Megan wanted to do. I didn't understand why, but I didn't care. I'd always wanted to be friends with someone like Megan. I thought hanging out with her would make me popular and that would make me happy.

But just being Megan's friend made me happy. The other stuff didn't matter anymore.

Months later, Megan and I were talking about the day my dad wrote on my car windows. "I was so jealous of you," she admitted. "People think I have this great life, but I have struggles too."

I nodded because now that we were friends, I knew the truth about Megan's life.

"But you know what? I decided something that day," she said. "Rather than feel bad that I don't have a dad that would do something like that for me, I decided to hang out with your family." She looked at me, determination in her eyes. "Someday when I'm married, I'm going to have a family like yours. My kids are going to feel so loved."

I realized in that moment that many things in this life are beyond our control. We can't change the family we were born into. Whether they're terrific or completely dysfunctional, we can only do our best to learn from what we're given.

Megan did that. And she showed me that I was the lucky one after all.

~Diane Stark

15

My Second Love

Music inflames temperament.
~Jim Morrison

One of my closest friends, Adrian, made me a mixed CD of songs after I had a harsh breakup with a girl. Each song was meant to summarize points of my life, and the feelings and exchanges I'd had with different girls. He had written some not-so-kind things about her on the CD with pink marker, and it made me smile. Smiling with sincerity was difficult for me then. I spent my days hiding away in the practice rooms of the music center and skipping classes with my friends. I had become so numb that I could hardly even feel, let alone pretend to feel. Adrian's mixed CD was a temporary release.

At the end of my senior year in high school, I spent the majority of my time continuing to try to escape. That's when I fell in love again. Her black and white keys were smooth, and the mahogany body was beautiful. I would occasionally skip English class to meet "my love" in the theater. My understanding English teacher would spot me through the windows, sitting at the eight-foot Steinway grand piano in the orchestra pit. He'd smile and wave.

I had music theory class at eight o'clock every morning. It was my science, my philosophy, and my escape. Every day after class, I felt like I had accomplished something. My other classes felt like child's play compared to music theory. Transposing keys, figuring out major thirds and chords, and remembering to hold my fermatas were a completely different feeling. I had been playing piano and guitar for years, but I never really understood them until I learned theory.

At the end of the year, Flan Man, what we called our music theory teacher, asked me to meet him in his office. I had this overwhelming feeling that I had done something wrong, like I had cheated on homework or failed the exam.

"PHILLIPE... AIR-NANDESS!!" Flan Man always greeted me with a handshake and his crazy smile. "Phil, remind me where you are heading off to school next year."

"JMU," I answered. "I plan on doing the business program there... or maybe something with law."

"Listen. I hear you every morning practicing on the piano. You've really got something. A certain je ne sais quoi!" He was always a little over the top, but he wouldn't have been a very good conductor if he wasn't so quirky. "Just promise me, whatever you do with your life, you keep music close by. Keep practicing some theory. I wouldn't want to see your talents go to waste." I just nodded and he showed me the A I got on the final exam. I never walked into the music room again.

There I was, barely eighteen, and deep in my heart, I could feel that shadow of emptiness pressing my shoulders down. Flan Man's words had thrown me a curve ball. It was the epiphany I had been waiting for, and all it took was someone else telling me I was good at something.

The first time I ever snuck into the theater and unveiled the piano, I felt relief. I felt relief from my failed relationship, relief from the fear of leaving high school, relief from my own complacency. There is a sensation that overwhelms me when I touch the keys of a piano. It's as if my feelings transcend my physical body and are released through song; the notes on each page are the ups and downs of my own emotions. And now, thanks to my teacher, I realized that music had become my purest passion.

~Phillip Hernandez

Fitting In

If you don't control your mind, someone else will.
~John Allston

I wasn't the most popular kid my freshman year... not even close. In fact, I was awkward. I wasn't into fashion, preferred reading to sports, had difficulty talking to boys—the whole deal. As a result, the first year of high school had not been kind to me. I had no close friends. I mostly kept to myself with my head buried in a book. Which is why I was so surprised when Ashley and I became friends the summer before sophomore year.

Ashley was very different from me. She was outspoken and fashionable. She listened to bands I had never heard of and was very artistic. She was quite popular and she had been for as long as I could remember. These were qualities I knew nothing about. We had always been in the same classes throughout school, but had never really talked much. I was always intimidated by her.

During summer school, we were both taking classes in hopes of graduating early. The teacher paired us up on an assignment. Ashley seemed reluctant to work with me at first, but she relented, I imagine, because none of her "cool" friends were in the class. We met at the library to work on the project and really hit it off. Ashley did most of the talking. We sat by each other the rest of the summer and when classes ended we continued to hang out. We went shopping, listened to music, went to movies and to the beach. Everything that you could imagine a great summer with a new friend would consist of.

I looked up to Ashley, idolized her even; she was all of the things

I thought I wanted to be. I began listening to the music she listened to, wearing the clothes she wore. I quit reading and started watching the TV programs Ashley watched. I even tailored my sophomore year schedule to her interests. I decided to take art class even though I had really wanted to take theatre. (Ashley found acting dull.) When we started school again, Ashley introduced me to her group of friends, the "cool girls." She was the leader of their group; I would hang out with them on lunch breaks and take classes they were in. I would tag along to football games and I joined art club after school so I could hang out with them even more. Finally I fit in. I followed them around, laughing when they told jokes, agreeing when they had opinions—most enthusiastically at the ones I disagreed with. I didn't say much. I wouldn't want them to think that I was being rude by disagreeing. This continued for several months.

One day, I skipped out of my last class a few minutes early so I could get a booth for our group at the diner across from school. This is where we would meet before our Friday afternoon art club. I slouched down in the seat and began working on some homework, awaiting their arrival. Concentrating on my paper, I didn't notice that they had sat down at the booth behind me. Before I could say a word, I realized what they were talking about.

I listened silently. "She's such a loser," one girl said to the group.

"I know, Ashley. She just follows you around trying to be you. She copies you; she doesn't have a personality of her own," another girl added.

Then the Queen Bee herself replied, "I know, I wish she would leave us alone. We were in summer school together and now she thinks we're best friends or something. Get a life."

I was mortified. This was the moment I remember feeling heartbreak for the very first time. My hands were shaking, my face felt hot, and my eyes began to well with uncontrollable tears. How had this happened? I thought we were friends. I didn't know she thought of me in that way. Had I always been a burden to them? I couldn't stay there and listen anymore. I got up and ran out the door. The girls sat in the booth silent as they realized I had heard the whole conversation.

I ran home and told my mother what had happened. She just held me while I sobbed for hours. I felt so alone and betrayed. I wanted to curl up in my bed and stay there forever, but I knew I would have to go back eventually. The advice my mother gave was so simple. I had heard it a million times, but this time it felt so profound: "Just be yourself and people will like you for who you are." Then and there I decided I was going to stop crying and discover who I was. That is exactly what I did.

Ashley and I didn't speak anymore after that. I always thought she felt bad and didn't know how to express it. We would pass in the hall, as if we had never been friends at all. Over the next month, I went through a lot of changes. I bought new clothes, the clothes that I wanted to wear. I dropped art class and joined theatre. I began making new friends who liked me for who I was. I rediscovered reading, and developed my own opinions. I never again just followed the crowd.

I built up the courage to audition for the school play, and actually got a part. I was in every play for the rest of my high school career, landing quite a few lead roles. I had the opportunity to compete at the local and national level, taking many first place ribbons. The friends I made in theatre are still my great friends to this day.

I had an incredible school year. When I look back, I think of it as the year I discovered the person I was going to be. Despite the pain I felt that day, it was a gift they had given me. They opened my eyes. The things that they said about me were true. I was just following, trying desperately to fit in. If I had not been given the chance to realize it, I might have been too concerned with "fitting in" to experience some of the best times of my life.

~Brianne Monett

The Girl in the Polka-Dotted Dress

Gratitude is the best attitude.
~Author Unknown

"A perfect summer evening lost to a bike ride," I thought crossly as I pedaled halfheartedly down the busted sidewalk.

A family bike ride to the local park. Basically, the equivalent of social suicide if I was caught riding my floral bicycle in a line of family members, just like ducks.

Finally, we arrived at our destination. After parking our various bikes, my younger siblings dashed away to glide across, climb upon, and dangle on their beloved playground equipment. I silently craved the innocence of a child again. Where the world was all just one immense playground and the perils of high school were not anything to be concerned with yet. I trudged over to the swing set in the center of the enormous park. I did my best to appear reluctant, but secretly I still loved the sensation of slicing through the air, defying gravity and soaring through the sky. But there was always a point when you had to fly back down. That was how my teenage life felt lately. For every high point there was a low to follow it. This thought flooded my mind with recent memories and I was left sitting solemnly and still on the swing.

Suddenly, I become aware of a presence. I glanced to my left and saw a small child on the swing beside me. The little girl looked up at me, her almond eyes shining in the bright sun.

"Will you push me?" she asked innocently.

I followed her obvious gaze to my mother propelling my sister up in the sky. There were families off in the distance, and I wondered which was hers. Didn't she have a loving mother to push her on the swings, too? And I didn't want this girl's parents to think I was trying to abduct her or anything. But how could I refuse her sweet smile, revealing two tidy rows of baby teeth?

"Sure," I replied with a grin.

I had attempted to match her smile's own sweetness, but my metal-mouth grin most likely fell short. I hopped off my swing and began to push her.

"What's your name?" she asked gingerly as she flew backwards.

"Claudia," I grunted, pushing her forward.

"My name is Chloe," she informed me as her golden hair danced in the steamy air.

I nodded and continued to thrust her forward, looking down at the pink polka-dotted dress she was wearing, tag sticking out.

"I like your dress, Chloe," I said.

"Thank you," she answered considerately. A silly grin began to cross Chloe's round face. "I love swings. We don't have swings, only a slide."

"I like swings, too," I agreed. "They've always been my favorite."

Chloe began to ask me questions that I would normally not answer with a total stranger. Questions about my family, friends, where I lived, and others. Answering, I became amazed at the pleasant conversation I was having with this child.

After a long while pushing Chloe on the swings, I glanced around the park. There were still no parents around claiming her.

"Chloe," I inquired. "Where are your parents?"

Chloe looked me in the eyes gravely. It was an odd way for a small child, who shouldn't have a care in the world, to look.

"They're gone," she answered timidly. "My grandma's here, but my parents are gone. I miss them."

I continued pushing Chloe, my heart shattering inside my chest for her. I wasn't sure what "gone" meant exactly, but it didn't sound like she was saying they dropped her off to be babysat for a while. I looked at my family further down the park. What must it be like to have no parents to push you on the swings or help you finish your homework or simply be there for every stage of your life? Yet, Chloe was happy. The sweet, silly smile of hers returned and she was happy. Eventually, our conversation was interrupted. I had to leave the park. Chloe's smile vanished for only a second when I told her I had to go.

"Bye," she chirped, rewarding me with one last flash of baby teeth.

She skipped off to be with her grandmother all the way across the park. I made sure they were reunited before I left. Riding my bike home with my family surrounding me, I couldn't stop thinking about Chloe. How sweet and joyful she was, even though she knew her parents were no longer with her. How she looked past the pain in her life, to be grateful for the little blessings, like going on the swings. I knew right then that I wanted to be more like the little girl in the polka-dotted dress.

~Claudia Connors

The Votes Are In

Oh, my friend, it's not what they take away from you that counts.
It's what you do with what you have left.
~Hubert Humphrey

At the end of my junior year, nominations for student body officers caused quite a stir. It appeared that Debbie would run unopposed for president. Talking amongst a group of disgruntled girls, I muttered, "There must be someone who'd run against her."

Suddenly Liz focused her attention on me. "Why not you?"

"Me? No way. I work after school. I can't stay for all those meetings."

My closest friend, Linda, vetoed my protests. "Why not? Just think how great our senior year would be! You could get a real senior trip approved and get better bands for the dances. You could even get celebrities to speak at our assemblies!"

My little group continued to ignore my now feeble protests as they speculated on the wonderful changes I could make. By the end of the week, they'd gotten enough signatures to put my name on the ballot.

Debbie and I had very different campaign styles. Because I was always hopping around, I'd earned the nickname "Bunny." Signs soon popped up around campus with perky rabbits and the slogan "Make your votes multiply with Bunny!" My platform aimed for more fun and less restrictions. We wore uniforms and I advocated more free dress days and a broader interpretation of what accessories were acceptable on regular dress days.

My opponent, on the other hand, avoided any hint of silliness on her posters. Catchy slogans and cuddly critters had no place in her serious campaign. What she offered was the opening of Senior Lawn to all students and an alphabetical reformatting of the yearbook that would intermingle ninth through twelfth graders rather than highlight seniors in oversized portraits. Gone would be a dedication of nearly half the yearbook to seniors, their quotes and their many exciting activities.

Underclassmen loved Debbie's ideas; her equality among the grade levels held a magnetic appeal for them. Would-be seniors, however, were livid. The lawn we'd gazed longingly at for three long years as our own private paradise was now to be shared by all? Outrageous! Senior portraits to be lost in a sea of lowerclassmen? What was she thinking?

My classmates rallied behind me and I was confident they could sway enough underclassmen to vote my way. Each day I got reports of a few more freshmen and sophomores seeing the light, however distant, of senior perks.

On election day, I felt fairly confident. I was even looking forward to quitting my job and focusing on school politics. The vote was to take place during homeroom but before any ballots were distributed, the principal's voiced boomed from the PA system.

"A special congratulation goes out to Debbie Hart who put our school on the map with her outstanding science fair project."

My head began to throb as I tuned out additional details the principal just had to share about the honor and glory this one science project had heaped upon our school. The details grew fuzzy but I got the feeling that Debbie's entry was equivalent to the invention of penicillin or the polio vaccine.

At the merciful end of the principal's tribute, the ballots were, at long last, passed out. I knew my peers would not be swayed by the announcement, but what about the rest of the school?

By the end of the day, the votes were counted and Debbie was declared the winner. A friend who helped with the counting let me know I'd lost by only twenty votes. Almost winning felt just like losing... actually it WAS losing... and I got depressed. All I'd been hearing for the past few weeks prepared me for the thrill of victory, not the agony of defeat.

Avoiding my group of friends, I sat on the steps that led to the Senior Lawn. Just staring at what would soon be shared space, I didn't notice Mr. Laskey, the cool young teacher with long hair and a beard. He sat down beside me sharing my view of the grass.

Turning to me, he smiled. "Congratulations!"

"No, I didn't win," I replied.

"Yes, you did. You won the time and freedom to do whatever you want next year." He went on to tell me he'd lost an election in high school too and it was the best thing that ever happened to him.

Honestly, I thought Mr. Laskey was nuts at the time. I didn't want to hurt his feelings though, so I didn't argue with him. What I didn't realize then was how wise he truly was.

Debbie's campaign promises came to fruition in September with the renaming of the Senior Lawn to the People's Lawn. Once the underclassmen invaded, my class of seniors lost all interest in eating there. When our yearbook came out in the spring, the only thing that set a senior apart from a freshman was what the seniors wore for their portraits. Size and placement mattered to us and there was a chorus of complaints about being buried alphabetically amidst students of every grade.

As the proposed changes became reality, I was the recipient of complimentary remarks from my fellow graduating classmates. The message was always a wish that I'd been elected to maintain the senior tradition of being set apart as both special and privileged.

As for me, I kept my job and took nine units at our state college while completing my high school classes with my friends. It took some juggling but I managed to fit everything in, a feat I could not have accomplished with all the extra meetings and activities required of a student body president.

I guess Mr. Laskey knew what he was talking about.

~Marsha Porter

19

Lesson of the Silent Hall

Youth is a wonderful thing. What a crime to waste it on children.
~George Bernard Shaw

I stand in the silent hall,
Almost terrified.
I've stood here for years now
But it's time to go.

Finals are over and done with;
The real world calls.
And I watch ghosts chase each other
And fade into the wall.

I've spent a lifetime here —
It's all I know.
This is where I grew up,
Where I became who I am;
This is my world,
This school ground —
These buildings that I love to hate
Are my second home.

But now I am grown.

I see children running,
Running past me and fading to mist.
Oh, I wish childhood was not like that.
I want to grab hold of innocence
And bring it back.
Let me return to kindergarten —
Is that too much to ask?

I stand alone in the hall,
Alone but for memories.
Class has started but not for me.
Am I now an interloper,
Not knowing my place?

But I was here first,
Thirteen years ago.

And now the end has come.
Where did time go?
Just yesterday I was a little girl
And now I'm a woman grown.
I can't curl up in Momma's lap
And Daddy can't throw me high —
And is it almost time to say goodbye?

I see kids running towards me.
Is it us, who we were, back at the beginning?
So happy, with childlike faith,
The belief that nothing could happen to me.
But I know the truth,
Standing here in the silent hall.
I've grown and learned
The real world waits for us all.

And I turn, a sad smile on my face,

Watching who we were race back through time.
I slowly go down the stairs, leaving for good,
One last time.
Someone else can have the silent hall
Because I am gone.

I'm gone from that world;
Time for something new.
I learned all I could
And the halls have nothing else to say to me.

~Laura Williams

Just for
Teenagers

101 Stories of Inspiration
and Support for Teens

Chapter
3

Liking Yourself

*It's not who you are that holds you back,
it's who you think you're not.*

~Author Unknown

20

Bald and Beautiful

*Be who you are and say what you feel, because those who mind
don't matter and those who matter don't mind.*

~Dr. Seuss

"**H**ey!" Mom's startled exclamation stopped me cold. "You have a bald spot on the back of your head!" She came over to take a closer look. "It's about the size of a quarter," she continued in a worried voice, peering into my hair.

I tried to shrug it off. It was probably just some weird fluke. "It'll grow back." I worked to sound nonchalant and confident. I was seventeen.

At first, the loss was minimal. I checked the spot with my fingers every day. No new hair, smooth as an egg. A few weeks later, I realized that the spot was a little larger, and there was still no sign of any bristles poking through the scalp. I began to worry, but continued to try and be cool about it.

It only took a couple of months for me to wake up in the morning and find hairs all over my pillow. I was devastated. I'd always wanted long hair as a child, but had always had to keep it short. Now that I was a teenager, I was finally allowed to grow my hair. And it was all falling out.

As the days went by, my hair started to fall out faster and in larger quantities. Brushing my hair or running my fingers through it would dislodge an alarming amount. I would stare at the tufts in my hands, analyzing how much I'd pulled out this time. Willing this to not be happening to me.

I began using my remaining hair as a cover for the bald areas, maneuvering it to hide my scalp and clipping it into place. When I went to a dance with some friends, a guy who had a crush on me (and who didn't know my secret) commented that the way my hair was clipped, it almost looked like I had a bald spot. I nearly hyperventilated.

I felt like an utter freak of nature.

Finally, I no longer had enough hair to fully cover the smooth areas. It was time to look at getting a wig. We went for the more expensive ones. Beautifully made, but hot and sometimes very itchy. At that point I still had some hair above my ears so I slicked it back and clipped it to the wig's hairs, trying to make the hairpiece look as natural as possible.

We went to see a dermatologist, who diagnosed my condition as alopecia. He recommended a cortisone injection to try to make the hair grow back. The injection would be administered to the head. We agreed to the treatment, and I underwent about six injections over a period of a few months. Each syringe was administered to several different areas, so that, in the course of one injection, the needle would slide into the scalp three to five times. They gave me a numbing cream after the first two sessions, but it didn't help much.

The cortisone began to double my monthly menstrual cycle, and we finally had to stop the procedure. My hair still didn't grow back.

I was a really, really shy kid. I didn't have many friends growing up, because I wouldn't talk to anyone. When I started high school, it was a chance to start over. I forced myself to be friendly and approach people.

I made a lot of friends in the first two years. My hair started to fall out in the third year. As the bald patches on my head became larger, I started worrying about the social implications. Even if I wore a wig, what if it slipped one day? I realized that I would have to let at least some of my friends know what was going on. I was scared to tell them, because I didn't know how they would handle the information.

What if they thought I was a freak, too, and didn't want to be my friends anymore? Slowly, hesitantly, I told them what was happening. To my surprise, they all seemed to take it in stride, even the boys. This was a miracle for me.

I came to realize that what had happened was not my fault, and not something I should feel ashamed of. I learned (and am still learning) that I should not let this condition have any impact on my sense of self-worth. Being bald doesn't change who I am, and if I don't let it affect my self-acceptance then other people are much more likely to accept me as I am, too.

There are still times when I look at someone's hair and ache a little for not having any. Once in a while I'll look in the mirror and feel a little down. These times are becoming fewer and farther between.

I am bald, and I am beautiful.

~Monica C. Webster

21

Bigger than My Body

It took me a long time not to judge myself through someone else's eyes.
~Sally Field

I have always been a big girl. I am comfortable with my body but there is a price to pay for being different.

In primary school, I was an enthusiastic gymnast and was actually team captain in my final year. I was not brilliant and had to make up for my inadequacies by hours and hours of extra practice. Long after the other girls had left I would still be in the school hall going over every routine. It took months to master the clubs and in the early days, I always managed to get my ribbon in a terrible knot. However, I persevered and I improved so much so that in 2002 I was in the Zimbabwe National Gymnastics Championships Final.

Whenever I went up in a competition, I always got the sense that the crowd did not expect much from the overweight child before them. The crowd never expected the little hippo bursting out of her leotard to have the talent, grace or control required to be a rhythmic gymnast. This crowd was no different. They commented loudly about my weight. One man even said, "That is the ugliest leotard I have ever seen and the elephant inside it isn't much better!"

I was mortified. As I tried to blink away the tears, I wanted to tell the man the reason I was wearing a leotard that resembled elephant hide was that I could not find any other in my size. Pretty does not come in extra-large. Instead I let my ribbon do the talking. I had worked particularly hard on my ribbon work and it showed. On the first beat I knew it was going to be great. The notes seemed to twirl along with the ribbon. I was gliding on the music, each crescendo echoing the exaltation in my heart as I executed the moves. Soon the sniggers of the crowd turned to cheers. As I went into that last split leap and cascaded the ribbon in a waterfall entering my final pose, the crowd went quiet. My ribbon ceased to flutter and all was still. Then the crowd erupted. I turned to face them and found each one on their feet, applauding. It was incredible.

I was crowned National Champion that year, but that was not the best thing I got from hours of grueling practice. The best thing was the knowledge that my body does not dictate what I am capable of. Society seems to assume that all overweight people are unhappy with their weight and have low self-esteem, so they never amount to much. I do not believe that. My body does not define who I am and should never limit what I can do.

I know that I can achieve anything I put my mind to because I am bigger than my body. Who wants to be normal anyway?

~Chido Muchemwa

The Bikini

Never violate the sacredness of your individual self-respect.
~Theodore Parker

Summer was just around the corner and I was going through a really self-conscious stage. I wanted to wear a great bikini and look great in it, so I asked my boyfriend Jack to go shopping with me to pick one out. He was always really helpful, telling me what looked good and what didn't.

At the mall I picked out several bikinis and retreated to the changing room. I emerged a few minutes later wearing a little black bikini. I really liked it.

But Jack wasn't so sure. I could tell by the look on his face he didn't like it so I tried on several more. But each time I came out of the changing room he had the same disapproving look on his face.

"You don't like any of them?" I asked.

He hesitated a moment. "I just think you should lose a few pounds if you want to wear a bikini."

I was depressed. I felt really fat. I put all the suits back and left without buying any of them. On the drive home Jack had a suggestion for me.

"I bet if you went to the gym and worked out for a few weeks you'd look great in a bikini."

I figured he was right. So the next day I found a gym near my house and walked in, ready to sign up, ready to do anything to look good in a bikini. I wanted Jack to be proud of how I looked when we hung out at the beach.

A really cute guy my age walked up to the front desk. "Can I help you?" He was adorable. I could tell he worked out, but he wasn't too beefy.

"I want to join the gym. I need to lose a few pounds so I can wear a bikini this summer," I explained, a little nervous about telling him why.

"You think you need to lose weight to wear a bikini?" he asked, surprised.

"Yeah. My boyfriend thinks if I work out for a few weeks I'll look better."

He just looked at me for a moment, then shook my hand. "I'm Brian."

"I'm Christine."

"Nice to meet you," he said. He smiled at me. I felt a tingle go down my spine.

For the next few weeks I went almost every day to the gym. Brian showed me how to use all the machines. Even though I was feeling more toned and happier about how I looked, I realized something. I wasn't doing it for Jack. And Brian was right. I didn't need to lose any weight.

A funny thing happened during those few weeks. Brian and I became great friends, and when I broke up with Jack for making me feel bad about myself, Brian and I began dating. He never once told me I needed to lose weight. He just supported what I wanted. Most importantly, he liked me just the way I was when I first walked into the gym.

~Christine Dixon

Clear Vision

I've never seen a smiling face that was not beautiful.
~*Author Unknown*

s a child, I distinctly remember watching the PBS cartoon character Arthur get glasses; the poor aardvark was then ridiculed, shamed, and teased by his peers. I silently thanked God for my good eyesight—but I spoke too soon.

When I entered the sixth grade, I could no longer decipher writing on the whiteboard or overhead. So, I received my first pair of glasses. I only wore them in the classroom, and didn't mind them too much. I was at the age of innocence when stuffed animals still had personalities and books were a girl's best friends. Self-image was not important.

My freshman year in high school, I began to miss basketball shots in games—more so than usual. My eyes were re-examined, and the doctor determined that my eyesight had become worse. I would either have to wear glasses full time, or try contact lenses. Being the avid athlete I was, I bypassed the nuisance of glasses and began to wear contacts. My entire world was transformed. Trees actually had leaves. The faces around me radiated individual expressions. And I could see the basket a whole lot better now. I was overjoyed with my newfound sight—and appearance.

When my junior year came along, I began to have trouble with my right eye. Once in a while, my right contact would irritate me, almost to the point where it was unbearable. It would take me thirty minutes just to get the lenses in comfortably, and I always ran the risk of the lenses bothering me later in the day. Determined to wear them and see clearly without the obstruction of glasses, I endured the discomfort. But the pain only got worse.

It got to the point where whenever I wore my contacts, my right eye would flare up with an intolerable, stabbing pain, forcing me to take the lens out. It was physically impossible to wear them. I would be in the optometrist's office at least three times a month, trying to solve the inexplicable mystery of the problem with my eyes. I was beginning to get frustrated. I didn't mind wearing my glasses to see the board in school, but all the time? At football games? At dances? On dates? No. That was not okay with me. I hoped and prayed the doctor would find the problem soon. That hope was soon crushed.

Finally, after another marathon of optometrist visits, my doctor declared me a medical anomaly. He found nothing wrong with my eyes, and had tried countless medications, ointments, and drops to ease my pain. Nothing had worked, and there was nothing left to try. He advised that I wear my glasses full time. I was not just disappointed; I was devastated. I had spent a year of my life steadfastly trying to cure my eye problem. And now the doctor was saying it was incurable? I could not believe it.

I despised my glasses. Whenever someone walked up to me, I would immediately rip the glasses off my face, self-conscious about the ugly obstruction covering my eyes. My self-confidence plummeted. I hated the way I looked in them, despite my friends' compliments. I hated the way my glasses fogged up in the cold, or how they were pushed crooked whenever someone gave me a hug. I felt worthless in them. So, I began to wear my glasses as little as possible. I accepted the consequential headaches, squinting, and loss of sight. My self-image was too important. I struggled with this internal war for a year, but eventually, I came to terms with the fact that I had to wear glasses. I still felt worthless, but I did it anyway.

The summer entering my senior year, I volunteered for my second consecutive year at a church camp called Camp RAD, hosted by the Diocese of Santa Rosa in California. One of the other leaders in my small group, Anne, also wore glasses. Anne was kind, spiritual, fun and full of wisdom; she didn't let wearing glasses get in the way of her outer — and inner — beauty. That epiphany made me feel a little better, and my confidence began to grow. Later that week, during a session of affirmations, one of the middle school campers sat me down and told me I was the prettiest girl she had ever seen, and how much I had changed her faith for the better. It hit me then that it wasn't my friends or my peers at school who were ridiculing me. I was the one passing judgment on myself. I was allowing my glasses to hold me back from the confident, happy person others perceived me to be. I needed to start looking at myself differently, and realized that I was only as beautiful as I believed myself to be.

I learned to be comfortable in my own skin, no matter what — and I can see clearly now.

~Gabriella Carroll

24

You Know She's a Dancer

It is not the mountain we conquer but ourselves.
~Edmund Hillary

With the grace of a dancer,
So tiny and small.
Pushing herself,
Trying not to fall.

Turns, smiles, pointed toes and tears,
Leaping gracefully throughout the years.
Trying to keep perfect form,
She dances on through the storm.

Putting on a bright smile for the stage,
She learned at such an early age.
She impresses the audience with her talent and poise,
But she's really just trying to block out the noise.

Cake or candy she dares not touch.
She knows one piece is far too much.

To fit in her pretty little leotard and baby pink tights,
No one knows how hard she fights.
She sighs and tells herself that this is right,

Always striving for the perfect weight and height.

She tries not to laugh when she hears someone say,
That they would trade places with her any day,
Because she sometimes thinks she'd give anything to dance
Away from this blur, this life so insecure.

Always asked about her hopes and her dreams,
She silently answers, "To be heard and not seen."

She accepts it all, her lifelong fight,
But she can't help praying every night,
"Please let me see the graceful girl everyone else can see;
The mirrors seem to be hiding her from me."

She builds up hope that her wishes, prayers, and dreams will
        come true someday.
And in the meantime, she'll continue dancing the days away.

~Jennie Hartstein

25

The Catch

The only sure thing about luck is that it will change.
~Wilson Mizner

Thoughts of fear and failure were going through my mind as I stood in right field staring at the plate. I just stood there, hoping that the ball would not get hit anywhere near me. Winning the game wasn't even that important to me at the time—I just did not want to be the one to lose the championship for the team.

Unfortunately, the only goal I ever had playing baseball was not to make an idiot out of myself. After all, baseball was not really my sport, I never really liked it, and I just played it because I felt like I had to. My confidence was low. I was a physically underdeveloped fourteen-year-old playing baseball with kids a few years older than me. I was a timid kid who was often the victim of bullying by my peers and consequently I had very, very low self-esteem. My playing right field did not help my confidence. In little league it is a well-known fact that the weaker and less skilled players get put in right field, simply because the ball gets hit there the least.

My team was playing in the league championship game. We did not have a very successful regular season, but somehow we squeaked into the playoffs and started winning games. And at this moment, my team was one out away from being league champions. Even more surprising to me was that my coach still had me in the game at such a crucial moment instead of on the bench. The other team's big hitter was up and this batter had already crushed several big hits in this game. The count was one strike and two balls. To make the situation even more gut-wrenching, the bases were loaded, my team was up by only one run, and there were two outs.

The pitcher delivered the pitch and with a loud "crack" the ball began to sail towards me in a hard, line-drive fashion. The other team's fans began to cheer and scream loudly. I instantly began to backpedal faster than I ever thought possible, thinking that I was at least going to make it look like I tried. Then, as the ball sailed over my head, I leaped up as high as I could with my glove open, just hoping by some miracle that the ball would find its way in. A split second later, I heard this big sigh from the cheering fans and I thought that something had landed softly in my glove, but I was unsure if I was just imagining it. I stayed on my feet as I landed and just about cried when I looked into my glove. Sure enough there was a shiny white baseball in it and my team had won the championship. As I was jogging back to the dugout, I gave the umpire the ball back and he gave me this look of disbelief. Shortly after, our pitcher, who had oftentimes made fun of me, ran up to me with a look of relief, hugged me, and said, "Thanks for saving my butt."

To this day I will always believe that God sent an angel down to lift me up in the air to make that catch. I felt better than Aaron Rogers winning the Super Bowl, or Tiger Woods winning the U.S. Open, after making that catch. Even though I would go on to win more trophies in different activities, the trophy from that season means the most to me. It reminds of the day that a little underdeveloped fourteen-year-old boy was the hero of the season.

~Ben Mueller

26

Food Should Be Fun

You do it with your own two hands, so there's a sense of pride.
You really do forget all our problems, because you're focusing on the food.
~Rachael Ray

I am not your average seventeen-year-old. This is epitomized by the Christmas gifts I got this year. In addition to the usual teenage girl stuff (a Katy Perry CD, jewelry, really cute mittens), I also got a stainless steel skillet, a square griddle, a ten-speed hand mixer, a baking spatula, and rubber prep bowls. And they thrilled me to no end. As you can tell, I love to cook.

Sitting here now, I smile as I think about the day before that Christmas. On that Christmas Eve, I spent hours in the kitchen, up to my elbows in flour and sugar. I scooped peanut-butter cookie dough onto baking sheets, then popped a Hershey's Kiss in their center right when they came out of the oven. I used a wooden spoon to roll out the sugar cookie dough I had prepped the night before and cut out cute little snowmen and stars, before rubbing them with egg wash and sprinkles and placing them in the oven. Later that night, I sautéed a handful of chopped onion in butter before adding spinach, artichokes, and cheese to the pan to make the most delicious dip ever. I loved every second in that kitchen, my nose filling with warm aromas and my ears attuned to the sizzle of vegetables. Cooking is pure bliss.

A little more than a year ago, I would never have said that cooking was anything other than a danger to be avoided. But I have grown a lot since then.

You see, after Christmas when I was fifteen, I made a New Year's resolution to lose weight. It started out innocently enough. I cut out chocolate milk and juice in favor of water, and scaled down my portions. I already loved running and was a member of a gym, but I kicked my workouts up a notch. I began to lose weight slowly but steadily. I was pleased with the results but wanted my ideal body to come more rapidly.

I should have seen that coming. I am, and probably always will be, a perfectionist. I do not like to settle for being in the middle or doing "well." To be the best, the brightest, the fastest, and now, the skinniest—I jump into projects full force to obtain my goal.

Calories became my obsession. The calories I ate, the calories I burned. It seemed logical to me that I should attempt to burn off every calorie I ate. So I stuck to a strict 1200-calorie-a-day diet (which in reality amounted to probably less than 1000), and burned over 800 calories a day in cardio. I hoped the remaining 400 would be burned from forty-five minutes of full-body strength training.

I panicked if my diet changed even a little. I remember one time when my mother, trying to coax me into being less anxious about food, made me a baked potato with grilled chicken and steamed broccoli. I could not finish it. How was I supposed to know how many calories were in it? Most of my diet was centered on frozen meals and packaged foods that had very precise serving sizes and calories. This plate of food was sheer madness!

Oddly enough, it was during this time that I began to watch cooking shows. My thought was if I could not enjoy the taste of food, at least I could enjoy the sight of it. So Rachael Ray, Giada De Laurentiis, and Bobby Flay became my regular viewing buddies.

I really think I can attribute a good portion of my recovery to those cooking shows. The hosts had such a light and passion in their eyes when they talked about this meat they were searing, or how wonderful the crusty bread would taste when spread with this tangy sauce. Rachael Ray was particularly influential. She was always smiling! I'll never forget something she said on one episode—with great sincerity, she insisted to the camera: "Food should be fun!"

Wait a second. How could food be fun? Food made you fat. Food was very scary.

But gradually, that message began to sink in. Maybe my thoughts about food were skewed.

Other factors played into this realization as well. I was called down to the nurse because my teachers were worried about my rapid weight loss. I got into fights with my mother over the state of my body. I began to have panic attacks when I could not go to the gym. My best friend showed me a text conversation she had had with another one of my friends about how I looked like a skeleton.

Then, slowly but steadily, I began to catch on. I realized that I was hurting my body. I had no period, I had trouble sleeping and, worst of all, I was causing my family and friends anxiety. It took some time, a lot of support from my loved ones, and therapy, but I finally accepted the idea that I needed to gain back some weight.

I also began to put some techniques I learned from my cooking shows into practice. Not necessarily cooking techniques at first, but how the hosts savored and appreciated the food in front of them. Enjoying every bite, appreciating a food's texture and taste, really brought home the idea that food was a good thing. Then I could put the actual cooking techniques into practice.

For what I believe is the first time in my life, I have achieved a healthy balance. I still love to run and work out, but now, if I have a very active day, I know I need to eat more. I eat very healthily, but I do not count calories as much. I recognize that I need to put nutritious food into my body, but I also know that the occasional pizza and the more-than-occasional piece of chocolate will not hurt me.

Now, I am hungry. I think I will make an egg white frittata with any vegetables I can find, and serve it alongside a freshly sliced tomato and a healthy scoop of salsa. Yum!

~Fallon Kane

27

Building Me

Make the most of yourself, for that is all there is of you.
~Ralph Waldo Emerson

Growing up and moving on,
As the years fly by so fast.
Living life and looking back,
On all the things now in the past.

Planning ahead and making decisions,
As I find my own way.
Gaining respect and earning trust,
As I mature more each day.

Trying hard and persevering,
To make my family proud.
Standing strong and staying true,
While others follow the crowd.

Making memories and having fun,
While I enjoy life's many pleasures.
Building blocks and paving paths,
As I discover new treasures.

Taking steps and learning more,
Of what my life can be.
Falling down and getting up,
As I build a better me.

~Janell C. Evans

28

The Beauty of Self-Esteem

Always act like you're wearing an invisible crown.
~Author Unknown

There comes a point in every girl's life when her fragile self-esteem is dropped—no, hurled—from a twenty-six-story building and smashed on the unyielding cement below.

It happened on a Monday, as dreadful things often do. My friend Petra Green and I were sitting with our mothers in the Civic Center, awaiting the start of the Novi Youth Assistance award ceremony. I looked out of place among the immaculately groomed guests, dressed as I was in faded jeans and an old blue shirt, my hair pulled into a haphazard bun. Ratty sneakers weathered by almost 500 miles of running adorned my feet. They looked like twin beggars next to Petra's sequined designer flats. Petra and I were like fire and ice, diamonds and coal. I was an inferior rock to her flawless diamond, and it never failed to confound me that Petra, with her perfect hair and tasteful outfits, would associate with the likes of me.

As I surveyed the crowd of impeccably dressed award recipients, I balanced my chair on its back legs, glanced down at my own outfit, and shrugged, almost tipping my chair over in the process. Instead of casting my eyes downward, I let out a loud, unladylike guffaw. A tiny line creased Mrs. Green's forehead. Her silver earrings clinked as she leaned toward my mother.

"I envy you, Linda," she whispered loudly. "My Petra is glued to her mirror every morning, meticulously curling her hair and applying her lip gloss. But your daughter..." She paused to give my sloppy outfit a perusal, her eyebrows raised in two haughty arches. "Truly Linda—you have it so easy! Oh, to have a daughter who doesn't care about her appearance...." Mrs. Green trailed off as her gaze lingered on my scuffed shoes.

My eyes, stinging as if I had poured a gallon of shampoo in them, were also fixed on my beat-up sneakers. My cheeks burned bright crimson as the veiled insult sank in. Out of the corner of my eye, I saw Petra shoot me an apologetic look. I tried to muster a smile, but it wavered on my lips before dying a quick death. My self-esteem had splattered painfully on the pavement.

For the rest of the ceremony, I sullenly kicked the toe of my sneaker against the chair leg. Each time my toe connected with the metal, I became agonizingly aware of every one of my shortcomings. I was a tomboy, a slacker when it came to fashion, an undiscovered contestant for a makeover show. I was guilty of throwing on old cross-country T-shirts and frayed track sweats while most of the female population primped in front of their mirrors. I wore the same pair of battered sneakers year-round, my hair was perpetually frozen in a ponytail, and the only "make-up" I owned was ChapStick. My failings did not stop there, however. I laughed too loudly. I smiled too much. I put my feet up on far too many tables. And before that fateful Monday, I could not have cared less.

That evening, I sat morosely at my desk, my legs crossed primly at the ankle instead of gracing the tabletop. Parametric equations swam before my eyes as Mrs. Green's jibes ran through my mind. Doesn't care about her appearance... you have it so easy....

I finally threw down my pencil in disgust and pulled on my sweats. Yanking my hair into a ponytail, I stormed outside, avoiding my reflection as I passed the mirror. I had spent sixteen happy years as a shameless tomboy. Hadn't I reveled in the fact that I owned enough sweatshirts to stock a homeless shelter for a year? Didn't I secretly scorn the girls nearly stabbing their eyes out with their mascara wands in the school bathroom?

I dashed into the cold evening, my cheeks welcoming the whipping wind. Rounding the corner, I passed a runner clad in an oversized sweatshirt and baggy sweatpants. Her ponytail bobbed cheerfully as she shot me a smile that lit up her entire face. I was taken aback by how similar it was to the toothy, unladylike grins I was known to give.

I flew down Nine Mile in a bewildered haze, my eyes fixed on my sneakers, dual blurs of gray and red. My gaze traveled to my pant leg, where "RUNNER" was proudly emblazoned, and finally rested on my sweatshirt, big and loose and utterly comfortable. And then, on an otherwise uneventful Monday evening, smack dab in the middle of Nine Mile at precisely 8:52 p.m., I came to a momentous realization: this was me. This sweatshirt-clad, sneaker-wearing girl who broke into inelegant smiles that took up half her face was truly and unquestionably me.

When I returned home, I did not avoid the mirror. Instead, I stared unflinchingly into it. As I noted my flushed cheeks and sparkling eyes, I realized that there was no point in slathering eye shadow onto my eyelids or smearing blush onto my cheeks. I would not become a wax doll with painted eyes and a thin, strained smile. I would be a living, laughing human being. I would break into toothy smiles that were horrifyingly wide and I would laugh from the depths of my soul. I am what I am—a ponytail-sporting, ChapStick-wearing tomboy—and I do not need to mold myself into someone I am not just to appease the rest of the world.

Self-esteem may be one of the most fragile things on Earth, but it is also one of the most resilient. No matter how many stories it falls—one, two, twenty-six, or a thousand—it has an incredible ability to dust itself off and walk away stronger than ever.

~Lucia Chen

Dear Ex

Never be bullied into silence. Never allow yourself to be made a victim.
Accept no one's definition of your life; define yourself.
~Harvey Fierstein

I am writing this to you because I am officially exhausted by you, and I want to start putting myself back together again. You single-handedly turned me into a crazy person.

I actively avoid you. I cringe when we have to interact and you pretend like nothing is wrong. Maybe you don't know this, but what you have put me through over the past two months has destroyed over two years of work on my part to believe that I am worth more than what some boy will think of me.

Just think! With little to no effort at all on your part, you have reminded me of all of my own insecurities and fears.

Are you proud to have used me, and then discarded me? Do you grin just a little bit to see me clenching my fists and staring blankly as I stand in the corner at parties we're both attending?

I met a new guy in class the other day. As the bell rang and we said goodbye, I almost finished thinking the words, "Well... I'm not good enough for him anyway" to myself before I realized what an incorrect statement that was.

You did this to me. Bravo, sir.

You should know that many of your friends have read this—let me rephrase that—many of the people that you think are your friends. Also, most of the girls you have systematically destroyed have also read this. I have shared it freely with almost everyone I thought would care. Everyone except you.

I didn't do this to brag about how fashionably tragic my love life was. I could care less about my reputation within the walls of this school. Perhaps that was already obvious, because becoming involved with you was social suicide. Really, the purpose of these words is to make you feel as insignificant as you have made me feel with every empty promise, ignored phone call, or lie that you've told me.

I would like to think that this letter has, in part, actually helped me to get over you. I also hope that other girls see this as a cautionary tale about a boy who can neither be fixed nor understood. I am sad that you have fallen so short of my expectations for you. I really thought that beneath your insecurities and faults, I would find a true friend. I'm sorry that I couldn't be the simple, uncomplicated, empty shell of a girl that you wanted me to be.

Somewhere, there is a guy who will want me. All of me. Unconditionally, and fearlessly.

I hope that you take my words to heart. I chose them carefully.

~Lia Peros

Sweaty, Red-Faced, and Beautiful

Anyone who ever gave you confidence, you owe them a lot.
~Truman Capote

Sweaty, yet happy, I walk off the court, grab my volleyball bag and stumble over to my mom. "Good Game, Reg!" she says with a smile. I feel anything but thrilled. I am a small setter who did some not-so-great passing tonight, and you can see that on my face. All red with a sweaty shine. But we won, and that's all that really matters.

What the crowds in the stands don't know is that I made the varsity team during my first year of high school. Shocking? Yep, I think so. But what they also can't see is the loneliness it brings. All my friends are on junior varsity, which leaves me with all the twelfth graders.

My mom and I begin walking out the gym door and into the hallway. My team is spread throughout this hall, on their way to the outside world.

As I recap the game with Mom, I hold the door open for a boy. Not particularly noticeable, but semi-cute, curly blond hair, with a skater boy look.

He says thanks, and then something that I don't really catch.

"What was that?" Mom asks the guy.

"Could I talk to you alone?" He is looking directly at me.

My heart starts to pound and my breath quickens just a teeny bit.

Mom and I look at each other for about an eternity of two seconds.

Be cool, Reg, be cool. "Sure," I say, feeling like I already blew it.

Mom walks away and the boy slides his hands in his pockets and looks at me, directly into my eyes. Be still, my heart.

"Hey, good game," he starts. I am wondering how I should play this. Flirty? Coy? Sweet? I really don't know though. This has never happened to me before.

I manage a thanks and he says, "Uh, can I get your number?" He flips out his cell phone. And I am sure my eyes pop to unrealistic sizes.

My heart beats harder and random thoughts go flying through my head. I am trying not to make a big deal out of this, but failing miserably. What should I say?

"No," I say. That's it? Just no? "Sorry, dude," I continue.

Dude? Really?

A flash of something crosses his face—pain, embarrassment, maybe genuine sadness? I smile a bit and shake my head. One part of me is feeling embarrassed for my pathetic word choice, the other is feeling a little bad for the guy.

"Okay. See ya," he says.

"Bye."

I find myself walking outside. It is over. The very first boy to ask for my number... and I said no.

What was his name? Why did he ask me? Of all the beautiful girls on the team, he picks the red-faced, sweaty, short girl? Oh and why did I say no?

I am left to wonder.

Part of me thinks it's a scam, just a big joke to him and his friends and they thought I'd be dumb enough to fall for it. But the other part thinks that maybe he saw something in me.

Either way, I walk with a smile on my face, my heart feeling kind of warm. In some ways, he was the first to really tell me that I'm beautiful. That I have value, that some guys may actually want my number. And just out of the blue, during one of my less-than-perfect moments. He didn't even know me.

I look back but find the hall empty.

But what did he see? I know what he saw. He saw what God sees, and that is beauty. I am beautiful, and this boy saw it.

I smile at this thought and walk out into the darkness.

So thank you, boy whose name I will never know. Thank you for the realization that I am beautiful, thank you for putting yourself out there, not knowing how much it would make me smile.

~R. Kooyman

Just for Teenagers

101 Stories of Inspiration and Support for Teens

Chapter
4

Love and Relationships

Love—a wildly misunderstood although highly desirable malfunction of the heart which weakens the brain, causes eyes to sparkle, cheeks to glow, blood pressure to rise and the lips to pucker.

~Author Unknown

31

Sissy

I'm so in love, every time I look at you my soul gets dizzy.
~Jaesse Tyler

I was a pretty normal teenage boy, just a lot more quiet and independent than other students in my school. I didn't find a lot of friends I liked, or girls who stood out to me. But that all changed when a new student was introduced to our class one day. Her name was Sissy.

Sissy was a beautiful girl with lily-white flawless skin. Her auburn hair shone with brown highlights. She had big, innocent blue eyes that sparkled in the light. Unlike all of the other girls in my class, she didn't wear make-up. All of her beauty was purely natural.

"Class, this is Sissy. She came all the way from Russia and is happy to be here at our school," Mr. Fisher, our English teacher announced. "Why don't you go sit in that empty seat in front of Jonathan?"

My heart raced. She was going to sit near me? Sissy smiled and sat down. Her teeth were a bright, pearly white. After the teacher discussed the terms and schedule with Sissy, he went on with the class. I noticed that Sissy had a light Russian accent. Her voice was just beautiful. As Mr. Fisher went on talking about the biography of Shakespeare, all I could look at was Sissy's hair in front of me. It smelled like fresh sunflower petals. I couldn't tell if five or sixty minutes went by when the bell rang. I was in a daze.

All of the twenty-five students got up and raced out of the class, but Sissy was the last one to leave. I was sure she had a boyfriend already. What guy wouldn't grab her the second he saw her? She had only been in the building for thirty minutes and she was already my dream girl. The way she smiled made nothing else in the world matter.

After English class was over, I met up with my friend Mark in Science. Class began, and I sat there daydreaming about her once more. Mark pushed me by the shoulder.

"Hey, are you alright?" he asked.

"Oh, huh?" I said, startled. "Yeah, I'm alright. I was just... nothing. Let's start the assignment."

Mark looked at me in a puzzled way. "Jonathan, Science is over. It's time to go to lunch."

"What?" I asked. "But we just got here!" I looked up at the clock. It was 11:35. Class was definitely over.

As I walked to my locker to put away my books, what I saw next shocked me. Sissy was walking alone in the hall with her head tilted to the floor, her tote bag dragging. She looked so depressed.

Later, in the cafeteria, I noticed that Sissy was not eating and she was sitting alone at a table writing in a journal. I finally got up the courage to approach her. When I went up to her, I thought she would move or not notice me. But she looked up at me with her innocent eyes.

"Hi," she said. "You were the boy I sat in front of this morning, right?" I nodded. I finally got my voice back. "Yeah, I'm Jonathan. I noticed you were sitting alone and... I was just wondering if I could sit here. I don't have much of a group to sit with either," I said. She told me that would be fine as she flashed her blinding smile.

Minutes seemed like hours as we talked about everything. She told me about Russia and how she was nervous to come here to America to live. It seemed like we were long lost friends. When she told me she had never had a boyfriend, I was struck in the head. I had never had a girlfriend. To make it casual, I started another conversation before bringing up the school spring dance. "My friends will be there. Would you like to go with me and them?" I asked. Her lips opened slightly, as if she couldn't believe someone was asking her.

"I'd love to," she whispered. The bell rang. I told Sissy that I would see her in three days at the dance.

Three days passed. The night had arrived. I cleared my anxious mind and looked at the clock. It was 7:30 p.m. I looked in the mirror. I wore a black short-sleeved dress shirt, and had in my contact lenses. I combed back my brown hair with my hands. I still couldn't quite absorb the fact that I was taking the most beautiful, kindhearted girl in my entire middle school to the dance.

After my father drove me to the dance, I met my friends inside. Most of the girls were wearing skirts and had their hair perfectly in place. But they were nothing compared to Sissy. I sat down with Mark and some other classmates.

"So who is your date, Jon?" the guys asked. I paused before answering.

"Sissy."

They all widened their eyes. "Whoa. She is one pretty girl," they all said. Just then, the double doors opened. And Sissy walked in. She was wearing a black and white patterned sleeveless dress. She was even more beautiful that night then when I first saw her. I proudly walked up to her. I told her that she looked amazing. Everyone started to dance in the center of the floor. "Do you want to dance?" I asked her. She hesitated at first, but then she agreed. I led her to the dance floor. Sissy was a little confused about dancing, so I told her where to put her arms and where to step. It began to go smoothly. My heart felt so warm.

"Jonathan?" she whispered.

"Yeah?" I said.

"Thank you."

"What do you mean?" I asked.

"I've always been so lonely. And you showed me how to open up. I know I came here only a few days ago, but it seemed like we've known each other forever." I knew Sissy was lonely the first day I saw her walking the school halls all by herself. Just then a tear rolled down her cheek. She looked up at me.

"I'm sorry... I just..."

Without thinking, I lightly kissed her. What was I doing?! But to my surprise, Sissy didn't draw back. My friends made noises behind us. We both smiled and laughed. Sissy once again revealed her beautiful white smile, and we both had a perfect night.

~Jonathan Diamond

32

Nothing's Sweeter than Summer

You learn to like someone when you find out what makes them laugh, but you can never truly love someone until you find out what makes them cry.
~Author Unknown

I was a summer person, a true believer that good things happened in the summer. It's a season meant for love and happiness and change. It was the season I matured and found myself. It was the season I overcame all my insecurities because someone told me I was beautiful. It was the season I met Tyler. It was the season I fell in love for the first time. It was the season when a boy had my heart and I had his. It was the season that changed my life.

It all began the night *Harry Potter and the Half-Blood Prince* came out. I was working at the local movie theatre saving for a trip out west to visit my brothers. That's the night I met Tyler. All the soon-to-be twelfth grade guys came to my cash before their movie. I was self-conscious to be seen in my work uniform by the popular guys but I made the best of it and tried to play it cool. After all, I was only a soon-to-be tenth grader.

Tyler was the last in his line of friends. I was trying not to seem like a total loser so I attempted to make conversation with him. I asked if he actually liked Harry Potter, to which he laughed and replied, "No, there was just nothing else to do tonight." I smiled at him and said I happened to love Harry Potter and couldn't wait to see the movie. He gave me that perfect smile of his and said, "I'll let you know how it is then."

As promised, he messaged me on Facebook that night and told me the movie sucked. I told him that was impossible. We teased each other back and forth until I went to see it and admitted it wasn't the greatest. We talked all the time after that. We seemed to really click and never ran out of things to say. But of course being the guy he was, he had a reputation for breaking hearts and I didn't want to be just another girl to him. I wanted to be the girl that stole his heart and made him fall in love.

Over time we really began to trust each other. I told him about my troubled childhood with my dad. I told him how it affected me and how to this day it still does affect me, even after the divorce. He told me how his father died and how his mother had a terminal illness. We helped each other through whatever life threw at us and it brought us even closer together. All my friends told me I was wasting my time. "He's never going to change Chels, that's just how he is. He isn't a good guy. He's only going to hurt you...." I won't pretend that we had it easy. I spent countless nights crying over this boy and sometimes it seemed like he didn't care. But I knew that was just the anger speaking and I meant the world to him. The truth was no one seemed to know him like I did. I knew that he was a good person straight to his core, even if he made mistakes sometimes. Just like I knew he never meant to hurt me.

Summer rolled around again and I was in love for the first time. We spent a perfect summer together, learning from each other and falling even more in love every day. Days were spent driving around in his old red pick-up truck with the windows down, my hair flying everywhere, and singing along to whatever was playing. Nights were spent going out for dinner and watching movies. We would cuddle under a nice warm blanket and make popcorn with white cheddar seasoning. I loved his arms around me, and the tender moments when he would kiss my shoulders and softly whisper "I love you" in my ear. I'll never forget the way he smiled around me. Whenever I did something he thought was cute, his face would light up with the most amazing smile in the world. It was a smile that could make any girl fall in love; it was the smile that made me do just that. I gave Tyler my heart with no hesitation or guarantee that he wouldn't hurt it, and he gave me his in return.

There are moments from that summer that I will remember for the rest of my life. I'll always remember lying on the beach with him, looking across the water at the fireworks while he held me in his arms. I'll always remember when he danced with me in his room because we never got to go to prom together. I'll always remember the night with him spent lying in the back of his rusted pick-up truck gazing out at the stars. But most of all, I will always remember the things Tyler taught me. He showed me what a real friend was. He showed me that loving someone with all your heart is never a mistake. He showed me that no matter how impossible it may seem, I should always follow my heart.

We spent our last two weeks together enjoying the end of summer and the end of our time together. The last week was hardest for us, because we knew that our goodbye was coming and it broke our hearts. I had given Tyler a piece of who I was; my heart was his. He was and will always be my first love. We had been through so much together and come so far, it felt wrong to end it. But time couldn't stop for us, no matter how much we wished it would.

The morning he left for university he came to say goodbye to me. With the promise to always stay in touch, he kissed me for the last time. We pulled away from each other reluctantly and said I love you with unsteady voices. With tears slowly sliding down my face I watched him walk away from me, get into his truck and drive away to start a new chapter in his life, taking my heart with him wherever he went.

~Chelsea Murphy

One Lone Tear

Singleness would be recognized as a vital stage of the journey to maturation, a time to learn about who we are, to learn responsibility and self-sufficiency, to identify our true desires, and to confront our inner strengths and demons.
~Harville Hendrix

"**Y**ou're so difficult," Michael grumbled at me. We sat on my couch, aimlessly arguing about what we should do. He wanted to stay in and watch television; he was tired and grumpy. I was excited and energized; I wanted to drive to the beach and look at the stars and hear the waves crashing against the rocks. He was not inspired by my plan, but sick of arguing, he angrily agreed. We walked to the car and drove in hard silence. Some sad melancholy music of love lost played in the background, teasing me, willing me to connect the lyrics to my own strained relationship. Tears wet my cheeks. This night, I knew, would end badly.

Michael and I reached our destination, both of us too stubborn to break the silence. He turned off the car, and we sat. The moon and the stars shone bright; the waves sounded like thunder. I felt no peace. The boy made me crazy. A couple so unhappy amid such a beautiful setting must be headed for failure. He finally turned to look at me. I turned away. For three years, our relationship proved so solid, so easy. I could not fathom what had changed.

I gingerly willed my mouth to speak. "What," I mumbled, "has changed?" He refused to break his silence. Instead he climbed out of the car and opened my door. We stood outside, the smell of the salty sea filling our noses and the California night air surrounding our bodies. I was chilly. He wrapped his arms around me like he did when we were happy. But I sensed a difference.

Michael and I used to be perfect together. We used to have so much fun. We used to laugh together, smile together, love together. We used to discuss everything. We used to bend over backwards to make each other happy. Was it all in the past?

Too cold to stand outside any longer, he headed to the car and motioned me to follow. We drove off into the darkness, and he finally spoke. "Kaylee," he started, his handsome brown eyes filled with pain, "I'm angry. I know I'm harsher with you, and I don't want to be. But I don't know how to change it. I know you don't understand. I don't even understand it myself." He hesitated, nervously fiddling with his strong brown hands. And then he uttered those four little words a woman never wants to hear: "I cheated on you."

My mind raced. I had not even realized that we were parked, that tears were streaming down his face, and that he was staring at me, waiting for a response. For a few moments, I was speechless and out of breath, like the wind had been knocked out of me. When I did not respond, he continued to speak. His words faded away. My mind had gone to another place.

I could not yell. I could not scold. I could not hit. I could not move. His words had arrested me. The sound of the CD player awakened me, and ironically, the sounds of "Emotional Rollercoaster" filled the car. My theme song, I thought, dejectedly. He reached for me. I pushed him away. "Don't touch me," I croaked, not even recognizing my own voice.

One lone tear fell from my eye. He brushed it away. His eyes pierced my soul; his steady gaze frightened me. I love him, I thought. I swallowed and closed my eyes. I love him. Tears flooded my eyes. I could not see straight any longer. I turned away. Frantically, I reached for the handle and shoved the door open. My slow walk turned into a wild, sobbing run. I heard him calling my name, screaming that he loved me and was sorry.

As I approached my house, I wanted to turn around and run

into his arms. Tell him I love him and ask him to make it all better. I wanted to forgive him for hurting me, forget that anything happened, and kiss him. I actually hesitated at my doorstep and almost turned on my heels in pursuit of love. And the easy road—back to him.

Instead, with one dramatic sob, I turned the key, raced upstairs, and collapsed onto my bed. Three years. Three years I loved him. Three years I gave him everything. He was my best friend, my confidant, my love. No one could make me happier, I thought. Until he broke my heart. I buried my face in my pillow.

My phone rang a dozen times. I wanted to talk to him, to hear his voice, to be comforted. Instead I cut it off and threw it on the floor violently.

I tearfully clicked on my computer and impulsively changed my Facebook relationship status to single. Three years ago my girlfriends and I used to throw around the term jovially. It was our right to be wild and have fun. Live life. Now the word made my heart drop into my stomach.

Yet, somehow my heartbreak revealed a strength in me I didn't know I had. I was able to stand tall and confident despite my struggle. It's amazing when you realize that you are not dependent on anyone but yourself. And right now, "single" for me means strong rather than unhappy.

~Kaylee Davis

Awkward Me

A kiss is only a moment, but that moment forever lasts in your heart.
~Author Unknown

When ninth grade came around and I still hadn't had my first real kiss, I was embarrassed. Although my personality was loud, I was shy when it came to boys. I stealthily avoided the topic of boys at sleepovers and when I had to, I flirted like I knew what I was doing. Yeah, I had had boyfriends before, but that was in eighth grade, when holding hands and being extremely awkward around each other qualified as dating. I was that innocent little girl who thought that there was this special secret method to kissing that everyone knew but me. There was something wrong with me, no question about it.

September arrived and I began the boring and annoying daily routine called school. After seven periods of torture I would head to the library for my forty minutes of freedom. I became very close with a small group of guys who shared the same free eighth period as me. Lounging on the sofas, not doing homework, and talking too loud was our specialty. Eighth period was no doubt the highlight of my school day. I had been friends with these guys for years, but one of the guys, let's call him Jordan, I had just met that year. Our personalities meshed well and we became friends very quickly.

Before I knew it, Jordan was working his magic on me. Every eighth period Jordan would subtly flirt with me and I soon found myself blushing at nearly every word. Jordan was older than me and I still hadn't had my first real kiss, which worried me because I was pretty sure he was interested in me. I could only guess how many girls he had kissed already. This anxiety made me even more awkward than normal.

One cold February Saturday morning I woke up to a power outage at my house. A huge snowstorm had hit while I slept, cutting off the power in the town. As I dragged myself out of bed, I looked out my window to see a wintry mess of blinding white. "Great," I thought. "My parents are not going to drive me anywhere. There goes my Saturday." I cursed the snow as I stumbled downstairs. As I ate my breakfast with my family, my mind drifted to Jordan, wondering what he'd be doing on such a snow burdened Saturday.

My thoughts were rudely interrupted by the thunderous sound of my cell phone vibrating on the counter. I jumped up from the kitchen table to check who was calling me, only to see Jordan's name lighting up the screen. My heart skipped a beat. He had never called me before! What could he want? What would I say? My mind flooded with so many thoughts that I almost let the call go to voicemail. Just catching the call on the last ring, I said hello in the least nervous voice I could conjure up (from what I recall I wasn't too successful).

"Hey Erika," I heard his smooth voice say through the phone. "I have practice down the road from your house and I was wondering if you wanted to hang out after."

My heart skipped another beat.

"Yeah I'd love to!" I responded, almost too eagerly.

"Great, I'll pick you up at five. See you later, Erika." As he hung up, his voice saying my name was still ringing in my head.

Jordan was older than me and he had his license. When he picked me up, I felt so cool sitting in his car. As he pulled out of the driveway, he asked me if I wanted to hang out at his house. Of course I said yes, so we headed to the opposite side of the lake. On the way there, the thought occurred to me that Jordan might not have power too, so I suggested he call his mom to check. He thought it was a good idea so he pulled into the parking lot by the steamboats. As he talked to his mom I took a look around outside. It was such a miserable day; no one was out, the street was empty. Suddenly it hit me like a fist to the face that we were alone! My heart started to pound—surprisingly, it was not visible though my chest. I could feel my hands becoming moist. When I heard him say "bye" to his mom I panicked.

"We're still out of power so I think we should go to Queensbury and get something to eat," Jordan suggested.

"Good idea!" I yelped.

"Hah, alright." He laughed. He stopped and smiled at me.

The kiss was coming! I had no clue what to do! While I tried to look calm and well... normal on the outside, I was panicking on the inside! But after a few seconds he broke his gaze, shifted to drive, and pulled away from the curb. I breathed a huge sigh, half of relief, half of disappointment. All I knew was that I had successfully been really awkward (that seemed to be happening a lot). Most likely, the last thing on his mind now was kissing me.

We drove down to Panera to grab a bite to eat. After ordering food, we sat down at a booth across from each other. Joking around and flirting, I finally felt comfortable around him, like we were in eighth period again. And, surprise surprise, I was blushing. Making me blush was clearly not a hard feat to accomplish. As we finished our meals I was bummed because that meant it was unfortunately time to go. Walking out of Panera, I felt something gently brush against my hand and then interlock between my fingers. Before I knew it, Jordan and I were walking to his car holding hands. At that moment, all awkwardness had emptied from my body. When we stepped outside, the sky was dark but full of stars. The only light outside was from the streetlamps lighting up the sidewalk. "This dreary Saturday couldn't have turned out more perfectly," I thought as we stumbled slowly and dreamily to his car. As we passed under the last streetlamp, I felt Jordan's hand stop me from walking any further. Standing under the streetlight, under the starry sky, he pulled me close to him. Finally, my first kiss.

~Erika LaPlante

Love and Wisdom

It was brief, swift, and then it was done. It was a professional job. I needed to be kissed, and I was kissed.

~Uma Thurman

In my early teen years, I was the toughest, most independent, most unromantic girl in school. Boys shrank away from my lashing tongue, and all the girls knew better than to gossip about boys in front of me. To me, love was a symptom of the weak, low-esteemed, and dependent. Because of this, my favorite quote of all time was by Bob Dylan: "You can't be wise and in love at the same time."

Being a critic for my high school's *Viewette* newspaper meant I was often forced into uncomfortable situations. I was ridiculed for my hammering of the local Macaroni Grill restaurant, and glared at by nearly every girl when I slammed the *Twilight* series. Movie reviews were by far my least favorite because it meant bringing along a fellow staff writer with me to discuss our opinions and collaborate. I was a free spirit and hated working with others on reviews, so when I was forced to accompany high school senior Danny Chay to the movie *Valentine's Day*, I almost balked.

I sat next to Danny, uncomfortably alert, feeling as if a surge of electricity was crawling up my feet, through my legs, and all the way up my arms. I'd accompanied boys to movies before, but never to one this... romantic. I was all too aware of Danny's hand on the seat next to mine, and I wanted to squirm away, at least five seats down. Nearby, couples were kissing, making goo-goo eyes at each other, and holding hands. I tried to ignore them, holding my pencil and notepad with a white-knuckled grip, doing my best to concentrate on the movie. Nothing seemed to work. Danny seemed to be perfectly relaxed, his ice-blue eyes staring attentively at the screen. Finally, in the midst of the awkward cinema crowd, I stood up.

"I'm going to get a Coke," I announced, taking a purposeful step towards the exit, planning to run as fast as I could to the parking lot once I got out of sight.

He looked up at me. "What is it?" he asked, his too-blue eyes boring into mine. "Seriously, you've been skittish the whole movie."

"It's just..." I began.

"You're uncomfortable, you can't concentrate on the movie, and you feel out of place?" he asked.

I was about to lie, but then nodded. "Yeah—and I'm sorry, but maybe next time we should watch some other movie—like *Star Trek* or something." I felt my face growing hot as another kissing scene covered the screen. "Really..." I trailed off.

Suddenly, before I knew it, his hand had pulled me into my seat, and he was kissing me straight on the lips. My eyes widened but I made no effort to move, as if in some kind of a trance. When we broke apart he grinned at me, in the darkness of the theater.

"There. Feel less out of place now?" he asked.

Instead I just sat numb, paralyzed by what had just happened. My lips tingled and I reached to touch them tentatively. I'd never expected such a thing to happen, and for some reason, I felt happy and tingly all over—not ashamed, nor angry.

"What was that for?" I asked quietly.

He shrugged as I sat in a daze, too stunned to leave the theater now, too numb to concentrate. Danny returned to staring back at the screen while the events went over and over in my mind. I had just had my first kiss... with a senior two years older than me. I'd never expected it to happen. I was the strong, independent, unromantic, unbeautiful... my thoughts trailed off.

After *Valentine's Day* finished, we walked out of the theater, the stars twinkling brightly.

"Got your notes?" he asked unfazed, holding out his notepad, which was scribbled across.

"My notes?" I asked vaguely, realizing that I had dropped my still-blank notepad when he had kissed me.

"Oh well," he replied. "It wasn't that great a movie anyways."

He tore out the pages of notes and stuffed them in the nearby garbage can. "Besides, it was worth just going there with you."

My heart seemed to soar, despite how hard I tried to hammer it back into reality. I realized that I'd experienced my first taste of love—never mind how small.

As I drove home that night, I recalled my helplessness during the movie, and how I hadn't written one useful note the whole time. I finally understood what the true meaning was behind the quote, "You can't be wise and in love at the same time." Right then, wisdom didn't seem important anymore.

~Christine Catlin

36

Crushed

You may not realize it when it happens,
but a kick in the teeth may be the best thing in the world for you.
~Walt Disney

I watched the seams of a perfect friendship tear apart, the pieces frayed and jagged, never to be sewn back together quite the same. I watched as the boy I knew slowly turned into a stranger, each step widening the gap that had already grown between us. But mostly, I felt the ache in my heart as I watched my best friend walk away from my last attempt to mend things between us.

Charlie was a little odd. Although he was always smiling, or cracking a joke that was so ridiculous it was funny, I always felt he was a bit different than the average high school boy. Charlie had a lovable personality and hordes of adoring friends that made him seem normal, but I always knew something was special about him. He wasn't like his immature friends who treated girls like objects and cheated on math exams. Charlie had a certain vibe that caught my interest, and it was hard for me to ignore my strange fascination with him.

I wanted to see the boy behind the shield of jokes and smiles.

We had a few mutual friends, but we never really crossed paths. It was Jessica who was close to him at first. She'd laugh as we walked to her house and recall all the funny things Charlie texted her; I'd giggle along and secretly wish I had hilarious texts from a guy like him. Charlie wasn't the boyfriend type—girls purely saw him as a friend—but my longing for a guy friend nagged at me until I finally approached him one gym class.

It wasn't awkward starting a conversation with him, considering our mutual friends, and our friendship quickly blossomed. We'd laugh together as he pelted balls at our opponents during dodge ball, and he'd cried with amusement when I tripped over the ball in soccer. Jessica, who was excited about the mutual friendship, began inviting him along whenever we hung out. His jokes and his weirdness always put a smile on my face.

But I should have seen the warning signs. I must have known what was coming, yet I tried to deny it. I tried to brush off the subtle flirty texts he sent me as jokes. I laughed when he suggested we hang out without Jessica. I saw the disaster stretch out ahead of me, and although I knew I was heading for heartbreak I couldn't stop it. I couldn't end the friendship I had built with Charlie. I knew it was selfish, but I needed him. His smile lightened my days and his jokes filled me with joy nobody else could create. Although I wasn't attracted to him physically, I loved him. I just didn't want to know he loved me too.

It was harder to act natural around him after Jessica told me how he felt. I guess he was finally done keeping it a secret. I acted like I didn't know, because I couldn't accept it myself. The friend I had always counted on was now crushing on me? It had to be a phase he was going through. Perhaps a quick lapse in judgment. Soon he'd laugh it off, tell everyone he was joking, and we'd go back to being just friends.

But things began to get worse. Our school's Winter Formal was approaching and everyone was scrambling to find a date. I myself was a little concerned; I had no idea who I was going with. And then it happened. As he stood by my locker and waited for me to retrieve my books for Chemistry, he asked me to the dance.

I didn't know what to say. I really should have been more prepared, considering that everyone told me he was going to ask me. But I'd ignored the thought, laughed it off and plastered a smile over my empty, hollow face. Because the last thing I wanted in this world was to go to Winter Formal with Charlie.

He was my friend. My best friend. And I knew he had feelings for me that I could never reciprocate. To go to Winter Formal with him would only hurt him more when he realized the feelings he felt were not mutual. But I did the worst possible thing I could have done: I said yes.

I made it clear we were going as friends, but the shine in his eyes and the smile on his lips tore my heart out of my chest because I knew how cruel I was being. I couldn't spare his feelings because I didn't want to lose him.

Of course, I couldn't let the poor boy have his night of happiness. I had to ruin it the week before the dance. It was something that needed to be said, but it couldn't have been worse timing.

It happened one night at my friend Isabelle's party. I was talking to a guy, Jackson, whom I was interested in. Jackson's eyes sparkled when he saw me, and a coy smile slipped across his lips as I pulled him to the dance floor. We danced for a while, our bodies swaying to the music, until out of nowhere Jackson said, "Carmen... I have to tell you, nothing can happen between us."

I stood in the middle of the dance floor for a minute, and my mouth hung open in shock, before I spoke.

"Why?"

But I knew why. The look on his face as he shrugged and walked off, leaving me alone and rejected, told me exactly the reason. And that reason was Charlie.

Rage fueling my body, I grabbed Charlie by the sleeve and told him we needed to talk. As we walked to the front door, I heard people cheer and the rage I felt grew stronger as I slammed the door and turned to face him. That shut people up.

I took a huge breath and told him everything. How someone I was interested in refused to talk to me because they thought we were an item. How I loved him as a friend, but we could never be more than that. How I needed him so badly, and I couldn't stand to lose him. He stood there bravely, listening to every word, until he finally spoke.

"Why didn't you just rip my heart out? It would have hurt less. I guess I'll be finding a new Winter Formal date."

I stood there, in shock for the second time that night, and suddenly burst into tears. I cried as I watched him walk away, back towards the house, feeling our special bond disintegrate. But suddenly I realized something; we were both free. Charlie could finally move on and find a girl who deserved him, and I could find a boy I liked back.

A smile played across my lips that night as I walked back into the party. Although I knew our friendship would never be the same, I laughed at the times we shared and the memories we created. I'd finally revealed the boy behind the shield of jokes and smiles, and he was everything I hoped he would be.

~Carmen Ang

37

Wanting Jason

Macho doesn't prove mucho.
~Zsa Zsa Gabor

When I was in high school, I liked two types of guys. The first kind included guys like my boyfriend, John. He was sweet and sensitive, good at sports but not a jock, kind, and loyal to me. John was an all around good guy who was a good friend and boyfriend.

The other kind I liked, well... let's just say he didn't have any of those qualities.

Jason was in the band with me, a saxophone player with a cool jazz mentality, whose dexterous fingers moved swiftly along the pads of his instrument and whose sound was smoothly seductive. He was gifted at his music, something that I have always found dazzlingly attractive, but he was aloof and separate, moody and in his own world. He had a bit of a reputation for experimenting—with girls and other things. He was one year older than me and drove an expensive red car, and when he dated one of my friends I heard more than I ever needed to about their torrid, explicit love affair.

When I was a junior and he was a senior, he and my friend broke up. Newly single, rumors swirled about him, a clarinetist, and sessions in the band closet that soon became legendary. As the marching band season kicked into high gear, we were spending a lot of time together. He was always teasing me, glaring at me with his blue bedroom eyes peeking out from his shaggy hair, making me blush and rendering me speechless. When the bell would ring at the end of the day, signifying that jazz band was over, my heart would ache as I tried to calculate the next time we had seventh period together. It was never soon enough.

For a while, I pushed that ache aside. My sweet boyfriend was all I needed, right? I loved him, not to mention he was the sensible choice. Plus, Jason thought of me as a lame wallflower, who didn't ever have a witty comeback or an interesting thing to say to him... or so I thought.

One cold October night, the more adventurous members of the marching band decided to do some drinking behind the bleachers at a late-night band competition. Jason was one of them—most likely the ringleader. On the bus back, he crawled into my brown leather seat, practically sitting on top of me.

"You're the prettiest girl in the band," he said, taking me by surprise. "Really." He was so close, closer to me than he had ever been before. "You are."

I shuddered and tried to laugh it off, but I knew. I knew because of the way he looked at me and toyed with me, that this was a moment of alcohol-induced honesty.

After that moment, I could hardly function around him. I dressed in the morning, lying to myself that the reason I wanted to look my best was not for him, but for my own good. If he missed class, I denied the fact that my heart felt like it was plummeting down an elevator shaft.

When Jason went to college, high school lost a shimmer of excitement it couldn't quite regain. I learned to be happy as I was, and I no longer lived in fear that he would—or wouldn't—speak to me.

That all changed one Thursday night during senior year. A message popped up on my computer from a screen name I rarely heard from—Jason's. He said he was in his dorm room drinking with his friends, and he was thinking of me. I knew this conversation was trouble, knew that it would only shuffle my emotional playing cards and make me question everything, but I couldn't help it. For a girl who used to scan the roads just to catch a glimpse of his car, I could hardly stop myself from having this conversation.

He talked to me for a few hours, getting progressively drunker. After the beginning small talk, he said he missed me. My hands shook on the keyboard as I tried to figure out the correct response. Next, he told me how attractive he thought I was.

Finally, as his spelling got worse and the time ticked by, he confessed to me: "I have always wanted you," he typed. "You are perfect for me, and I want you."

The summer after my freshman year of college is when my Jason obsession came crashing down. Through a text message exchange, a few friends and I ended up going over to his wealthy friend's house, where it was just Jason and a few other guys, an empty house, and a swimming pool. I was newly single and this, I knew, was it. This was my chance. I couldn't believe I was hanging out with Jason.

Later, he and I sat on the couch in the pool house, watching TV. It was very late, and it was just the two of us. I snuck looks at him every now and then, confused. After years of back and forth, we were alone and hours had passed without anything. He hadn't even moved to hold my hand. Jason, the guy who was brave enough to flirt endlessly with me when I was in a relationship, who had said such forward things to me online that one night, was now sitting to my right, practically ignoring me. Where was the womanizer I thought he was? How on earth could he just sit there, ignoring the years we had spent building up to this moment?

We sat on the couch, just like that, until the sun came up.

After that night with Jason, I lost it. My self-esteem was a mess, because I wondered how he could like me so much one second, and then have no interest in me the next. I was a basket case, analyzing that night every spare second I got. Why didn't I just tell him how I felt? Could I have changed the course of this story? Could Jason and I have done then what we had always wanted to do?

It took me a year to get over that night. It sounds extreme, but it required a rebuilding of confidence for me to finally realize what Jason represented to me, and what broke inside me when he failed to live up to my expectations. I was enamored with Jason, the fantasy, not Jason, the reality. In reality, he was a skinny, shy boy, who was all talk and no action. My cool fantasy was actually totally lame, and once I saw that, I no longer had any interest.

Today, I'm comfortable enough in my own skin to know that I was too good for the way Jason toyed with me. He was actually more insecure than I ever wanted to believe. I learned a valuable lesson from my crush on Jason, one that changed the way I think about relationships forever: In the end, Jason wasn't a bad boy. He was just a human being.

~Madeline Clapps

My Rock Star

True love stories never have endings.
~*Richard Bach*

Chad: the best acoustic guitar player I'll ever know, and the boy I fell hard for. Me: the shy girl he called Firefly. Who knew we'd fall in love this way? Who knew it'd all just crash and burn?

Chad was the funniest, most handsome boy I think I'll ever know in history. He had brown hair, he was tall, and he had eyes and a smile that could light up anyone's soul. He made the funniest faces, and he was always a comfort to have around. He was tall, and sometimes he could be too self-confident, but that's how you knew it was Chad. That was his trademark.

Chad and I met in sixth grade, thanks to our friend Seth. Going from elementary school to middle school as a shy girl was never easy, so of course I stuck to Seth. I don't think either one of us expected me to fall for his best friend. Seth was walking me home from school one day when Chad met up with us and we were introduced. We both said little to each other, but that smile of his caught me right then and there. From that day on, he walked home with us.

Eventually, my feelings for Chad grew. I never spoke up about my feelings until one day when Seth couldn't walk home with me, and Chad offered to walk me home himself. We walked in silence, and I was nervous about telling him what I had to say, but I just blurted out that I liked him. He had a girlfriend, so I knew nothing was going to come of it. He did admit that he liked me back, though.

The way that he spoke to me and treated me was just phenomenal. We'd spend hours on the phone together talking about life and nonsense. He'd give me piggyback rides and the best bear hugs ever. Soon after, we drifted apart a little, and I found myself a boyfriend, Chris. No one, including Chad, was very fond of my new boyfriend. He was controlling, he tried to fit in way too hard, and he just wasn't what my friends thought I deserved. Chad was still there, though. He told me constantly that he didn't like Chris, and I could kind of understand why.

After about nine months, I broke it off with Chris. I didn't leave Chris just because he was controlling, or because of my friends' opinions. I left Chris to win Chad's heart. And that's just what I did.

I was ending my seventh grade year, meaning Chad would be moving on to high school that coming fall. I was a little disappointed, but something unbelievable happened that summer. Chad and I couldn't really deny how we felt about each other anymore, so I asked him out to dinner with my family. We went out for Japanese to celebrate my sister's graduation from college. I had been toying with a ring on my finger I had gotten from my mom. I put it back on my finger, and then Chad asked to see it. Puzzled, I started to take off my ring until he told me he wanted to see my hand, not the ring. He grabbed my hand and held it under the table for the rest of the night, each of us eating dinner with only one hand. From then on, we were inseparable.

Chad and I kept our relationship a secret the whole time we went out. We'd kiss when our friends weren't looking, and when we were alone, it was magical. Chad and I would take long walks together, we'd dance under the moonlight and just hold each other, or he'd serenade me with songs on his guitar. He let me steal his clothes, so I took home two shirts and a sweater, just to feel like I had him near me all the time. He loved my hair, and he'd always take the ponytail out and run his fingers through it.

Chad took me to homecoming. He even went dress shopping with me, making me feel pretty while my brother was making mean-spirited jokes and comments about the dresses I tried on. I stormed out of the store, and Chad caught my arm, whispering to me how pretty I was.

After a while, Chad just drifted away and became a faint memory. My blisters that formed while I tried to learn guitar from him healed, and there were no more late-night phone calls or funny pictures. Everything faded.

Occasionally, I miss Chad. But even though I don't hear that guitar anymore, I still remember his smile and his eyes, and I know he's still my rock star.

~Rebecca Thomas

I Deserve Better

He that respects himself is safe from others;
he wears a coat of mail that none can pierce.
~Henry Wadsworth Longfellow

When Taylor came along, it changed my life. I wasn't even expecting it; it all happened very fast. One minute I was with a guy and the next, I was with a girl. Some people might have a problem with it, but for me it seemed perfectly normal.

Before I was with Taylor I was with this guy, Corey. I really didn't want to be with him anymore. Every time I tried to end it he would threaten to kill himself, so I was afraid that he would do it. One day I got up the courage and ended it with him. I no longer wanted him to be in my life, I was done with him and wanted to move on. Eventually he stopped calling.

After Corey, things changed a lot. Taylor and I had known each other since elementary school. We had been friends on and off for years, but around this time we became good friends and began to write notes back and forth in class. She told me how much she liked me and we started to talk every day. We were always hanging out together. Then, one day, we started holding hands in the hallway. I didn't really care what other people thought—I knew it was what I wanted. Our friends didn't care that we were two girls who liked each other, but the other kids at school seemed to have a problem with it. They thought that it was sick and wrong, but I didn't. I thought that Taylor was the best thing to happen to me, and I was so much happier with her than when I was with Corey.

There was just something about Taylor that was different from other people. It was weird because I had never felt that way about anyone before. Really, I had never thought of dating a girl in my life. But Taylor changed all that.

I found out the hard way that Taylor wasn't everything I wanted. We broke up a lot, but always managed to get back together somehow. Taylor was also into drugs and drinking. I had never done any of that stuff before, but when I started doing it because Taylor did, I couldn't stop. I was being stupid, thinking that getting high wasn't so bad because I had friends who did it more often. So I kept doing it every night, until I realized it wasn't good for me and I stopped. I haven't done drugs since.

I wanted so badly to tell my parents but I knew it wasn't the right time. My parents raised me to be whoever I wanted to be and told me they would always be behind me one hundred percent. But when they found out that I had been lying to them for over a year about being with a girl, my world came crashing down around me. I was told I could never see Taylor again. My parents refused to have a gay daughter. Because of my relationship with Taylor, I got into more trouble than I'd ever been in with my parents. Regardless, I didn't listen to them. I kept on seeing her, because I really thought I loved her.

Taylor and I did what we could to make it work, but in the end we went our separate ways. I don't regret dating Taylor. It was a time in my life when I was very vulnerable and confused. Taylor helped me get out of a bad relationship with Corey. If it weren't for her, I think I might have stayed with him. What I had with Taylor was something that was so special in many ways. I've found it hard to find the same feelings that I had for her in someone else. I know that Taylor and I will never be together again because I've got plans for my future and she doesn't; I want more out of life than a party every night of the week and getting drunk and high. But being with Taylor did help me realize that I deserve more than a guy like Corey, that I'm a special person and one day I will find that special someone I'm meant to be with.

Dating Taylor changed my relationship with my parents. In some ways, it brought us closer together, and in other ways it pulled us apart. But I learned not to let anyone's judgment affect me.

The number one thing being with Taylor made me realize is that I'm truly meant to be with a guy, and not with a girl. I loved Taylor, but it didn't feel right. I now know that waiting for the perfect guy can take longer than you expect, but I'll keep on looking until I find him. In the meantime, I am proud of who I am and where I come from, and I will always feel comfortable being with who I want to be.

~Brittany Neverett

Loving and Letting Go

How lucky I am to have something that makes saying goodbye so hard.
~Carol Sobieski and Thomas Meehan, Annie

"Brazil," Dan told me over the phone. "I'm going to Brazil next year." I can remember those words flashing through my mind. It's hard to say what my first reaction was. I think it was a combination of sadness, anger, and confusion. The only words I could say were, "That's cool," which came out in sort of a choking manner. Dan was so excited that he completely missed my response.

Dan continued to talk while I listened halfheartedly. I struggled desperately to gain control of my emotions. "You're leaving me," was the only thought that crossed my mind. Dan was the first boy I had ever loved, and I couldn't imagine life without him. I really wanted to be happy for Dan. I knew this was a dream; a dream that was actually going to come true for him. This was a chance of a lifetime, yet it was so unfair. After I hung up the phone, I went to my room and cried. As time passed I gradually accepted it, but there was always a little voice in the back of my mind that wanted to scream, "Don't go, please don't leave!"

Dan and I met when we were fourteen years old. The first night we met and slow danced, we could see eye to eye, but that didn't last for long. Since we lived in different towns and attended separate schools, we usually saw each other a couple of times per year.

The funny thing was that we could go without seeing each other for months and immediately pick up where we left off. We were friends for a long time before we started dating. Dan was easy to hang out with because he was so smart, quick to laugh, and a good listener.

We lost touch for a year, but Dan popped up in the strangest of places. In my sophomore year, I attended the county finals for the cross-country team. Since I had been injured earlier in the season, my job was to play timekeeper for the team. After the race, as I walked towards the bus, I turned a tight corner and ran smack into a white racing jersey. I nearly dropped the clipboard as I tripped backwards. A big hand reached towards me and pulled me up. As I was apologizing for my klutziness I caught sight of the brightest blue eyes I had ever seen. Dan broke into a huge grin as he introduced himself to me again. I was stunned. This young handsome guy could not have been the chubby kid that I slow danced with so long ago.

Once again, we slipped into our easy pattern of hanging out and chatting like it was yesterday. Over the next year, Dan and I became close friends who hung out together at dances, school trips, each other's houses, and sporting events. We took refuge in each other when dealing with the stresses of school and home, with trying hard to fit in, figuring out our own identity, and dealing with our parents.

I remember the thrill of kissing Dan when we first decided to date in my junior year. He was taller and filled out—now I barely reached his shoulder—and his short spiked hair had grown into floppy red bangs. Our relationship was so easy because I didn't feel any pressure to hide my true personality. It wasn't unusual for us to play one minute and then go for a quiet walk around the neighborhood and stare at the stars the next.

Over that year, my love for Dan changed from romance to friendship. The depth of my feelings did not change, and I didn't love him any less, but the intensity and focus of that love had changed. Dan broke up with me in early spring. It wasn't a harsh breakup, but I was heartsick and cried as he hugged me to his chest.

That summer, I decided it was time for me to get a fresh start by working at a summer camp. I needed time to slowly distance myself from Dan before he left the country. Then, something funny happened—we decided to share letters of our misadventures at camp. These letters showed a new and deeper relationship developing. We were becoming best friends, laughing at our stupid mishaps while clinging to each other through the storms of growing up.

It was a warm August night when I returned from camp. Dan was having his going away party. I was shaking in fear wondering how Dan would react after seeing me again. I know it was foolish, but I had secretly hoped that maybe he would have forgotten me. When I turned the corner to his house, Dan scooped me up in a big bear hug. "Do you know how much I missed you?" he whispered in my ear and then tossed me over his shoulder.

The carefully crafted walls around my heart were smashed to bits that night when I realized I still loved Dan. It wasn't losing Dan that scared me; it was my fear of being hurt when I had to let him go.

One of the hardest days I ever faced was saying goodbye to Dan at the airport when he left for Brazil. My heart cracked in half as we said our goodbyes and I watched his blue eyes fill with tears before he turned and headed to the gate. As his plane took off, I knew our relationship would never be the same. I quietly understood the meaning of love that day... if you truly love someone, you want what is best for them, even if it means letting go.

Dan and I followed different paths in life after that year. I am forever thankful that Dan taught me about unconditional love. His lessons have had an extraordinary effect on my life and have helped me to form many rewarding friendships. Our lives still cross on occasion and we pick up our old rhythms of where we left off, sharing tales of adventures and many bad jokes.

~Lisa Meadows

Louder than Words

I have always thought the actions of men the best interpreters of their thoughts.
~John Locke

I was babysitting—super, super late—for these two little girls, Sara and Nicole. I woke in the night to a sound that got my heart pounding wildly. Just as I started getting worked up about a possible burglar, Sara and Nicole's older brother Riley walked in.

"Riley? What are you doing here?" I asked, straightening the blanket I had over me on the couch.

"What am I doing here?" He raised his eyebrows. "This is my house. What are you doing here?" He grinned, obviously knowing the answer to the question. "I was camping, but then it started raining."

He picked up my teen magazine, thumbing through it. I held my breath, hoping he wouldn't notice the quiz I'd taken about having crushes on childhood guy friends.

"You know, you're a really sound sleeper," he said, still looking through the magazine.

I blinked. What did that mean? How long had he been here? Had he been watching me sleep? Did I snore? Drool? Ack!

He peered up at me, gazing at me like he sometimes did his Barbie doll girlfriends.

It was weird when he got like that, when out of nowhere he seemed to notice I was a girl. Maybe it was my new lip gloss. Or maybe I looked kind of pretty just waking up—maybe he liked my hair all tousled and full of popcorn.

Or maybe—Oh my gosh!—maybe he read my diary! Suddenly I noticed it sitting open on his family room desk. It was angled precariously, just as I'd left it. Still, seeing it, I could hardly breathe. Did he read it while I slept? Was that why he was looking at me like that? I tried to calm down and not look at it. It was possible he hadn't noticed the tattered thing. It was halfway covered under my shamble of schoolbooks.

He straddled the chair at the desk, looking at me, bemused. "Remember when we used to be best friends?" he asked. "We used to tell each other everything. Remember that?"

"Yes," I said with a sigh, knowing what he was getting at. "We are still friends Riley. I'm sorry, okay?"

"Yeah. I just can't believe you were back three days without telling me."

"Well..." I really didn't know how to explain it to him without sounding like a dork. But the thing was, he was wounded and somehow just knowing he cared enough to be hurt made me want to be slightly honest. I mean, absurdly, his pain touched me. "I specifically sought you out the first morning I got back—I did. But then, when I found you, you were with some blonde on the bleachers—I would have felt stupid interrupting."

"Yeah, but three days?"

"Well, every time I saw you, you looked busy. You were either with a girl, or with a bunch of guys. I just never had the chance...."

"I don't get it. We've been friends all our lives—we took naps together—and you can't even bother to stop me in the hall and say 'Hey Riley, look, I'm back?'"

"Well... I just felt kind of shy about it."

"Shy?" He looked perplexed. "Why would you feel shy?"

He's a moron. I hate him. "I don't know. I guess I was afraid you wouldn't care. I mean, since last year we've barely spoken. I was afraid that I'd be all excited, and tell you I was back, and you wouldn't care. That would have hurt, you know?"

He gazed at me a moment. "Why do you always think like that? You're the one who always acts so cool, like you couldn't care less. I never act that way."

"Yeah, but when I do it you know it's an act. And how should I know how you act these days anyway? I have no idea how you act anymore. It's been a long time since we've actually had a conversation—I mean, besides 'Hi, how was your weekend?' And every time I saw you this week you were with a different girl."

"What, you were spying on me?"

"Kind of."

His expression changed at that. I couldn't read it, which was strange because I knew Riley pretty well. "You must have like, been hiding from me," he said. "I mean, you don't exactly blend into a crowd."

"Apparently I do."

"Man, if I hadn't seen you Wednesday in the cafeteria you would have just let us graduate without ever telling me you were back. I mean, they would have announced your name to come up and get your diploma, and I would have sat there like a jerk, wondering how you were able to get it from our school when you'd spent the last year in a convent."

"It wasn't a convent. It was an all girls school."

•••

Instead of sleeping in his bed that night, Riley unrolled his sleeping bag and slept on the floor, beside me on the couch. He started snoring immediately, but I couldn't go back to sleep—not just due to his snoring, but also because of a feeling of despair I couldn't quite shake.

See, the thing was, I wouldn't have even seen Riley that night if his camping plans hadn't got axed. I mean, he could say he missed our closeness all he wanted, but as the stupid saying goes, actions speak louder than words, and well, let's face it, the guy had put out zero effort. Basically, I was out of sight, out of mind. When I wasn't in Riley's sight, I was completely out of his mind. At best, I was like a stray dog to him. Whenever my pathetic existence reached his attention he threw me a bone.

•••

Monday, I was contemplating the whole Riley conversation at school, when suddenly he was there, hovering over me as I shut my locker. "Want to get a hot chocolate?"

"Can't. I have a test."

"You're studying during break? That's so boring."

"Yeah, well, you know me..." I headed towards the library.

"Yeah, I do."

The way he said that made me turn back to him, a shiver of dread running through my body.

He grinned. "I have something of yours."

Suddenly, I felt sick. "What?"

He handed me my diary—I forgot it at his house. I burst out, "Ahh! You didn't read it, did you?"

He nodded that he did, explaining quickly he didn't know what it was at first. "It was just this ratty notebook on our den desk," he said. "But then I started reading it... and it was about me... so I kept reading."

He grinned, "You really think I look like Zac Efron?"

"I hate you."

He raised his eyebrows. "That's not what I read."

• • •

That night, Riley came to my house to apologize for reading my journal. He even wrote me an "apology poem" and brought me flowers... and asked me on a date. I was still kind of mad, but I forgave him. Because he was doing that effort thing—coming to my house in the middle of the night, giving me flowers, gazing at me all puppy-eyed—you know, actions speaking louder than words.

~Melanie Marks

The Art of Using Someone

Talk not of wasted affection; affection never was wasted.
~Henry Wadsworth Longfellow

He pretended a hanging potted plant was yuletide mistletoe. We were in the children's section of the library for our volunteer Christmas party, playing a mass game of hide-and-seek in near darkness. He'd tagged me and now I was helping him look for the others. He chose this time to flirt with me.

"You didn't bring the mistletoe?" he'd asked.

"No," I'd said. "I don't have any."

Once in the children's section, he quite purposefully stepped below a hanging plant. Seeing what he was up to, I smirked and said, "I'm not going anywhere near you."

He walked right up to me, so close my heart started thundering.

"I'll really kiss you," he said.

Nervous, I insulted him—called him a "creeper" or something—and laughed it off. I started walking away but somehow he ended up standing in front of me, close to me. The kiss was brief and I don't really remember it. I just know I was nervous, wondering why he was kissing me, and also feeling excited because now I could add another name to the very short list of boys I had kissed. The taste of chocolate lingered in my mouth after our lips parted. He must've stopped by the dessert table.

Once the game was over, we parted ways and I rushed off to tell my friends what had happened. I was excited but also confused. My love life had been virtually nonexistent since my boyfriend and I had broken up in the summer. After months of feeling depressed, I'd gone to a party with my sisters and realized that being single could actually be fun. I was free to receive attention from males. And now David, the boy who kissed me near the hanging potted plant, only reminded me further of how much I could enjoy the single life. After all, I was only seventeen. Why would I want to commit already?

Over the next few days I talked to my friends who volunteered with David and I—friends who had known him much longer than I had. I asked people if they thought David liked me or if he'd just kissed me for the heck of it. I guess they asked him the same thing, because before long he asked me out on a date so we could "talk about things."

Now I have to admit I didn't really like him a lot. I didn't know him very well and only thought he was "kinda cute." But I wanted some excitement in my life, so I went out with him.

We spent the afternoon walking all around, from store to store, and mall to mall, making out in dark hallways and elevators. He seemed to really like me. And by the time I got home, I felt very guilty. I knew I didn't want anything serious, but I had a feeling he wanted something more.

That night I e-mailed him, telling him I'd really enjoyed our date but didn't want to lead him on. I told him very honestly why I wanted to date him and that I didn't want anything too serious. In return, he got very upset and said that he didn't want something casual. I had to respect him for not being one of those guys who's just after a good time. But I was also annoyed. I'd been honest with him and in return he said very nasty things to me. So it surprised me when things continued.

He e-mailed me every day and kept asking me out, wanting another chance. I told him I'd see him again but I insisted I wouldn't change my mind about wanting to keep things casual. Our e-mails were more like debates than anything else. Finally, after a couple of weeks of this, we started seeing each other again.

He was very sweet in many ways. He told me I was beautiful and he could see himself falling in love with me. He had many opinions that I respected and valued; he thought drugs and alcohol were stupid things to get into, he disagreed with casual hook-ups, he cared about the environment, and he was a feminist. It seemed like he was everything I'd ever wanted in a guy, but I just couldn't stand him. He was loud and immature. I didn't understand his sense of humour. He was clingy and invited himself over to my house. And he was severely jealous of my best friend Sam.

One day Sam called me. He found out his girlfriend had been cheating on him and I convinced him to break up with her. The next day he came over to my house so we could talk and I could comfort him. As soon as David found out, he got very jealous and started sending Sam threatening messages. He insisted he was "only joking," but I knew he was genuinely jealous. He knew I'd had feelings for Sam for a long time. And he knew that since we had an open relationship, he couldn't trust me not to act on my feelings for someone else.

Later that night, Sam confessed his feelings for me and I confessed mine for him. I knew I had to break things off with David—for his sake and for mine. Now, I believe that in a committed relationship, breakups should be dealt with honestly but tenderly. No phone call or text message breakups, no beating around the bush or making up excuses. But what David and I had wasn't a committed relationship. We had something casual that he'd chosen to believe meant much more than it did. So I sent him an e-mail and told him I "just couldn't do it anymore." He chose to believe that I left him for Sam, while the truth was that whether Sam liked me or not, I would've broken up with David sooner or later anyway.

Sam and I dated for four months and then went back to being friends. Now I have an amazing boyfriend who treats me wonderfully and may not be the dream man I always envisioned, but is in many ways something so much better—because he isn't a dream. He's real.

I still see David once a month at our volunteer meetings. And he avoids me for the most part. In turn, I avoid him, except for a brief word of acknowledgement, which isn't always returned. Do I still feel bad about hurting him? Sometimes. Do I still feel guilty? No. I realize I didn't do the most wonderful thing to him, but I can only take responsibility for my end of it. I was honest with him about what I wanted from the beginning.

He is a good person and he treated me well in many ways. But he isn't for me. Perhaps he has a girlfriend right now who he loves, or perhaps he'll marry a girl someday and be her dream man. But to me, he is a boy I dated who made me feel good about myself for a little while, who helped me evolve into the person I am today. And for that, I am thankful.

~Marady Owens

43

Just the Beginning

Don't worry about losing. If it is right, it happens—
The main thing is not to hurry. Nothing good gets away.
~John Steinbeck

I have never been kissed. Whether he knew that or not, I didn't know. But I sure didn't tell him, so there's a good chance he's still clueless about that little personal fact of mine.

I officially met Ryan on the long journey to Ithaca. We were in the same Advanced English class freshman year and were assigned to the same group for our project on the amazing Greek poem, *The Odyssey*. I never really paid attention to the other students in my classes besides my friends, so I hadn't acknowledged his presence before.

I'm not quite sure what it was, but after working together, there was just something about him that made me feel nervous and self-conscious whenever I was around him. At the time, I wasn't sure what this meant so I quickly shoved the feeling aside.

We immediately become pretty good friends. Our teacher made all group members exchange cell phone numbers, and after the Odyssey project, we texted regularly. As the year flew by, he became my best guy friend.

It was the following summer when I really began to develop feelings for him. A few days before I went away to summer camp at Stanford University, my dad got me a brand new phone, with both a touch screen and a keyboard. Along with one of my best friends, Danielle, he was the main person I texted during camp. We would talk about what we liked and made imaginary plans such as see the upcoming Harry Potter movie together. When I got back from camp, I was surprised that that particular plan came true. And as I sat in the movie theater, my brother already fallen asleep to my left and Ryan sitting to my right, laughing at inappropriate moments in the movie, I realized I liked him.

When school started our sophomore year, he got a girlfriend. There went my chance to tell him how I felt. Later that year, Danielle found out my little secret. From what she told me, she had already had a feeling. Even though she encouraged me to tell him, we agreed to keep it a secret until the time was right.

I waited eight whole months. After he broke up with his girlfriend, he was, of course, down in the dumps. The moment it happened was a complete blur. I had been casually texting him when, after all this time, the ultimate question popped up on the screen of my phone.

"Do you like me?"

The text literally took my breath away and I just couldn't stop staring at those words. My heart had been pounding faster than I thought a heart could ever pound. While this conversation was going on, I had been texting Danielle simultaneously, and she was coaching me throughout the whole thing and telling me, in all caps, to just do it. So I did.

About a week or two after my confession, we officially became a couple. We texted nonstop, we went to the movies multiple times, and he even met my parents. But through all that, we never kissed. Not once.

"You guys have been dating for a month and you haven't kissed yet?" a classmate once asked me.

"Nope," I replied nonchalantly, not wanting to make a big deal out of it. I mean, it wasn't a big deal, right? At least, that's what I thought.

I believed I loved him, I really did. But I wasn't ready for my first kiss. I wanted it to happen when the time was right. And though I tried so many times to deny it, something told me the time would never be right.

Summer had approached and I was off to camp at Stanford again, followed by a week with my other best friend, Beth, in San Antonio. Ryan and I typically texted each other every day just like we had the year before, but once I was in Texas visiting Beth, I became busy and wasn't able to text him as often. After all, I only got to see Beth once a year and I wanted to make the most of it. When Beth flew back with me to my house for another week, I had received the text that was the beginning of the end.

"Why aren't you talking to me?"

"I'm just busy," I texted back. And when he asked why I wouldn't kiss him, I panicked, but thankfully Beth and I were at the amusement park and I had the excuse, "I'll ttyl, I'm about to get on a ride."

"All right," was all he said. After that, we didn't speak to each other for a week, both of us too proud to be the one to text first. Then one day while lying in bed, I got the very last text I would ever get from him: "Hey, I'm breaking up with you."

I stared at the text, waiting for the impact. But there was nothing. I didn't feel a thing. My heart was still in one piece, beating at a normal pace. It was when a big grin formed on my face that I had realized I wasn't in love. I was in love with the idea of being in love.

I immediately hopped on the computer and did what any other teenager would do. I changed my relationship status to "single" on Facebook. Next, I threw away the birthday card he had given me. On a roll, I threw away a majority of the giant chocolate bars he gave me as a birthday present, saving three bars for Danielle since I knew she'd like to have some. And then there was his shirt. I decided to be nice and just give it away to charity instead of simply tossing it out.

Of course, doing all those things didn't erase him from my mind. In fact, I thought about him every day for a while. But I knew he was only the beginning. I'm glad he was my first love and my first mistake, but I know there will be plenty more loves... and plenty more mistakes.

~Sara Bechtol

Make a Wish

*All love that has not friendship for its base is like
a mansion built upon the sand.*
~Ella Wheeler Wilcox

I never had good luck with boys. I always seemed to wind up with the same types—a bad boy, a player, or someone who was just generally careless. I would devote my heart and soul to these boys, only to be walked all over. You could say that I was lonely, which is why I always gave more than I received. But because of that, I constantly settled for whoever waltzed my way. I never took the time to realize what—or who—was right under my nose.

His name was Ashton and he was a year younger than me. He was a total cutie and lived just down the street. He was always my first choice when it came to hanging out with someone. I thought of him as my best guy friend—nothing more. When summer rolled around and school was out, we became inseparable. Of course, my very outspoken best friend Stacey had something to say about our tight-knit friendship.

"Oh come on, Jess!" Stacey said. "I know you like him!" I crinkled my nose and shook my head.

"He's my best guy friend, Stace. I do not like him and I never will," I insisted stubbornly, flopping onto my bed. Stacey huffed, unsatisfied with my denial.

"Fine. I'm asking him what he thinks then," she said snootily, whipping out her phone.

I rolled my eyes. "He's going to say that he doesn't have feelings for me. It's a waste of your time. You'll see," I said stubbornly. Stacey ignored me and continued to text. Who was I to think that she would listen to me?

Soon after the controversial text had been sent, Stacey and I fled to the hot tub for a few hours. It was a beautiful, early summer night. The blanket of stars above was gleaming and illuminating the dark earth. Stacey was chatting away about the latest gossip, but all I could think about was the text she had sent Ashton. "Could you ever have feelings for Jess?" is what the life-changing text read. Originally I thought nothing of it. However, the longer we soaked, the more my curiosity grew.

After the hot tub, we went inside and plopped down onto my bed. I smiled and closed my eyes but was quickly disrupted by a sharp gasp.

"Oh my goodness, Jess!" Stacey shouted, shooting upward into a sitting position. My heart rate sped up and my eyes widened when I realized what she was gasping about. She was staring at her cell phone, her mouth wide open.

"He said yes! He has feelings for you!" Stacey screamed, bouncing up and down on my bed. "Look!" she exclaimed stuffing her phone in my face. Sure enough, written simply across the screen were three letters: Y-E-S.

I tried hard to swallow the lump in my throat. My mind was a complete vortex of scattered thoughts. My best guy friend was in love with me? I felt dizzy and sick to my stomach. I was officially faced with a tricky situation. I could pretend that I never saw the text and continue on as friends with Ashton, or I could risk losing my dear friend and take a chance with him. Many say that the best relationships are born from friendship. Did I have the guts, not to mention the right feelings for this boy, to go through with this?

Over the next week I kept my distance from him, but we spent more time than usual texting and talking on the phone. I pretended to be oblivious to the entire situation and luckily Stacey managed to keep it secret that I knew about his feelings.

Ashton and I ended up hanging out a week after the truth had gotten out. It was a beautiful night. The air was warm and fresh; the stars were so bright that it was hardly dark. We sat on a hill in front of my house, talking about pretty much everything. After a moment of awkward silence, he spoke softly. "Jess, look... I need to tell you something," he said, and paused for a second. "I have feelings for you. I have for a while now." He bowed his head bashfully.

I smiled and looked at him. Despite the darkness I just knew he was blushing. I considered acting surprised but giggled instead. "I know," I said shyly. He looked at me and grinned, getting up to walk me to my front door.

Once we got on my porch he stood facing me, a wide smile plastered across his face. "Goodnight, Jess," he whispered, squeezing my arm. He leaned in and planted a kiss on my mouth, then turned to head home. When I stepped inside I couldn't stop smiling and almost fell over with happiness.

The next few weeks were spent with Ashton as we grew closer and fonder. We spent most days together and nights were spent stargazing until the wee hours of the morning. After some time he asked me to be his girlfriend, and I gladly agreed.

Ashton and I developed a habit of saying, "make a wish," every time the clock struck 11:11. This habit originated during our days as friends but became something else while we were a couple. Before we were dating, we both used to secretly wish for things to work out between us. Whether we had fate to thank, or our strong belief in 11:11, things fell together perfectly. There isn't a moment that I regret falling in love with my friend.

~Jess Bunbury

Just for Teenagers

101 Stories of Inspiration and Support for Teens

Chapter
5

Family Ties

The family is a haven in a heartless world.

~Attributed to Christopher Lasch

Life Lesson

Other things may change us, but we start and end with the family.
~Anthony Brandt

It took me longer than it should have to learn to appreciate my family. Up until I was seventeen, I considered my life perfect. I had both parents who were still madly in love even after twenty-five years, two older brothers who have kept me out of harm's way, an older sister who spoiled me rotten, and a little brother who I adored. I had the best of friends, lived in a great neighborhood, enjoyed school, and was the first in my family to get a car bought for me at just sixteen. I found myself expecting more and more from my family and didn't appreciate them for the things they did do for me.

I'll be the first to admit that I was more spoiled than most. The older we all got the worse I became. Once my two older brothers and my sister moved out, I felt the "power" of being the oldest sibling in the house. I was also becoming too self-centered to be as close to my little brother as I used to be. He was just a freshman, and outside of home, I didn't care to be around him. Over time, my brothers moved farther away, I spent less time at home, my little brother became more rebellious, and we all grew apart. I could have cared less.

Then one day, everything changed. My dad always woke us up for school with a simple yell of our names every five minutes, which eventually motivated us to get up and get ready. This particular Monday, however, was different. There was no wake-up call. I was lying on my bed, making shapes on the rough textured ceiling, waiting for my personal alarm clock. After a while I got up on my own, woke up my little brother and got ready for school. I brushed the unusual morning off and went about my day with an uneasy feeling. Before I knew it, I was in the Salem Hospital waiting room, watching the clock tease me with the annoying "click" noise it made as each second passed. My dad had suffered a stroke and had to be flown to OHSU hospital in Portland. My brothers kept assuring me he was okay. I even chuckled at the fact that he was going to be in a helicopter because he was so terrified of flying. Once we arrived at the hospital in Portland, the severity of the situation really hit me.

After a very long Monday and Tuesday some of us went home for the night, questions still unanswered. But something told me not to go to sleep that night, and I knew why once I saw my older brother's picture pop up on my caller ID at 2 a.m. By the tone of his voice, he didn't have to tell me the news because I already knew. As I got into the car, ready for the longest forty-five-minute drive of my life, I tried to prepare myself for goodbye. All I could think about was myself. My graduation, my wedding, my future kids growing up without a wonderful grandpa—how all of this was going to affect me.

Then, before I could grasp what was happening, it was over. My world came to a complete halt. I stared in a daze as my fourteen-year-old brother lay across my dad's peaceful, lifeless chest, promising him his own world. The pain behind his eyes wrapped around and suffocated my already shattered heart. And as I wrapped my arms around my broken baby brother, every selfish thought I ever had left my head and never returned.

Losing my dad taught me a life lesson that everything you have can be taken right from under your nose quicker than a hiccup. I can truly say my life took a complete turn for the better. My days are no longer spent living in my own world. I never leave without reminding my family that I love them, and I've learned to appreciate the things I have in life. I even enjoy taking care of my little brother, now seventeen and not so little. I love the things he depends on me for, and how much of an impact he has on me. It took losing one of the most important people in my life to realize I needed to cherish the ones I have. Even though I would give the world to have my dad back, I thank him every day for helping me learn to appreciate God's greatest wonder, my family.

~Latrice Holmes

46

It Takes Three to Tango

To the outside world we all grow old. But not to brothers and sisters.
We know each other as we always were. We know each other's hearts.
We share private family jokes. We remember family feuds and secrets,
family griefs and joys. We live outside the touch of time.
~Clara Ortega

I stand outside waving at the car pulling slowly out of our driveway. I can't see the person I'm waving to but I know that she's waving back. As the car gets smaller and smaller, a boomerang joke comes into my head but I know that there isn't going to be a punch line this time. The only thing that comes back to hit me now is that she's gone. I force a smile, hoping it will cover up my tearing eyes, but I know it's not working.

I run into the house, slam the door behind me, and begin crying. It's just occurred to me that this is the last time I'll see my sister, Monsura, for the next four months. I ask myself why it is that I'm crying when I know she's doing something good for herself. College is a time for independence, but I'm not ready to be independent from her.

I feel selfish for thinking it but I'd be lying if I said I was happy for her for choosing to study in a university in Boston. When my brother, Shafat, left for college it was different. I still had one sibling at home to call me the stupidest person alive on a daily basis. I hated her now for leaving me to do that myself.

I am reminded of all the things we did together as kids. Like the time when we struck a deal with Shafat to play *Beauty and the Beast* with us if he got to teach us about the solar system. I can't remember whether we actually got to the lecture but I know for a fact that for a while we were all unbelievably happy — even me, starring as Gaston.

I come to the conclusion that growing up isn't all that it's made out to be. In our old two-bedroom apartment, our parents succumbed to our constant begging and traded rooms with us for one night. It was like being part of the circus; using our parents' gigantic squishy bed as a trampoline. That was the first night that I witnessed a full moon. My sister and I believed my brother when he said that the reason it was so yellow was because it was made from cheese. We made elaborate plans to visit the moon so we could melt a part of it and make cheese dip. Back then I was convinced that one day in our grown-up lives we three would get our own big bed. But now I laugh at myself for being so naïve and not realizing that the big bed would be for one person, and not the three I was accustomed to.

But of course, it wasn't all fun and games. When we weren't busy reenacting Disney movies together, we'd be butting heads, bickering over the smallest things: accusing each other of passing the imaginary line that marked "our side" of the bed, or writing on the walls that we hated each other. There were the extreme times when we threatened to kill the sibling we were currently mad at in their sleep. But thankfully, we always managed to wake up the next morning, alive and forgetting what we were mad about in the first place.

Sitting in front of my computer, playing our shared iPod, I listen to songs that remind me of my two best friends. I come to terms with the fact that there's no longer anyone here to laugh uncontrollably with me or to go to at night when I have a nightmare. I'm shaken into reality by the sound of my cell phone ringing. Shafat is calling. I pick up and he immediately says "Thank you for such a great childhood." Those few words mean the world to me. We three-way call Monsura and spend the next hour reliving memory after memory, and by the end, I forget that I'm alone at home. I hang up, reassured that my siblings are only a phone call away.

~Samaira Sirajee

47

Chicken Soup
for the Soul

A Father's Love

Any man can be a father. It takes someone special to be a dad.
~Author Unknown

Sweat dripped its way down my forehead and into my eyes quicker than I could wipe it away. Attempting to conquer my cottonmouth, I spat onto the red clay near first base and swept over it with my cleats. It was hot. The dugout thermometer read 109 degrees, but the air was still and the humidity was rising from the previous night's rain.

This was it, the last out. One final play and the State Softball Championship was ours. The pressure was on. The bases were loaded, their leadoff hitter was at bat, and we were only two runs ahead.

I glanced towards the crowd, searching for familiar faces. Sure enough, I found my mom braving the heat to cheer me on. It was only a routine thought to wish my dad were here. The farm demanded his full attention, but I did not care. I was selfish, always resenting him for choosing his work over me.

Out of the pitcher's glove and into the catcher's. Strike one. Again, only this time she swung and missed, just under the pitch. I could taste the sweet victory on my tongue as the pitcher stepped onto the mound.

Her wind-up was perfect, flinging a fastball right down the center. The bat cracked from the impact. An in-field fly to third sent us all scrambling for our bases, ready to protect our title. I worried that she would not catch it. The yellow ball was hidden in the sun, and the glare was overwhelming. Treading circles around the bag, the third baseman shaded her eyes with her glove.

She caught it.

Euphoria swept over me. State Champs! A scream of delight caught in my throat as we stormed the mound, interrupted by a wave of tears when I looked back at the crowd. My mom was there, giving me a thumbs-up and smiling. I smiled back at her through blurry eyes.

We all received medals, plaques—the works—but I cannot remember any of it. I focused my thoughts on my dad, who was not there. I ran to my mom, begging for her cell phone. I had to tell my dad about the happiest day of my life, and rub in how he did not care enough to come and watch me play.

The phone rang twice, and then went to voicemail. My heart sank with disappointment, but I tried again anyway.

"Hello?" My dad answered, the sound of a combine shutting down in the background.

"Dad!" I cried. "We won State!"

Silence.

"Dad?" I could hear him sobbing on the other end. "Are you—crying?"

"I'm just really happy for you, Meggie," he said. "And I'm sorry I couldn't be there."

An apology was all I needed. I hung up the phone feeling perfectly at ease, and I began to understand how it must feel to be a father. My resentment dissolved as I forgave him for never being there. He worked so I could play; it was as simple as that. My father loved me enough to let me experience life's happiest moments without him.

That is a father's love.

~Megan Thurlow

Ongoing Battle

No law or ordinance is mightier than understanding.
~Plato

We finally sat down in the crowded restaurant when my brother shrieked, flailing his arms wildly. "Can't you control your son?" remarked the ladies sitting next to us. As my mother explained my brother's condition, I saw an expression on their faces that I had seen many times. The ladies didn't understand and kept looking over and frowning the rest of the evening.

Since then, the same situation has been replayed many times throughout my life. It's come down to the point where I don't even mention my brother, to save myself from the torture of seeing the expression of the confused person's face. I can count on one hand how many times I've seen my brother be accepted by people. I, as well as my family, have explained over and over—but in the end, it's useless and I end up feeling embarrassed and low.

My brother has autism, a disorder of neural development characterized by impaired social interaction and communication. It's quite easy to spot in the infant years if you know the symptoms. Children with autism show little or no signs of interaction with peers and adults from the very beginning. They are into doing things alone. They may show compulsive behaviors such as repetitively stacking objects in order. Also, they show physical signs like hand waving, arm flapping and body rocking. It ranges between mild, moderate and severe and usually brings along loss of hearing and speech. A person with mild autism may show the anti-social behaviors of the disorder, but can hear and speak very clearly and can be very intelligent. Someone with a severe case may show all the signs of impaired social development and the physical signs.

From the early age of three years old, we started to notice my brother becoming stagnant and not as alert as he always was. I can recall many hours sitting in doctors' offices and waiting rooms with my parents, watching my brother and unaware of what was going on. When we finally found out he had autism, we felt a sense of relief, and then disappointment. I was only six at the time, so I didn't know exactly what was wrong except that he couldn't talk or hear and made weird movements with his arms and hands. But, as my parents explained it more and the embarrassing situations started happening, I got the picture. Life wouldn't be easy at all.

There are many controversies as to what the cause of autism is. Whatever turns out to be the cause, it won't matter to me. I've said many times that having a brother with autism, and all the experiences that come with that, is my inspiration, and it's true. With him, it's an ongoing battle every day from morning till night. He challenges my family's faith and patience. The best moments are seeing my brother smile and catching a glimpse of the innocent little boy lost behind the mask. I would never want to live without him. Nothing could take the place of his laughter and smile.

~Teresa Silva

Fireworks

Rejoice with your family in the beautiful land of life!
~Albert Einstein

I was fast asleep the first time my father almost died. It was the middle of the night, and while he was clutching his chest suffering a major heart attack, I was lost in a dream that would last me long after his rush to the hospital.

I was fourteen when it happened, and at that tender age, I initially thought the incident was no big deal—a mishap that my family was being overdramatic about. In the days that followed, I remember feeling so irritated that everyone was in a constant panic. My house phone would not stop ringing, people at school asked how he was feeling, and family friends kept showing up to our house with casseroles. I was confused as to why everyone was acting so paranoid; my dad was the one who was sick, but everyone around him was on edge. I thought he would get better, and we would move on with our lives, plain and simple.

I soon learned how very wrong I was.

In the weeks that followed his heart attack, my family sort of sprung away from each other in separate directions, the way fireworks do when they explode in the sky. My mom was at the hospital, my sister clung to her friends, my brother confided in his wife, and I kind of just hung around, waiting for things to get back to normal. I remember eating out at different restaurants every night with my aunts and grandparents, a way for them to distract me while my mom spent time with my father.

In the midst of my teenage angst, I remember complaining to one of my friends that I felt like I didn't even have a family anymore. I couldn't remember the last time we were all in the same room, and instead of being understanding, I was a little annoyed with the situation.

At this point, I hadn't even visited my father in the hospital. I talked to him on the phone almost every day, but because he was sick and on all sorts of medications, I didn't really want to see him. I thought it would be too hard to face him in such a sickly, vulnerable state, especially because it was so opposite of his normally energetic personality. I figured he would be home in a few weeks, and I could just see him then.

Like I expected, my father finally came home. The rest of my family was overjoyed, and while I was so happy to have him back, I couldn't help but gloat, with an I-told-you-everything-was-fine attitude. It was then I learned that his heart attack wasn't just bad luck; his father, whom I had never met, suffered heart conditions that ended up taking his life in his early forties. Hearing this, I came to realize how serious the situation really was. But, still I thought, it was fine; he was healthy, and we could all just move on.

I spoke too soon, because just after he returned home from such a good recovery, his heart suffered another battle, and once again, he was in the hospital for a major heart attack.

The second time around rattled everyone much harder, including me. It took the second heart attack for me to realize that my father might really be sick. The fact that he could be dying kept running through my head; I just couldn't shake the thought. I realized then that at any moment my father could possibly slip away from me. While it was a grim thought, it was also enlightening, because it made me realize how important spending time with him really was.

This time around, I visited him multiple times in the hospital. I no longer accused everyone of being overdramatic, or treated the situation lightly. I swallowed what had happened with full force, and prayed, hoped and wished my father would come home safe once again.

He did, and thanks to medicine, and everyone's good thoughts, remained heart attack free for a long while. I would say that things got back to the way they were, but they didn't—in a good way, though. Post-heart attack, I spent a lot of time with my dad and appreciated all the moments with him.

Sometimes I feel guilty that it took the endangerment of my father's life for me to realize how precious the time I get to spend with him—and the rest of my family—really is. But I also realize that in the dark, scary reality of his heart condition, the sparkly silver lining in the story is that it opened my eyes to how quickly things can change.

As the months turned to years, my father got healthier and healthier, and eventually his series of heart attacks became just another family memory. Although we valued it deeply, his heart was no longer the subject at dinner. We had all developed a newfound love and appreciation for him, and though it was triggered by his heart attack, it was rooted inside us long after the attacks passed.

Years later, I am proud to say that my appreciation for my father is still alive and well. We recently took a family trip to Hawaii to celebrate my parents' twenty-fifth anniversary, and as we sat on the beach for the Fourth of July fireworks to begin, I looked up at my dad and couldn't stop thinking about how happy I was that we were there together. We have had countless fights and flaws in our relationship, but I know my dad is an irreplaceable part of my life.

As the fireworks began exploding in the sky, he kissed my head, reassuring me that he, too, was happy to be there as a family. With each firework that burst into an explosion of color, I could think of one more reason to love and appreciate my father.

~Audrey Mangone

My Hero

A grandfather is someone with silver in his hair and gold in his heart.
~Author Unknown

I sat in the uncomfortable chair in our living room, staring at my parents, who had just given me the news that my hero, best friend, and grandpa, had Alzheimer's. I did not want to believe it. Alzheimer's would slowly rob my grandpa of his intellect and his social abilities, severely enough to interfere with daily functioning. It has no known cure.

The thought of that happening to my grandpa scared me. How could someone who I love so much and who lived such a great life slowly lose his memories of everything around him? All I could do was cry and think of all the good times we used to have.

● ● ●

"Grandpa!" I call, as I run at full speed into his arms just like every Sunday afternoon before, my feet pounding on the gravel driveway. He opens his arms and braces for the leap. He is a strong man of about five feet five inches with welcoming eyes and never ending love. I am about six years old, and we have carried on this tradition every Sunday since I could walk. It is something I look forward to when Mom says, "Get ready, we are going to Grandpa's."

As we head inside the red brick house, I smell the sweet aroma of Grandma's cooking. Grandpa puts his arms around me and gives me a tight squeeze that is all too familiar. Since my dad works a second-shift job and someone needs to watch me, Grandpa is like a second father and we have a deep connection.

"I love you, Grandpa," I say.

"I love you too, my pretty Morgan," he replies.

The dinner table is not just a place where we eat a good meal, but also a place where we laugh together. Grandma tells us that what the preacher said today in church and Grandpa makes jokes. We gossip about the things that have happened since our last encounter and share stories of the past. Then comes my favorite part of any meal—dessert! This is one of the many things for which Grandpa and I share an equal love.

As always, Grandma has a baked good or mint chocolate chip ice cream. Grandpa and I head to the kitchen and prepare the dessert.

"I want ice cream, Grandpa."

"Now, Morgan, do you know why mint chocolate chip ice cream is green?"

"No, why?"

"Well, they put grass in it," he says with a wink.

"Oh, really?" I shrug. "I will eat it anyway."

We both start to laugh and share a moment no one else would understand. That is just the way my grandpa is, always trying to make me laugh or pull a fast one on me. My grandpa also has a serious side, and uses that to teach us grandchildren life lessons, like patience. He always says, "Now, Morgan, be patient and I will be right back."

At this, I close my eyes, put my arms across my chest, and wait. Being the curious little kid that I am, I ask when he is coming back at least five times. Grandpa always comes back and we head off to the garden or to the grocery store, places we can go by ourselves, with no interruptions.

• • •

As I come back to the present and reality, I am sitting across from him at the table, but our relationship is completely different. It has been six years since we first learned that he had Alzheimer's. He now has slouched shoulders and wary eyes. This disease is terrible. His long-term memory is somewhat normal, but he cannot remember what he did ten minutes ago. This makes it very difficult to carry on a simple conversation.

The role of grandchild and grandparent has switched, and when we are around each other, I am the one teaching him lessons. But the lesson in patience he taught me long ago is the one I value the most now. When someone you love has Alzheimer's, it is very hard not to lose your cool with them. Right now, he probably has the mind and ability of a four-year-old. It is so bad he cannot even go to the bathroom or enjoy a meal without having someone help him with the basics.

We don't know what the future may hold for my grandpa, but as he slowly fades away, we will always remember the good times before he was sick—the times of laughter, humor and lifelong lessons. This is how I want to remember him, because it is just too hard to think that, someday, he won't know who I am. But even if that does happen, I will always be his pretty Morgan and he will always be my hero, best friend, and my grandpa.

~Morgan Deich

51

Chase's Journey

Tis better to have loved and lost than never to have loved at all.
~Alfred, Lord Tennyson

When the news came, my parents were heartbroken and distraught. My dad and stepmom had been trying to have a baby for quite some time and had just learned that the chances were slim to none. That's when they decided to participate in foster care. The idea of giving back to a family and allowing ours to grow at the same time was exactly what we were looking for. After many months of classes and tests, a two-year-old boy named Chase entered our lives.

At first I was very skeptical. A stranger was coming to live in my house and become part of my family. I didn't know if I was ready for such a drastic change. With my sister at college, I was "big man on campus," the baby, and most of all, my daddy's little girl. I didn't want to have to compete for his attention, but what I didn't realize is that he would be competing for mine.

After the first month, I fell in love with Chase. He was very loving and filled with laughter. As soon as I got home I would run to find him and give him a huge hug. What were normally dirty chores, such as bath time and changing diapers, became extra time with him that I wouldn't miss for the world. He grew with us and learned from us. I taught him as much as I could and played with him whenever there was a chance. He became my brother, just like flesh and blood. Then social services called.

Chase left us in December of 2007. My heart was shattered. I was more hurt than I had ever been in my entire life. I remember the day as if it were yesterday. I sat with him in his room the night before, clinging to the last bit of time we had to spend together. Chase, oblivious to what was going to happen the next morning, smiled and laughed and then easily dozed off to sleep. The next morning I woke up and got Chase ready and held him as long as I could. When the social worker arrived and took him away, it seemed to happen in a blink of an eye. One minute he was sitting on my lap laughing and the next I was alone. There was no more time to be spent playing, teaching, or loving Chase.

I cried myself to sleep for the next week, but after a while, the pain started to ease. There are still times when I see his picture or walk by the room he once called home, that I feel sorrow and loneliness. I wonder how he is doing, and if his new family is treating him well. All I can do is hope and pray that he has a life full of accomplishments, success, and love. I never thought that a little boy would force me to grow up so fast. I now know to cherish the time you have with others and to show as much love and care as possible. I have also learned to look for the good things in a situation and appreciate them instead of focusing on the bad. Chase's journey helped me through my own and although there is still a bit of sadness when I hear his name, I know that I am a stronger person because of him. Chase came into my life for only a short period of time, but he shaped the person I am today and I am forever grateful.

~Ainsley Holyfield

52

My Real Parents

Biology is the least of what makes someone a mother.
~Oprah Winfrey

I don't look like the rest of my family. As a matter of fact, I stand out quite a bit with my olive skin and almond eyes. When people see us together it is clear that I am adopted. I am happy to have such a loving and caring family, but sometimes I wish I knew who my birth parents were.

My friends often ask, "Are you sad that you don't know your real parents?" I know that they are just curious and concerned about me—I'm fine, for the most part—but I feel like there's something missing in my life, like a giant hole in my heart. My mother listens when I tell her about my feelings, and she feels that it is important for me to be in touch with my culture. Because of this, she and I go to Chinese Heritage Camp each year in Snow Mountain Ranch.

Chinese Heritage Camp is a two-day camp where hundreds of adopted kids like me spend time with each other. We talk about how it feels to be adopted, and we participate in fun outdoor activities. It's great because we can talk about our feelings without having the conversation get too intense. It makes me feel like I am not alone, and that there is someone out there going through the exact same emotions.

Whether we're talking, laughing, crying, or dancing, CHC is always an experience to remember. I adore all of the new people I meet, and I will keep them in my heart forever, because it always feels good to know there are people out there just like me.

Camp has changed the way I look at things. Each year seems to open up new surprises, adventures, and friendships. CHC taught me to learn that being adopted doesn't mean that I'm weird or strange, it just means that I wasn't born into the family I live with. Being adopted won't make my parents love me any less.

Thanks to Chinese Heritage Camp, now when people ask me, "Are you sad you don't know your real parents?" I can safely answer, "Maybe I don't know who my birth parents are, and that makes me a little sad. But I do know that I live with my real parents in a real house, with a real family, and I love my life just the way it is."

~Lilly Putsche

Just for
Teenagers

101 Stories of Inspiration
and Support for Teens

Chapter
6

Tough Times

When the world says, "Give up,"
Hope whispers, "Try it one more time."

~Author Unknown

53

Chicken Soup for the Soul

Five Minus One Equals Five

Death leaves a heartache no one can heal,
love leaves a memory no one can steal.
~From a headstone in Ireland

"I'm an expert, too!" I proclaimed at the ripe old age of two-and-a-half. I actually have no memory of this event, but the story—retold frequently, to my embarrassment—is ingrained in my brain. To hear the rest of my family tell it, I was in preschool and my two older, wiser, kindergartener brothers had come for a visit to demonstrate something to the class.

The teacher must have praised them and called them experts. Although I was always trying to keep up with them and often envious, I was proud of my brothers, proud to be their sister. I had fantasies of being a mother and showing them off to my children when they came to visit.

The minute I came out of my shell after getting to know someone new, they'd have to hear all about my incredible, talented brothers:

"My brothers are the best chess players."

"Did you know my brothers are taking music lessons? One plays the trumpet and the other the clarinet."

"I'm going to make one of those toy rockets you can actually launch; my brothers make them."

When they got older, it was all about the car they shared, the tuxes they rented for the prom, the colleges they were applying to.

And then, the summer after their freshman year in college, their plans diverged. Bill stayed home. Chad headed off for a semester abroad. For three weeks, there were only four of us at home. Even then, it was as though Chad were there. "I wonder what he's doing now?" we'd ask each other.

"It's been a while since he called," Mom worried. "Hope all is well."

At two o'clock one Monday morning the phone rang.

"Oh my god. Oh my god."

I don't know how many times I heard that drifting in through the vent from my parents' bathroom into my closet. At some point, I realized it was my mother sobbing. Wearily, I dragged myself out of bed. My chest felt constricted as my blood rushed in. Somehow, I knew someone had died. My mother's father was the oldest person I knew. Bracing myself for the news, I left my room.

My parents' light was on. I stopped in the doorway. My father stared at me from the far end of the room. "Chad's dead." Still in shock, he sprang the news on me. They were the worst words I had ever heard in my sixteen years.

For a moment, I did not react. The words traveled in warped slow motion from my head to my heart. "No."

But it was true. The phone call in the middle of the night had not been like the countless calls I'd learned to ignore from patients needing my father. This one had traveled nearly halfway around the world with news not meant for the phone, news not meant for a parent to have to hear, ever.

My mother appeared from the bathroom, face red and wet, eyes swollen. She held me tight.

"I'm going to wake up Bill," my dad said. I guess the sight of us made him realize that someone was missing. Well, two someones. Chad would be missing forever. Maybe he just wanted to hug Bill and pretend it was Chad. Having all four of us awake and crying at four in the morning did not soothe the pain. The four of us. Four survivors floating out in different directions as though the bridge that held us together had snapped.

The year was a year of firsts no parents or siblings ever want to face — like first birthdays and the first Christmas without my brother. My days of bubbling with enthusiasm over regaling the latest news about my brothers were over. And the following year, as I headed off to college, brought a new set of firsts: meeting new people.

"So," a fellow freshman — nervous and trying to make conversation — asked, "do you have any brothers or sisters?"

My face went pale and my hands turned clammy. "Sure," I mumbled. "Er, excuse me." I made up some lie about finding the bathroom or refilling my drink. Alone for a moment, I gulped in deep breaths. Small talk was no small matter at all.

What was I supposed to say? I have two brothers? No, I didn't, not really. One brother? That was wrong, as well. I grew up in a family of five. We lost one member, but we were still a family of five.

I spent those early days steering clear of social situations and avoiding small talk when I found myself with people as we waited for a class to begin or stood on line in the cafeteria. I learned to keep up an incessant flow of questions and feigned interest in everyone at my table.

When all else failed, I came up with other answers: "I came here because my brother's here." I had chosen to go to the same college as my brothers, even after Chad died. If someone told me they had a sister then I'd say, "Wish I had a sister."

Sometimes, I'd say, "I grew up with identical twin brothers," or "I had two brothers," and hope that no one would notice.

Unfortunately, someone was bound to ask, "Where are they now?"

"One of them is a junior here and the other is dead." Now there's a conversation stopper. My tone wasn't very kind either, clearly showing my resentment that this stupid small talk was like dragging sharp tacks across a wound that wouldn't heal.

This was no way to make friends. The resentment had to soften. It wasn't their fault. The weight of carrying my brother in my heart grew lighter. And then one day, it happened: Someone asked me, "Do you have any siblings?"

"Two brothers," I responded automatically. There was no hesitation, no catch in my throat, merely the statement of fact. One of my brothers may no longer be of this earth, but he is part of my family of five forever.

~D. B. Zane

54

My Home
Where the Brave Live

This nation will remain the land of the free
only so long as it is the home of the brave.
~Elmer Davis

The love-hate relationship I have with my brother is like a car: I hate that he gives me unexpected problems, yet I love him because I have no idea what I would do without him.

My brother, Jerod, prayed for a younger sister for four years, so when I finally arrived, I had open arms anxiously anticipating me. Since the day when he first cradled me in his arms at the hospital, we were practically inseparable. Occasionally, we butted heads and would get into full-on fistfights, but at the end of the day we both knew we would take a bullet for the other in a split second.

Jerod helped me rise above the vicious cycles of drama at school where the boys were jerks and the girls were sneaky. He helped me cure my boredom with games ranging from our own form of *Fear Factor* to action games where we ran wild through the tangled forest of pine trees in our backyard. He helped me train intensely for the upcoming soccer seasons so that I could outperform all the other girls flaunting their fancy footwork on the field. He helped me finish my chores for the sole purpose of freeing my hands to toss the football a few times outside before the sun disappeared behind the dense forest, sometimes practicing so much that I was better than half the guys on my school's football team.

Jerod helped bring up my spirits when I was down, usually from getting into trouble by my smart-aleck mouth. Most of all, he helped to assuage my fear of being alone in this big world. Jerod would improvise bedtime stories just to get a smile and a laugh out of me before the night ended. He used to take me mud-bogging, spinning "donuts" with his car in giant puddles of mud, in a couple of nearby neighborhoods. To this day, a glimpse of the red Honda splashing across the muddy field never fails to leave a grin on my face.

Not only were we siblings, we were each other's best friend, confidant, guardian, and support system—Jerod and I made the best team. When he told me that he was recruited into the Air Force and would be leaving for boot camp post-graduation, I felt like a helpless puppy left in the pouring rain, scared and confused. He was gone before I knew it. I was forced to become independent overnight. I knew then that things would never be the same.

My brother was the first person I knew to enter this foreign land of sergeants and salutes. At his boot camp graduation, I was his biggest fan, cheering for his squadron, The Wolfpack, in the graduation parade. Tears came to my eyes as I saw the fit and disciplined man my brother had become. I was finally at peace with his decision when I saw the confidence gleaming from his eyes as he marched among his fellow graduates in six single-file lines.

Shortly after I learned to accept his absence, I was indirectly informed of my brother's deployment to Kuwait, which was neighboring the Iraq-Iran war zone. To me, war was Death's four-year waiting list. Unsettling images came to my mind as I thought of Jerod in the midst of God-knows-what. Maybe he was facing the enemies, looking into the whites of their eyes like in Civil War pictures, full of rusty muskets and firing canons. Or maybe he resembled the characters in *All Quiet on the Western Front*, forever scarred by the torturous cries for help, lost in a foreign land. Or maybe he was being terrorized by monstrous, metal machines, the sting of mustard gas in the air, like in the stories I heard in history class. The months passed the slowest during this time, especially during Christmas.

I had never spent Christmas without my brother, or without my family together. Tensions were high within my family, and without my brother there to support me or reassure my fears, I felt extremely alone. Depression rendered me emotionless. The few instances when I was able to catch my brother at a time that was decent enough for both of us, I spoke with distance and remained selfishly guarded. I didn't fully comprehend his need to keep in touch; I felt ostracized from his life. Relief revived me when I was informed Jerod had returned safely to the States. Now that the terrifying knowledge that my brother was in a war zone had subsided, we were free to resume the closeness we had just three years before.

Jerod's deployment has transformed my view of military service. Now I regard it as the most selfless and courageous sacrifice someone can give to the American people. My brother carries a nation's worth of honor in every step and upholds the respect of every citizen in this country. Before this experience, my brother was a hero and a leader to me, but now he is a hero and a leader to all Americans.

~Kalie M. Eaton

A Mother at Fifteen

The willingness to accept responsibility for one's own life
is the source from which self-respect springs.
~Joan Didion

I ended up pregnant at the end of ninth grade. I knew I faced many difficulties—how I would tell my parents, if I should keep the baby, and if so, how the father, Ronnie, and I were going to take care of the baby.

I knew we were going to need plenty of help so I first decided to tell my mom. When I told her, I felt like I had completely disappointed her. She struggled with accepting my condition and telling my dad.

Soon after, my entire family knew about my situation. We began to have many discussions about whether or not I planned to keep the baby. After long debates, eventually I told them it was my responsibility, so I wanted to deal with it. At the time I was not sure how I would balance school and a baby. I thought I would have to drop out my tenth grade year because I could not imagine handling the responsibility of being a teenage mother and full-time student. After sharing my thoughts with relatives and close friends, they offered their support and told me they refused to allow me to give up on school.

Before Jaylen was born, we pre-enrolled him in daycare to secure him a place when he reached six months. Although this preparation was a relief, his father and I were still concerned about transportation; getting him to and from daycare. Daycare required infants to report by 8:00 a.m. but I had to be at school by 8:15 a.m. We were required to pick Jaylen up from daycare by 3:00 p.m. but I was not dismissed from school until 3:15 p.m. This frustrated me because I knew that there was no way for this arrangement to work. Again, I was at the point of giving up on school for a while until I could derive a workable plan that would coincide with my schedule, but Ronnie's father volunteered to take Jaylen in the morning and my mom decided that she could pick him up in the afternoon. With Jaylen visiting his father on the weekends, I had a little free time to complete school assignments and projects or just simply hang out with friends. Having "me" time removed some of the pressures of my hectic schedule.

Another obstacle I faced was how I would continue participating in school clubs and other organizations. The thought of not being an active member of the clubs I belonged to saddened me. Although at times I was not able to stay after school, teachers worked with me and held meetings during school hours or allowed me to catch up with the "happenings" of the organization during a later time. Many days I was unable to fraternize with the other students, so I appreciated the compassion and flexibility from my peers and teachers.

Currently, I'm a senior in high school and I'm glad that I decided to continue school for the sake of myself and Jaylen. Now the question in my head is, "What about college?" Taking on a higher education initially seemed like a difficult choice, because I wasn't sure if I was going to have dependable people to take care of my son while I went to class. Thanks to caring grandparents and Jaylen's father, I no longer have to worry about the care of my son since they have agreed to be full-time caretakers while I am at class.

I had to rule out going to college in another state, far from home, because this would mean I wouldn't have the opportunity to spend time with Jaylen. After doing research, I found an outstanding engineering school, Southern Polytechnic State University, in Marietta, Georgia—close to my home. Since Jaylen is enrolled in daycare, I will be able to take morning classes, have time to study, and still be able to spend time with him. Right now, I am planning to live on campus so that I am able to focus on my education and experience college life fully. With the awesome support from my family and Jaylen's father, I have the chance to accomplish my dreams of receiving a high school diploma, providing for my son, and getting a four-year-degree in computer engineering.

Being a teen mother has been one of the most challenging experiences I have faced so far. Just imagine a child, who is still growing up, trying to raise another child. It is tiresome and a very difficult task, but as a mother, you have to be strong, energetic, patient, and dedicated, because your child depends on you. Being a mother is not always stressful; it can be rewarding in its own way. When Jaylen began to speak and took his first steps, I felt so much gladness and unexplainable happiness because I knew I had something to do with his success. Knowing that he will grow up to appreciate me for the things I have done, the time I spent, and the hard work I put in to being his mom is gratifying.

Being a young mother has encouraged and pushed me to become a much better person. I overcame selfishness, opened up, and have become a stronger and more positive person because of it.

~Tracie Weaver

Stacy's Secret

The greatest gift God can give a person is another person.
~Franz Werfel

I t was the first day of school. My stomach was in huge knots and my face felt hot as I clutched my tray, scanning the lunchroom for a place to sit. Nearby, a table full of girls caught my eye as I headed for the empty table in the back. Chatting. Giggling. Eating. Everyone was surrounded by friends, all except for me. I was the new girl in school and I was feeling completely insecure and lonelier than ever. For a week, I felt this way every single lunch period.

The following Tuesday, I sat alone barely touching my salad and soggy French fries. I peered intently at the clock on the wall, imagining that it sprouted wings so that time would actually fly and I could catch a ride out of this place. Homesickness crept over me like a heavy fog as I thought of my best friend, Jessica. If only she were here...

"Hey, I haven't seen you around before. Are you new?" said a smiling curly-haired girl as she interrupted my thoughts.

"Um, yeah, my dad's job just transferred us here."

"Come sit with us," she said as she motioned me over to a table next to her raven-haired friend, Tabatha. For the rest of the lunch period, we sat talking and giggling. And for the first time in a long while, I felt like I belonged again.

From then on, Stacy was my best friend. We spent tons of time together, hanging out at the mall, watching movies that scared us silly, talking about the cute guy named Brent who played on the football team, and about basketball.

Stacy was the best player on the girls' team. She was good at everything she tried. She made straight A's in Algebra where I was struggling to maintain a C. She loved science class and someday wanted to be a nurse. Plus, she was pretty. Her life seemed so perfect that I often found myself feeling jealous of her.

Then one day she didn't show up for school. I thought maybe she was sick at home or had a doctor's appointment. I asked Tabatha if she knew where Stacy was and she didn't have a clue.

I tried to call her later that night, but no one answered. Again and again I tried, for the next week. It just rang and rang, and not even the answering machine picked up. Finally, her dad answered.

"No, Stacy's not here right now. I'll have her call you back, Kim." Then he abruptly hung up the phone.

I could tell by his tone that he was holding back and something was terribly wrong. So I called back to see if she was okay.

"Kim, she's out of town visiting her aunt. I'll have her call you when she's back home."

I didn't believe him. She'd never talked about going to an aunt's house. It sounded fishy to me.

A few days later the phone rang and I didn't recognize the voice on the other end.

"Hi, Kim."

"Who's this?"

"It's me, Stacy," said a raspy voice.

It was during that conversation that I learned something unbelievably upsetting. My best friend had tried to commit suicide.

Stacy had taken forty sleeping pills she'd found in her mom's medicine cabinet and crawled into bed. Her mom found her an hour later when she returned from work. Luckily, the sleeping pills were far past their expiration date. Otherwise, the doctor in the emergency room said she wouldn't have survived.

She was having a hard time talking because her throat was sore from the tube they put in to pump her stomach. She spent a week in the hospital so they could make sure she wouldn't hurt herself again. Her counselor was on call if she needed to talk.

As I sat listening to her, I wondered how I could have missed that Stacy was hurting inside. I choked back the tears and asked her why. She didn't say anything for a while. I could tell she was crying.

"Stacy, are you there?" I whispered.

"I'm still here."

Again I asked, "Why, Stace?"

"I just... I just didn't think I was good enough."

She explained how her dad pushed her so much to make good grades and be good at sports and that she lived in the shadow of her older brother who was off at college. She never felt like she was good at anything and she fought a lot with her mom.

"I'll be back at school tomorrow. I better go."

I sat on the edge of my bed. How could I have missed all the warning signs? She seemed so put together. I was her best friend, and I had no idea she was in so much pain. A sickening feeling grew in the pit of my stomach and somehow I felt partially responsible.

The next day I saw Stacy at her locker.

"I'm so sorry I wasn't there for you," I said swallowing hard.

I gave her a hug and she told me it wasn't my fault. She didn't want anyone to know what was going on at home. Not even me.

"The good thing is now I know that God's not through with me yet," she said. "There are things left for me to do."

Just then the bell rang.

As I walked to class, I remembered the day she invited me to sit at her table and how much that meant to me. I still wished I could have been there for her somehow when she needed a friend the most.

That's when it hit me. My eyes blurred with tears as a familiar gentle voice stirred inside of me. There was someone who was with her all along. It was God. He had never left her side. Not ever.

The years have whizzed by since my school days with Stacy. Instead of a nurse, she became a doctor, wife and a mother of beautiful twin girls. God did have things for Stacy to do in her life after all.

~Kim Rogers

57

Take One Step In

People are pretty much alike. It's only that our differences are more
susceptible to definition than our similarities.
~Linda Ellerbee

Take one step in
If you've ever felt alone,
That no one wanted you
And you were all on your own.

Take one step in
If your heart's ever been broken,
Shattered and destroyed
With nothing left to be spoken.

Take one step in
If you've ever cried yourself to sleep,
Eyes heavy with tears
Thoughts dark and deep.

Take one step in
If you've ever lost yourself,
You forgot who you were
You hid away yourself.

Take one step in
If you've ever been confused,
No idea where to turn
You felt worn down and bruised.

Now take a look around
Everyone took one step in too,
You're not going through this alone
We're standing right by you.

~Tiffany Chan

58

At a Moment's Notice

Dad, your guiding hand on my shoulder will remain with me forever.
~Author Unknown

I swung the door open and rushed down the stairs. My chest was palpitating and my vision was beginning to blur. I came around the corner, slipping onto the cold tile floor, losing my balance, and dropping everything I had in my hands. I grabbed a handful of hair and clenched my fist tighter and I began to feel the beginnings of a scream that had been building up all day long. Before I could let out a sound, I felt someone's gentle, yet firm touch on my shoulder. I used my sleeves to wipe the tears away and turned around to find myself staring up at my father. I could see the outline of my reflection in his eyes grow larger as I stood up and wrapped my arms around his thick waist.

"Bad day at school?"

I rolled my eyes, then nodded.

"You have no idea."

He let out a soft chuckle and then pressed his lips against my forehead. They were cold, and I felt the roughness against my skin.

"Well, do you want to talk about it?"

I pulled away from his arms and walked towards the steps. I sat down and shook my head. "You know Dad, I'm not so sure. I didn't think you would actually care to hear about my problems."

His jaw dropped and his breath blew out in a sharp gust. I felt the heat from his anger burn right through me.

My eyes were glued to the floor, and I knew that if I made one more sarcastic comment I would be punished for life.

"It's getting late. Go to bed and I'll see you in the morning."

His tone had calmed down, and the color of his face slowly returned to normal. He walked past me and headed up the stairs, hoping that I would change my stubborn ways.

I remember lying in bed that night and finding it extremely hard to fall asleep. I kept thinking about how much I had hurt my dad's feelings, and how guilty I felt for not apologizing. He had always been there to support me, and he helped me whenever I needed him.

He was there when my boyfriend Ryan passed away. It was July 10th, the day my brother Austin turned seven. I woke up to a surprise knock on my door, and it was my dad. I remember that day clearly because it was the first time I had ever seen my dad like this. I sat up in bed and turned on the light, blocking my eyes from the brightness. My dad was calmer than usual. His eyes were glossy, and it seemed like he had been crying for hours. He sat down on the corner of my bed and reached out to grab my hand. His hands were wet from wiping the salty tears off his face, and they were a bit colder than they normally were. I knew something was wrong, so I began to tear up myself. As my dad made his way through the tragic story behind Ryan's death, I became weak. My dad pulled me closer and continued to cry. I held my ear against his chest, and tuned out every sound but the calm beats of his heart.

"Angela." He hesitated, and took another breath. He continued on in a quiet, shaky tone. "As a parent I am so devastated to hear about Ryan. I would never be able to live without you or your brother."

Tears streamed down my face as I continued to listen.

"This was a freak accident, and shouldn't have happened. I'm really sorry."

It was then that I realized how much I needed my father in my life. He was there to protect me, teach me right from wrong, and more importantly, to love me as his daughter and first child. Every time I go back and look at how much he helped me through the pain of losing Ryan, I realize that my dad and I have a closer relationship than I think.

Remembering how much my father cared, I stared up at the clock wondering how I could apologize to him for the scene I had made earlier. What if he wouldn't forgive me?

After a few moments of silence, I jumped out of bed and threw my sweater on. I swung the door open, and saw my dad standing right before my eyes. It looked as if he was looking for a way to speak to me for hours as well. We both looked at each other in shock, a little frustrated.

"Angela, I..."

"Dad," I interrupted politely. "I am sorry about earlier, I was just upset and having a bad day. I didn't mean to take everything out on you."

His face relaxed and he sighed in relief.

"Angela, I want you to know that I only ask you to tell me what's wrong because you're my daughter. I care about you and love you way too much to ignore that."

I felt a rush of guilt as I continued. "I want you to know that I'm really sorry. I was always afraid to let you in and tell you things because I didn't want you to think that I wasn't strong enough. Now I know that all you've been doing is trying to help me and be the loving, supporting father that I need. I'm sorry."

He shook his head and began to laugh.

"You know, they do say guys are a lot stronger than girls for a reason."

I began laughing and playfully punched his arm.

"So," he began.

"What do you say? Up for a little one-on-one game of basketball?"

I smirked, and then replied, "You're on!"

I guess being around my father more and more each day helps us to build a stronger relationship. We both have our moments, but if we work together we find a way to make things work. I could never picture my life without my father, and I always want to make sure he knows that.

~Angela Brewer

Little Bit

The only real mistake is the one from which we learn nothing.
~John Powell

"Meow, meow, meow," is what I heard as I walked through the alley. I approached the noise, and I noticed a tail sticking out from under a piece of wood. Under the wood was a tiny black and white kitten. I picked him up and realized he must be freezing to death. I hurried home with the kitten wrapped in my jacket.

My new best friend, who soon became known as Little Bit, received his name because he was nearly weightless when I held him in my hands. He stood about five inches tall and his paws were the size of dimes. Little Bit's small size had a great advantage—he fit perfectly in the pocket of my jacket, which made taking him everywhere very easy. He would ride with me on my bike, play in the dirt with me, and catch frogs.

Little Bit was the best friend I had ever had. Any time I was home, he wouldn't leave my side. He was always eager to play with me. Anytime I ate cereal he would sit there patiently until I gave him my leftover milk. When I fell asleep at night, he would always curl up around my head to ensure that I was warm.

Unfortunately, I grew up. My teenage life weakened my relationship with Little Bit. I lived at such a fast pace that I stopped making time for him. My free time was spent with my friends instead. I would come in the house on my phone and not acknowledge him at all. His meows became an annoyance to me, but it wasn't his fault that he wanted his best friend back.

Time had taken a toll on Little Bit. His body began shutting down and by the time I realized something was wrong with him, he had already lost his balance. He lay there and looked at me, and to this day I still remember the sorrowful look in his bright green eyes. I took him to the vet, but there was nothing he could do. The last time I held him he wasn't the same tiny kitten I had found ten years before. He filled my arms now. Little Bit was put to sleep that day.

Little Bit's death made me realize how much he meant to me. I regret being so caught up in my own life that I never gave him the attention that he deserved. If I had been by his side all along, maybe I would have seen his symptoms and prevented them from getting worse. I'll always regret not being there for him. He was always there for me when I needed him.

I don't know why they always say that a dog is man's best friend—Little Bit was the best friend I ever had. I couldn't have asked for more from him. I regret our last years together, but I will always cherish the special memories we made.

~Steven D. Farmer

Mistake

Wisdom consists of the anticipation of consequences.
~Norman Cousins

Not a day goes by that I don't regret that day.
I knew it wasn't right, but what was I to say?
No thank you, not now, maybe another day?
It didn't matter he'd do it anyway.

The night was over; time to go home.
He didn't even say goodbye, I felt so alone.
My mom woke up and asked where I'd been.
"Oh just out with Kate and her little sister Gin."

A few months went by and my belly got big.
No, I couldn't be pregnant. I just ate like a pig.
I went to the store and got a test.
It didn't feel right, but I hoped for the best.

Ten minutes went by and it was time to look.
It was the hardest test I ever took.
I looked at the test and fell to the floor.
Next thing I heard was a knock at the door.

When I showed my mom she wasn't very proud.
When I showed my dad he screamed so loud.
There was nothing we could do, the damage was done.

But there were options that wouldn't be so fun.

We went to the doctor, they said it's a boy.
I felt a mixture of emotions—both sadness and joy.
My mom told me we have to put him up for adoption.
My dad said that this was my only option.

I chose a family who couldn't have their own child.
I learned their names, and the papers were filed.
The labor was hard and it hurt quite a lot.
But it all went away when I got the shot.

The doctor came in and said, "The family is here"
It was a long road but the end was near.
Caleb's new family came in, I didn't know what to say.
They promised they would write every day.

I wrote Caleb a letter,
Telling him this was for the better.
The new happy family left the room and I started to cry.
I was so sad I wanted to die.

I was only fourteen when I made a big mistake,
And it's one I hope you never make.

~Holly Rose Brumm

61

Living with Depression

The turning point in the process of growing up is when
you discover the core of strength within you that survives all hurt.
~Max Lerner

It all started when I was eight years old. My parents were going through a divorce and I was moving to a new state, leaving all my friends behind. For three years, I cried myself to sleep almost every night, overwhelmed with the pain of my life. We moved again when I was eleven, and then we finally talked about how I was feeling. My mom was a nurse, and has depression herself, so she knew what I was going through. I started seeing a counselor, who put me on anti-depressants. I felt like a freak for taking them, and often felt like they weren't working, so I stopped taking them. I lied to my mom when she couldn't understand why I wasn't getting better.

It was moving again that triggered the worst of my depression. I didn't like school and I never had many friends, so after moving and missing a few weeks of school I decided I didn't want to deal with it. I was numb to the outside world. I was so scared of going back to school that when my mom forced me to go one day, I went home and swallowed a whole bottle of Benadryl. I chickened out at the last minute and told my mom, who took me to the hospital right away. If we had gone an hour later, I would have died.

After that incident, my mom wouldn't leave me alone. A counselor started to come to the house every Wednesday. I still refused to take my meds, and I went on like that for another year.

I finally started to take my medication, and now I'm living life to its full potential. I learned that killing yourself is never the answer, and that there is always a light at the end of the tunnel. Depression is not a weakness and it's not just going to go away. Most importantly, I learned that my illness doesn't make me a freak—it's a common problem for teens everywhere.

~Crystal Haigh

Winner of M Magazine story-writing contest

62

Not Such an Easy Way to Diet After All

Don't dig your grave with your own knife and fork.
~English Proverb

I was a typical sixteen-year-old girl who read fashion magazines and listened to music. Like a typical teenage girl, I also thought I was fat. Standing at only five feet two inches and weighing 125 pounds put me ten pounds over what the health experts said was my ideal weight. I read every diet and exercise plan I could find, including ones in *The National Enquirer*, in hopes of shedding that ten pounds.

Then one day, while sharing weight-loss woes with my seventeen-year-old cousin, a miracle happened. My cousin had discovered a weight-loss secret that even *The National Enquirer* had not claimed.

"It's easy to lose weight," she said. "Just make yourself throw up after you eat."

Initially, I was taken aback by her statement. I thought it was a disgusting way to lose weight, and I would never share such a secret with anyone else. Besides, even though I wanted to lose weight, I cherished food. My family was poor, and food was scarce. I couldn't imagine wasting food like that. Nonetheless, I secretly held on to the idea, and a week later, I had my first binge and purge.

As much as I loved food, and as much as I respected the fact that food was scarce in a household of eight, I was desperate enough to try anything that would help me be thinner. So right after dinner, I went straight to the bathroom, turned on the overhead fan to create a noise distraction, stuck two fingers down my throat, and forced up my dinner. The next night I did the same thing, repeating this ritual night after night until it became an addiction.

I had finally found a diet secret that worked, or so I thought. Little did I know that what I thought was a diet secret had actually been acknowledged as an eating disorder called bulimia. No wonder *The National Enquirer* wasn't claiming it.

After several months of bingeing and purging, I got to the point where I would purge not only dinner but also any food I didn't want to enter into my digestive system. If I wanted to eat three doughnuts, I ate them, and then rushed to the bathroom afterward. If I wanted to eat a whole eleven-ounce bag of chips, a pint of ice cream, or a whole row of cream-filled sandwich cookies, I would, because I had finally found an easy way to diet without denying myself.

One day, however, I faced a dilemma. The trick to bingeing and purging is to get rid of the food before it is fully digested, or purging will be difficult. I had been on an out-of-town school trip, and on the way back, we stopped at a restaurant about an hour away from the school. I ordered my favorite meal, country-fried steak and gravy with mashed potatoes.

After enjoying every bite of the meal, I began to worry. How would I purge it? I had never purged in public, nor did I have a desire to do so. Purging was a private, messy ordeal that required a lot of cleanup afterward and sometimes left me feeling dazed and exhausted, depending upon how much I had eaten. I could never purge in a public restroom, only in the privacy and security of my own home. Panic set in as I sat through that hour-long bus ride, wondering whether my dinner would still be "purgeable" when I got home. The first thing I did when I got home was rush to the bathroom. I was able to purge, but it was the most painful purge I had ever experienced.

My obsession with bingeing and purging continued through my senior year in high school, so I was on my secret diet for about eighteen months. I knew enough about weight loss to know which foods to purge and which foods to keep in order to maintain a decent body weight. But what I didn't know was the other damage that this eating disorder was causing me, or could potentially cause me. For one, I had a persistent, painful sore throat. Also, I didn't realize that bulimia could have caused permanent medical damage and even death. Essentially, what my cousin and I considered an easy way to diet could have been an easy way to die.

I don't recall the amount of weight I lost over that eighteen-month period, but I do recall dropping from a size 8/10 to a size 5/6 by the summer after my high school graduation. I never told anyone about my shameful dieting secret, not even my cousin. I just allowed everyone to marvel at the fact that I was finally losing weight.

In the fall, I started college, and, to my dismay, the freshman dormitory did not have private baths. The restrooms and the showers were down the hall and were locker-room style. I thought about purging, but I knew I couldn't, not in a public restroom. According to the website, www.bulimiatips.net, "Bulimia runs on the same premise as other chemical substance addictions, it is ultimately left to fate and luck whether or not they are devastated by the disease." I could say that fate and luck saved my life, but I would rather call it the grace of God. What I thought was a curse—public restrooms—was actually a blessing that ended my addictive eating disorder.

I never purged again after starting college, because once the addiction was broken I never had the desire again. Unfortunately, I had developed another eating disorder that was not so easily broken. I was still addicted to bingeing. I had now become a compulsive eater. I gained twenty pounds my freshman year in college, eating anything from an eleven-ounce bag of chips to an entire medium pizza in one sitting.

My fad dieting, eating disorders, and yo-yo weight losses and gains continued for the next three years, until the summer before my senior year in college. I don't recall how it happened, but I do recall for the first time I stopped being overly concerned about my weight and became more concerned about my future career plans. Perhaps the distraction of trying to find a job took my focus away from food.

By the end of that summer, just before I entered my senior year in college, I found myself wearing a size 5/6 again, without even trying. I had finally lost weight and was down to what the experts said was my ideal weight. After all my weight loss attempts, eating disorders, and fad diets, I finally developed a healthy lifestyle, not based on what an expert said was ideal for me, but based on how I felt about myself.

~Linda Jackson

Was It Me?

Mom hates dad, Dad hates mom, it all makes you feel so sad.
~Kurt Cobain

My mother lives in one place and my father in another,
My sister's with my mother and my father has my brother,
One week I live with her and then the next belongs to him,
They want me to act happy but I find it really grim.

When all of this first happened, I didn't understand,
Was it me who made them angry, throw away their wedding
    bands?
I remember when they laughed a lot and hugged and kissed
    like mad,
But suddenly they stopped all that and everything turned bad.

I used to be real difficult and sometimes Mom would cry,
My dad would get so angry, off the handle he would fly
My brother and my sister seemed so perfect next to me,
Said I was just a tyrant with a different destiny.

When life became a place where both my parents lived apart
The sun went right behind a cloud and darkened my young
    heart.
The air I breathe feels thin and stale and fills my lungs with pain,
Every moment I am thinking that I caused them all their strain.

Oh God please help me get through this, help change the way
    I feel,
I'd love to wake tomorrow and find none of this is real.
People try and tell me that it wasn't me at all,
But they weren't here in this nest with me before I had my fall.

I had a home where Mom and Dad and bro and sis all met,
But now I have a suitcase piled high with sad regret.
I know that Mom had met a guy with whom she wished to be
But I still feel that they simply didn't want to be with me.

~Trudy Weiss

64

Chicken Soup
for the Soul

The Hardest Day
of My Life

The difficulties of life are intended to make us better, not bitter.
~Author Unknown

I was fifteen years old and a high school freshman when I started rapidly losing weight. I was 130 pounds and 5'8", and I was dropping ten pounds every couple of weeks. I couldn't understand why I was always hungry, always thirsty, and never satisfied. Every night I woke up five or six times to go to the bathroom, but I never actually had to go, I just always felt like I had to. Finally, we decided to go to the hospital, just to make sure nothing bad was going on. Nothing could have prepared me for what I was going to hear. I have a brief memory of my sister crying and putting her head on my shoulder, but I was so numb all I could do was crack a joke: "Well, at least now we're sure it's not a tapeworm."

Eight hours later, after being told nothing besides go to the hospital immediately, I found myself in a hospital bed, confused, hungry, and with a blood glucose level of forty-five. The hospital staff thought I might go into a coma, so they injected me with insulin and told me the worst news I could have imagined. I had been diagnosed with Type 1 juvenile diabetes. The only question I could think to ask was, "Am I going to die?" The nurse told me to go out, enjoy a meal with my family, and relax, because tomorrow my new, difficult life would begin.

I don't recall what time I had to be at the hospital, but I know it was early. Three nurses, one dietician, and a doctor all trained me, over the course of two days, to take care of myself. Every needle hurt, but in some way I began to feel stronger every time I was able to think about the needles without crying. I knew that, despite my new struggle, I would come out a more resilient and more compassionate person.

Now, nearly three years later, I still remember the feeling when the doctors told me I was a Type 1 diabetic. I'm thankful when I look back that I was able to be strong, and that my family and friends supported me. I am now two months shy of eighteen and have been on an insulin pump for almost a year and a half. To this day, I have had 3,438 needle injections, but every scar reminds me of my own strength. Surprisingly, I am grateful for my disease — it has made me the person I am today, and I would never change who I am.

~Kelsey Bard

Winner of M Magazine story-writing contest

65

Bump in the Road

A bend in the road is not the end of the road...
unless you fail to make the turn.
~Author Unknown

Life's path is not always smooth. Throughout our lives, there are always bumps that we have to overcome. My first big bump came at the age of fifteen, and it knocked me down, literally. I had a seizure.

The last thing I remember is cutting down trees with my parents. I was unconscious when the EMTs put me into an ambulance and took me to Great Falls. I didn't wake up until I was in the emergency room. I remember a white ceiling with the light shining on me like a spotlight, my parents looking down on me with tears in their eyes. The nurses told me I had to have some tests done, one being an EEG. I was taken into a room and was told to sit down. A nurse came in and started putting these little sticky pads that had wires coming out of them on my head. I felt like I was trapped in wires.

About halfway through the EEG, a doctor walked in, whispered something to the nurse, and walked out. At that point I knew something was wrong. A few minutes later the nurse took off all the pads and led me into the room my mom was in. We sat in that room for five minutes, both lost in our own thoughts. The doctor finally walked in. He sat down and told me that I had abnormal brain waves. He didn't explain at all what this meant. He prescribed medicine I had to take morning and night; then he walked out.

At this point I had no clue what was wrong with me. In fact, I was in denial that anything was wrong with me at all. After a day of lying to myself, I decided I needed to find out what I had and learn about it. It turned out that I had epilepsy and I went to see a more helpful doctor in Missoula, who explained that I had juvenile myoclonic epilepsy, which is a type that is characterized by muscle twitches.

Over the next few months, I was having five or six twitches every day. This slowed down everyday activities such as curling my hair, brushing my teeth, and eating. I poured cereal on people, stabbed myself in the face with a butter knife, and discolored my eyebrows by accident with mascara. I thought these were the most embarrassing things that could happen to me. I was worried people would make fun of me or get mad if I ruined something of theirs. To my surprise, I found that other people did not find my twitches embarrassing. They found them entertaining, and this helped me see that they were pretty funny! My friends came up with ways to help me see that. They called me Twitch and they have even tried to mimic my twitches themselves. I will always be thankful to them for helping me learn to laugh at myself.

By now, I have accepted my epilepsy. It flipped my life upside down but, strangely, I think it has been for the best. Epilepsy has changed my outlook on life. I used to take my health and life in general for granted. That has changed. Now I try to take time to look around and appreciate everything. Strength is something I needed a lot of when I found out I wasn't perfect. Now I know that my imperfections make me stronger.

When we meet a bump in the path, we can choose to get over it or turn around and never face it. I am proud that I faced this bump even if it did cause me to fall. I am thankful all the time that I don't have anything worse than epilepsy. I can live with this, and I will be able to live life to the fullest. I am happy to say that I have not had another seizure since the first one, but if I ever do, I will deal with it. I have made it over one bump in my life and I am ready for the next.

~Lexi Bremer

Just for
Teenagers

101 Stories of Inspiration
and Support for Teens

Chapter
7

Taking a Stand

Sometimes the biggest act of courage is a small one.

~Lauren Raffo

66

Breaking Boundaries

The time is always right to do what is right.
~Dr. Martin Luther King, Jr.

"**N**othing said in this room will leave this room. We are a family tonight, and this is an unbreakable circle of trust."

I laid my head down on my pillow and squeezed my stuffed animal closer to my chest, preparing for the pain and tears I knew were to come. I was going to spend the next few hours of the five-day leadership camp in an activity called Boundary Breaking, during which I would discover the dreams, fears, secrets and struggles of eighteen other high school students, all of whom I had known for a total of two and a half days. I would be expected to completely open myself up to these people, a thought that made me squirm with discomfort.

The questions started off easy, more like icebreakers than the deeply personal questions I was expecting. Yet with each question, I could sense my connection with the members of the group growing, and together we could feel the atmosphere in the room changing. As the intensity of our new relationship increased, so did the intensity in which we responded to the progressively more intimate questioning. Questions such as "What do you fear most?" and "What has been the most difficult time in your life?" began to draw tears from some members of the group.

However, it was the next question that brought out the most powerful responses of the night: "What is something that you wish everyone knew about you, before they could ever judge your character?" our senior counselor Jon asked the group.

A flood of stories was unleashed; stories of abuse, bitter divorce, suicide and depression caused even our strongest members to succumb to tears. I did my best to stop the torrent of tears flowing down my own face when it was my turn to speak. With little knowledge of what I was going to say, I began.

"What I wish people could know about me is that… I have three gay uncles. They have had so many challenges to overcome because of their sexual orientation. The last thing they need is for people to disrespect their lifestyle in their everyday language. I can't stand it when people call something "gay" when they don't like it. I wish people knew that their word choice hurts me, and it hurts my family." I choked out the last line through my renewed tears. Several people put their arms around me and patted my back.

I felt my previously shaking hands steady themselves as I realized what I had finally been able to share. I had never stood up against the use of offensive words before, even though they bothered me immensely. I had always assumed, as I still did for the next several days, that speaking out would make no difference; people would continue to use these words no matter what I had to say about it. However, this idea changed when I checked my mailbox two days later and found a note from a girl in my group who I had not spoken to very much.

"I want to thank you. You've changed my life and made me realize I have been offending people with my words. You've made it clear to me that I need to change and I'm going to."

I sat in stunned silence as tears once again filled my eyes. For the first time in my sixteen years I felt like I had affected change. I was able to stop one person from offending people with her words, and from that experience I gained the belief that I can stop more than just one person. I am no longer scared to stand up for what I believe in. I know now that all it takes is one story and one person willing to listen to make change happen.

~Heidi Patton

Drama Queen

Relationships are like glass. Sometimes it's better to leave them broken
than try to hurt yourself putting it back together.
~Author Unknown

I was never "that girl"—the one who started drama, who partied with friends, who flirted with boys, who fussed over her social life. I was another girl entirely, one who smiled at people in the hallways and drifted between the "preppy" and the "nice girls" group, the one who earned straight A's, did varsity sports, and had strict parents. Not that I didn't care about friends, fun, or boys, I was just content with myself. I didn't think it was worth investing large amounts of time and effort into changing how I looked, how I acted, and how I talked to boys, even as I started high school.

On the second day of freshman year, he was sitting in the back of my second hour Biology Honors class, lanky frame folded into a desk chair, dressed from head to toe in Nike apparel, which turned out to be his everyday outfit of choice. I took my seat in the front and wondered how on earth I had missed him the day before. He had sleepy blue eyes and close-cropped blond hair, and I spent every Biology class after that resisting the urge to turn around and look at him.

The following months were confusing but also wonderful. It didn't make sense that the sight of someone I didn't even know that well could improve my whole day, but I didn't want to question it. I didn't expect anything to happen between us, either, but the times we stopped to talk or laugh in the hallways, when he teased me and pulled my sweatshirt hood over my head—they were all golden.

After a month or two, some of my best friends guessed my secret, but I didn't mind—as long as my parents didn't know, his friends didn't know, and Marissa, most particularly, didn't know.

Marissa was "that girl"—fun to be around, good to know, but not to be trusted. Tiny and platinum blond with a high, sweet voice, she was dramatic to an extreme. We'd known each other since fourth grade, which is why we remained friends even though she constantly caused trouble in our friend group. Around her, I kept my mouth shut and hoped for the best.

We were at a sleepover one weekend, and though the conversations started out innocently, the topic soon turned to boys. Out of the four girls that night, Marissa was the only one who didn't know my secret.

"Irene, is there anyone you like?" she raised her eyebrows at me. I squirmed and laughed it off, but she kept pushing. "It's not a big deal!" she cajoled.

It was, actually, to me. To me, this was the first guy who'd meant anything substantial. But I knew she wouldn't understand, and not telling her, in that moment, would have immediately made things much worse.

"Okay... well..."

The following weekend, there was a birthday party, and everyone was invited. I'd been feeling a sense of impending doom since that night, but I told myself I was being silly and suppressed it. There was music; there was dancing. I went upstairs for a few minutes, and when I came back down, Marissa was lying on a couch with her head in his lap.

I survived the rest of the night on autopilot. I danced, I ate, I laughed, and I avoided looking at the couch in the corner with all my might.

The next week was better—I threw myself into homework, sports, extracurriculars—keeping myself distracted and my mind occupied. Only my very best friends knew what had happened, and they spent the week giving Marissa the cold shoulder.

I wasn't mad. No one, including me, could understand why, but I think it had to do with the fact that I wasn't surprised. Marissa was just that kind of girl. Of course, that didn't mean I was okay with what she'd done—I was disgusted and offended and hurt, but I was also wary. I didn't want to face it or deal with it, and I didn't want to talk to her about it. Eventually, one of my friends snapped at her, and she came looking for me.

"We really need to talk," she told me. "This is really important."

"Are you sure you want to, Marissa?" I asked. "Because... you might not be happy with what I have to say."

It was clear that she didn't understand what I meant, and that meant she didn't understand the significance of what she'd done. So I told her. I told her that actions spoke louder than words, and though she told me our friendship was more important than a boy, what she'd done told me the opposite. That I'd always been a good friend, defending her in front of others, and that she hadn't, if she was repaying me like this. That she rarely thought of anyone but herself, and that she thought even less about the consequences of her actions.

I told her that this attitude was going to destroy her someday, and that I didn't hate her, but I didn't think we could be friends anymore.

I spoke quietly and slowly, because the thoughts were coming so quickly and furiously that it was difficult to put all of my feelings into words. When I stopped, she was sobbing.

I wasn't trying to be mean or get even or bring her down. I legitimately wanted to show her what she'd done wrong so that she would learn from her mistakes, but my emotions filled me until I was drowning her in frustration and hurt.

She kept crying. I left.

By the end of the day, everyone had heard that Marissa had been crying, and that I'd had something to do with it. I just wanted it all to go away, or run away myself. I was drained, emotionally, mentally, physically, and I finally appreciated how uneventful my life had been before.

Marissa and I never talked about what had happened again, but I heard her version of the story that she'd told to other people. He never mentioned it to me either, though his name had been tied to it. At the end of the year, I made a decision I'd been considering for quite some time: I left my old school for a boarding school specializing in math and science, and haven't looked back since.

The whole fiasco left me with a fear of vulnerability, and a renewed determination to keep my feelings in check, because it was better than feeling uncertain. The next year, at that boarding school, I met a boy who both shattered those notions and brought me back to myself, to a place I'm very happy with now.

I haven't talked to Marissa or that boy since freshman year. I heard Marissa didn't change, despite what happened. I don't believe that telling her off like I did was the right thing to do, and so I still feel bad about it and I still feel bad for her. Maybe someday I'll figure out what I should have done. Maybe someday she'll learn those lessons I tried and failed to teach her. And maybe someday, she'll figure out how to be happy, too.

~Irene Jiang

Speaking Up

A time comes when silence is betrayal.
~Dr. Martin Luther King, Jr.

I never looked up when my friends were talking and joking about the "Retarded Boy" (as they referred to him) a few tables away. It didn't even cross my mind that he might feel bad when people whispered about him, or that he might be hurt when he saw the weird, disgusted looks from his peers. So I just let them talk, and I never intervened.

Then came the day I was standing in the kitchen helping with dinner, asking my mom about my brother's doctor's appointment. They were testing him for autism. My parents had told me there was a huge chance of it coming out positive, but I had never thought about him like that. My brother, Captain, four years old at the time, had always been my best friend. We would wrestle, play games and have the best of times together, even though we were far apart in age. My mom told me about the appointment, and when she got to the point about the test, she stopped. I turned around and she had tears in her eyes. I stared at her, wishing she would say something, when I realized what that silence meant. My eyes got blurry and my breathing got very ragged. "The test came out positive, sweetheart," she said with a calm voice. I broke down, crying and asking why it had happened to Captain.

My mom was trying to pull me together, saying that Captain couldn't see me like this and I had to be a big girl, when the front door opened, and Captain, our three-year-old sister Cali, and my father came in. I walked out of the kitchen. Captain was talking to our dad and then stopped, switching his attention to me. As he looked up at me with those huge blue eyes, I had to look away. I couldn't look at him. Everything had just changed. He was no longer that little baby brother who was just a normal little boy anymore. He was a little boy with a disease who didn't deserve anything that was going to come with it.

Over time, I was able to accept his disease a little more. We had to move a while later because Captain needed treatment and where we lived at the time didn't have the type he needed. So we moved to Maryland. Time passed and Captain and I both started at a new school. One day, I was standing in the bus line waiting when the "short bus" came and picked some kids up. The children in the other line started making jokes about the "retards" on that bus and I felt a strange feeling in my stomach. One that I had never felt before. As the other kids laughed about the cruel jokes, I said, quietly, that those comments weren't very nice. No one listened and I went on my way. I regretted it immediately, and wished I had said something else.

My family moved once more to a new school and I was given my chance to speak up pretty quickly. During band class, my teacher, Mrs. Young, stopped our playing to give us some feedback.

"Guys, we're playing like the kids on the short bus! Come on!" I felt that same feeling I had on the bus line, except worse. This was an adult, and I thought adults would be more careful about what they said. Apparently, ignorance comes in all different ages. The entire room was laughing when I raised my hand. I wasn't sure what I was going to say but I wanted to be heard.

"Yes, Alexis?" Mrs. Young asked. The class quieted down because the new girl was about to talk for the first time. I could feel my face getting red and was about to just say never mind, when my mouth opened and this came out:

"I don't think we should make fun of the short bus, because there are a lot of people on that bus who have great personalities and have the same feelings we do." I could feel my voice getting louder. "And also, I know some people on those buses and they are some of the most caring, sweetest, and smartest people so I would appreciate it if you didn't make fun of them."

The room was very quiet and everyone stared at me. Mrs. Young apologized for the comment and then started the song again. Everyone was a little on edge. At the end of the class, everyone was giving me weird looks and sizing me up. They looked like they were labeling me a nerd right off the bat, but I didn't care, because I knew three things: I had spoken the truth and what others in the class were probably thinking, I had taught everyone something, and while everyone in the classroom was being a follower, I had decided to take a different path. I want to become a leader and a positive role model and go on to teach others about people on the "short bus." I want to teach people about my brother Captain, who doesn't know that he's different. And really, he's not. He's just a five-year-old who loves baseball and eating cookies, and I never want to hear anybody make fun of him.

~Alexis Streb

Until She's Gone

Never let the hand you hold, hold you down.
~Author Unknown

Iain and I had been dating for a year, though I felt like I had known him my entire life. He was the only person I wanted to talk to when I was feeling blue. A shoulder to cry on at the end of a sad film. Someone who could quite literally turn my frown upside down by throwing me over his shoulder and tickling my toes. Everything between us seemed to be perfect; we were unbreakable. Until he transferred high schools.

Iain and I were already at different schools but they were relatively close and we often rode public transit home together. His new school was closer to his mom's house, and apparently had a significantly larger population of female students. At first I didn't worry. I didn't think I had a reason to; he was my boyfriend. My trustworthy boyfriend who loved me. Yet slowly we began to drift, and more fights began over Iain's flirtatious female study buddies. We were out at a coffee shop by my school when it happened. He looked up from his math homework and uttered the seven most excruciating words ever put in a sentence: "I want to break up with you." His face held no remorse, even as he watched a stream of tears erupt from my eyes. I walked home alone that night with the realization that I was now single. It was the most heartbreaking thought that I had ever had.

Surprisingly enough, a few days later Iain began texting me again. He said that the breakup was just as hard on him and that he was devastated. Though I was hearing several rumors about Iain flirting with other girls, I chose to believe he was changed. We became each other's support system through our own breakup. A few weeks later at a concert, he leaned in and asked me to be his girlfriend again. My immediate reaction was to say yes, but the thoughts of Iain with all those girls began to seep in. He noticed my hesitation and said, "You know Baby, I didn't know how much I needed you until I had lost you." I felt safe again, loved and in love. How could I not forgive him? Even if some of those rumors did prove to be true, Iain and I belonged together. I needed him.

Throughout the next year Iain and I became an on-again off-again couple. Our relationship was an emotional roller coaster and every time I thought the ride was over he'd throw me for another loop. On one of our "off-again" breaks, one of my friends told me that Iain and my best friend Danielle had secretly started to date. Never in my entire life had I felt more betrayed. Nothing Iain could say or do would ever mean anything to me again. Every "I love you" he said had been echoed in someone else's ear. I still cared about him, but I knew I couldn't forgive him for this.

A year later, I was in the very coffee shop where he first broke my heart when I saw him. I had heard from a friend that he and Danielle were recently broken up. He smiled and politely asked to join me and catch up. Twenty-five minutes into our conversation, he still hadn't mentioned his recent breakup. Instead, he looked up from his latte and searched my neckline for the heart-shaped locket I had once wore with such pride. When he discovered my collarbone was bare he looked up at me with defeated eyes and gently said, "You know, I never knew what I had until it was gone. I really miss you." I instantly thought of the night at the concert and how the same words had once made me feel complete. Only then did it finally dawn on me how much I had grown up since I left him. A year ago I thought that I needed him to be happy; no matter what he did to me I could always forgive him. Yet on this day, looking into his sad eyes, I realized that I'd experienced more joy on my own than I ever had with him.

Taking the last sip of my coffee I rose to leave the shop. Before I left, I said, "You know Iain, in my opinion, if you don't realize the value of something while it's still in your possession, then losing it is exactly what you deserve."

I walked home that day with the realization that I was still single. It was the most liberating thought that I have ever had.

~Kaity D.

Castaway

A lot of people are afraid to tell the truth, to say no. That's where toughness comes into play. Toughness is not being a bully. It's having backbone.
~Robert Kiyosaki

I gripped the spoon gouge to carefully shave off the rubber, following the pencil outline of the island. The moisture in my eyes evaporated like water in Death Valley as I refused to blink, perfecting the image I was creating. I glanced down at the calm, serene scene that was engraved on the pad of rubber. I imagined myself isolated on a deserted island, lying underneath a palm tree that hovered over me to protect me from the strong rays. The Caribbean waters crashed onto the white sandy beach as I lived in peace. In Key West, it was sunny every day, the warmth always lightened your mood, and the crystal clear waters cleansed all your problems away.

Then I blinked and was transported back to my first period art class.

I looked up from my art project and saw Becca's hands cupped around Alex's ear as she whispered something, with their glances directed towards me. I studied the thin and thick patches that made up the background of my stamp, my failed attempted at being an artist.

I asked Judy if she listened to the new Avril Lavigne CD, the album that replayed in my head every day.

"You would listen to Avril Lavigne. She's seriously the worse person in music," Becca snorted even though I wasn't even talking to her.

poser. Like, she thinks she's all punk, but she's not. So ...prised you listen to her."

...il's a poser? What did that make you, Becca? A spokesperson ...oxy and Billabong, I thought to myself. Of course, I didn't say ...ything because defending myself wasn't even in my vocabulary yet. I was fourteen, and my shell was as thick as ever, while my self-confidence was as thin as the patches on my rubber stamp.

You're worthless. No one likes you. You're so stupid. Your parents don't even love you. Those were the sentences running through my head, thanks to Becca and Alex. I just wanted out. I thought if I saved enough money, I could afford a one-way train ticket to the island I carved in the stamp and I could start a new life in Key West. Maybe I could really relocate to the land of serenity I dreamed about. I could sit in the shade of the palm tree, slap sunscreen on my pale skin, and feel the insecurities pour out in sweat.

I splashed on green paint, coating my finished stamp before I pressed it firmly on my blank canvas. I used all the force in my hands to make sure every speck of paint attached itself to the paper, perfecting my runaway landscape. The more paint, the more detail that would seep through on paper. The more detail, the more the stamp turned into my surroundings.

A shove yanked me from the white sand of Smathers Beach and pulled me back to the art room. Becca stood beside me with the corners of her mouth slightly curved upward. Instead of being on Key West beaches, I was thrown into a scene I had watched repeatedly in *Harriet the Spy*, where the kids in the class purposely spilled blue paint all over Harriet after she trash-talked them in her diary. I didn't trash-talk anyone in a diary. I hadn't even defended myself once, and now black paint was soaking into my favorite white tiger sweatshirt that I had only worn once before.

"Oops, sorry," Becca said, and took her seat as she snickered with Alex.

For the rest of the day, I walked with my arms crossed, hiding the black blotch that made me smell like a bottle of acrylic paint.

My confidence wore down, getting so thin that I could have

mistaken it for tissue paper. As I stared at the green stamp in front of me, I started to believe that the island I carved in rubber was just a representation of my life at that moment. The ocean in front of me was made of all the tears that had accumulated over a year. The palm tree hovering over me was Becca, stealing the sunshine that used to be in my life. Maybe my island wasn't a welcome haven—maybe I was just a lonely castaway there.

There was nowhere to escape. Every corner I turned, she was there—the hallways, the cafeteria, the art room, and even in my math class. I was trapped on this dark island, a thousand miles away from help.

One day she strutted into math class in a Billabong sweatshirt—a sweatshirt that I wanted to cover in black paint.

She stopped in front of me. "So I heard a rumor the other day that your parents don't even love you."

I could feel the wood from the pencil crack as I pressed my thumb harder into it, as if it were a stress ball. I had four and a half more years of this? Four and a half more years of her abuse? It would only continue if I didn't defend myself.

"If I'm such a worthless person, then why do you spend all your time talking to me?" I finally said, after a whole year of torment and anguish. "Seriously, grow up."

She scrunched her face in anger. "You wanna fight? C'mon, right now. I'll kick your ass!"

I laughed. "That's okay. I don't waste my time on people like you."

Four and a half years later, I walked down the steps of the stage, a sea of green and white gowns in front of me. I held my diploma in my hand, and passed by Becca. She gave me a small glare as if to threaten me. I wasn't fourteen anymore. I wasn't afraid of her. So I gave her the same grin she gave me after she spilled paint over me, but even more victorious.

I thought I was the only one in the world experiencing relentless bullying. In eighth grade, I wasn't able to comprehend that this stuff happens to all of us. Everyone at one point is stranded on an island, feeling like there's no chance of survival. In a sad way, dealing with kids like Becca is a part of growing up. They shove us just to see if we're strong enough to make it out alive. Bullies are weak people, weaker than their victims. It doesn't take a superhero to fight them off. All you need is just a little confidence and, just like magic, you won't be a castaway anymore.

~Morgan Miller

71

A Closed Door

Sadness flies away on the wings of time.
~Jean de La Fontaine

I had been staring at my cell phone for about two hours now. The number was completely dialed and all I had to do was press the talk button, but I couldn't bring myself to do it. My heart was beating out of my chest. I wanted so badly to be able to call him and tell him how I felt. I wanted to tell him how much I wanted to be with him again. Why was this so hard? All I had to do was call him and tell him how I felt. That's it. It didn't matter if he felt the same way about me, at least he would know and I wouldn't keep asking myself "what if?"

Another hour passed, and then another, and then another. Why couldn't I just do it? I looked at myself in the mirror and told myself that I could do this. I had to give myself courage. I got up off the bed and rummaged around in a drawer in my dresser. I found a picture of Jake and me sitting on a couch. He was giving me a peck on the cheek while I was laughing and staring at the camera. My mind flashed back to that night. We were goofing around on his couch with his camera. All we did was laugh that night. I couldn't help but smile when I thought of him. That was the night he told me he loved me.

We had been dating for a year at that point. Our relationship had been going great ever since he asked me out during our freshman year. It was March of our sophomore year when I received a text message from him saying that he had met someone else. "I think it's best if you just move on," he had said. I couldn't believe my eyes when I read it. I felt so many emotions all at once. I was angry that he didn't have the decency to tell me to my face, upset that he didn't love me anymore, and scared of what I was going to do without him. I came back to the present and felt a tear roll down my cheek. I wished I could crawl into his warm arms and have him hold me tight. I wished he would dry my tears and tell me everything was going to be okay. I knew I was wasting my time crying over him. I had always known, but I didn't mind. I wanted to waste my time over him. I didn't want to get over him.

I wiped the tears from my eyes when I heard the doorbell ring. I walked to answer the door and when I opened it I saw the face of the person who had caused me pain all these months.

"Hey Keri," he said awkwardly. All I could do was stare at him and give him a slight smile. "I know I have no right to come here and say this, but I made a huge mistake breaking up with you. I'm so sorry."

I just stood there trying to figure out what to say. I looked up into his beautiful blue eyes and something was missing. I wasn't getting that warm, giddy feeling when I saw him. And that was the moment I realized that through all the pain and tears I had suffered through the past four months, I had moved on. I changed. I grew up. I matured. Whatever you want to call it, I had gotten over him. All I said was, "Thanks for stopping by, but I think it's best if you just move on," and then I closed the door on him. In a way, I closed the door on him in my heart as well. I rushed back to my bedroom and hung up my phone and then tucked the picture of the two of us away in my heart forever.

~Keri Metcalf

72

Acceptance

The greatest oak was once a little nut who held its ground.
~Author Unknown

"Eighth graders rule," my friend Dee yelled to me as I left the school bus. "Yeah, we do," I shouted back. I turned to make sure the bus had rounded the corner and was out of sight, and I did a little conga step of celebration down my driveway.

I burst through the back door. "Mom," I said. "I've been nominated for the National Junior Honor Society."

My mother gave my shoulders a squeeze. "I'm so proud of you," she told me.

Mom and I sat together in the family room as I filled out the honor society application. I had to prove that I had all the characteristics required in a candidate: scholarship, leadership, service, character, and citizenship. I wrote that I worked hard at my honors math and science classes; I made the high honor roll most quarters. I listed my baking cookies for prison inmates and my singing with the District Select Chorus to raise money for the community. My mom had me put in that I was first chair in orchestra, to show leadership, and she also told me to include that I sold hand-beaded bracelets and crocheted purses to benefit St. Jude Children's Research Hospital and the ASPCA. Moms make you put everything on these applications!

The next day, I turned the paperwork into the advisor and didn't think any more about it.

Months went by, and I received a letter from the school about the honor society. As soon as the bus let me off that afternoon, I raced into the house. My mother was typing at the computer. "Mom," I said, "I didn't make the honor society."

She smiled and held up her hand to give me a high five. "You jokester."

I felt tears seep from my eyes. "No, really, they didn't pick me," I said and handed her the letter.

"Oh, honey, I'm sorry. I thought you were kidding," my mother said. "There must be some mistake." She grabbed the phone from the charger and dialed the honor society advisor.

He told her that no mistake was made, but he couldn't disclose the reason for my non-selection. The decisions of the faculty committee were final. There was no appeals process. However, when my mother perceives an injustice, she is like a German Shepherd with a tug toy; she contacted the principal. His answers were the same.

"It's not fair," I said that night at supper. My mother agreed. She proceeded to tell me a story about a high school friend of hers. "He was intelligent and had a good heart, but for some reason he wasn't chosen for the National Honor Society. He was hurt and angry." She paused for effect. "Do you know what he does for a living?" she asked. "He is a world renowned lung cancer specialist, and he saves lives every day."

I understood what my mom was trying to say. Not being a member of the honor society wasn't going to ruin my future, but it was hurting me now.

Nearly all of my friends were chosen for the honor society. One day, they went to a rehearsal for the ceremony. Afterwards, I heard that the teacher in charge called my name during attendance. "Oops! I forgot to skip the names of the non-selected students," she told everyone. On the night of the induction, Facebook was filled with posts about what dresses my friends wore and photos of the event.

I told my parents how difficult those weeks were for me. "This shouldn't happen to anyone else," I said. We discussed ways that the selection process might be improved. "I wish that teachers who knew me well could have shared their input with the committee," I said.

My dad, the engineer, was all about the process. "They should set up a concrete set of requirements for selection. For example, each candidate must have five hours a month of community service."

"It bothers me that I don't know why I wasn't chosen," I said. "The committee should give a reason, so the student can do better."

Not surprisingly, my mother wanted an appeals process put in place.

We arranged a meeting with the school principal to share our ideas. A few days later, he telephoned to say that the committee was going to use some of our suggestions. I felt proud that I had helped future students, like my younger sister.

As the weeks went by, I began to feel happier. Finally, the night of my graduation arrived. I wore a new dress. My older sister helped me do my hair, and I thought I looked somewhat sophisticated.

Everything was going well. Then, the principal announced the names of the honor society members—alphabetically. When he skipped my name, I felt a stab of sadness return.

When the applause quieted, the principal said, "One of our teachers nominated a student for a special New York State award in recognition of her scholarship and civic involvement. This award is given to Erin Miller."

I was so excited and surprised. I jumped up and ran onto the stage. I couldn't stop grinning. As soon as I sat down, I heard the principal say, "The award for the best German language student is Erin Miller." I popped out of my seat again, like a whack-a-mole.

This was turning into the best night of my life. After the ceremony, my friends gathered around to congratulate me. Dee was smiling, yet behind her glasses, her eyes looked sad. I knew just how she felt. She hadn't won any awards.

I rushed over to her and gave her my tightest hug. "Freshmen rule," I told her. "Yeah, we do," she said, and her eyes were smiling.

~Erin Miller as told to Marie-Therese Miller

You Decide
What You Want

*I am not in this world to live up to other people's expectations, nor do I feel
that the world must live up to mine.*
~Fritz Perls

y mom picked me up, and the whole drive home was
dead silent.

"What's wrong, Mom?" I asked, trying to break the
tension.

"I don't know. You tell me."

I told her I didn't know what she was talking about and she said
in a toneless voice, "You'll see when we get home." My eyes teared up
and I was getting scared. I didn't want to get home to find out what
was wrong.

When we arrived at home, we both walked into my room. There
on my bed were the recent love notes I had received from my girlfriend. I was done for. She had found out about my homosexuality
weeks before, and now this would only make it worse.

"I thought you said you weren't gay, and that you broke up with
her," she said.

I couldn't help but start sobbing. "I'm sorry! I'll break up with
her. I promise! Please don't be mad! I'm really sorry! I'm not gay! I
swear!"

She hugged me and said we would talk again when my dad got
home, but I didn't want to talk about it anymore. I looked at her with

angry eyes and ran out of my house. Hot tears were pouring down my cheeks as I headed to the park. Every person I passed stared, but I didn't care. What feeling could be worse than the one I was already feeling? It was a terrible feeling of losing trust in my parents because they wouldn't accept me for who I was. I sat on a rock at the park and cried. I tried calling my favorite teacher but she didn't answer. I felt alone. I walked back home and no one said a word to me. My sister finally asked if I was okay, but at that point I wasn't in the mood to talk to anyone, so I just walked past her, not looking at her.

That night, my parents sat me down again and talked to me. They said they wanted to help me and that they had made an appointment with a priest so we could talk everything out. Why would we need a priest? What were they going to do, perform an exorcism?

Soon, we were at church, sitting in the priest's office. We explained everything to him and then he told my parents to step out. Being alone with a priest made me feel a bit more comfortable. He asked me what was wrong and he wanted me to be completely honest because he knew I wasn't saying the whole truth with my parents there.

"How do you feel?" he asked in a calm, peaceful, comforting voice.

"I feel dirty and ashamed. I hate my parents. I don't trust them," my eyes started to fill up with tears. "I feel as if God is looking down on me and that He hates me. My parents keep telling me that if the rest of my family found out, I would be an embarrassment to them. They tell me that I don't know what I'm feeling because I'm really young, and they make me feel so stupid and powerless."

He looked at me and told me to relax and then he said, "God does not hate you. He loves you no matter what you do. You have to learn to accept yourself for the way He created you. I understand that having homophobic parents is a difficult situation, but you shouldn't hate. Hate is a strong word. You're just hurt and that's why you say you hate. Your parents are intolerant of homosexuality because it's something that they grew up thinking was wrong. You, however, are growing up in a different society."

I was shocked. The priest was telling me that it was okay to be gay? What? He finally wrapped everything up by telling me to keep my head up. He said I have to learn to make my own, smart decisions in order to be happy, because that's what God wants you to be — happy.

I stood up, he gave me a hug, smiled and said, "God bless you."

"You too, Father. And thank you," I said to him. I walked out of his office and I hugged my parents. I still held a small grudge against them, but something was telling me to hug them. We cried, and slowly let go of all the drama that had gone on in our house. Little by little, my parents began to gain trust in me again. Things were getting better.

My girlfriend broke up with me and went back to dating boys. At the time, I thought maybe I was just confused and my feelings would change, but it's been two years and they've stayed the same. My parents continue to believe that homosexuality is wrong, but I continue thinking it's okay to be myself. I know there are many kids out there who probably went through something similar to me, and so I want to say this: You're not always going to agree with your parents, because you're a different person with different opinions, so go with what makes you happy. In the end, it's up to you to build your life. You have friends and family to help you out, but you decide what you want.

~Adriana Tapia-Bernal

Just for
Teenagers

101 Stories of Inspiration
and Support for Teens

Chapter
8

Giving and Getting Kindness

Never look down on anybody unless you're helping him up.

~Jesse Jackson

74

Unforgettable Hero

A hero is somebody who is selfless, who is generous in spirit,
who just tries to give back as much as possible and help people.
A hero to me is someone who saves people and who really deeply cares.
~Debi Mazar

I can hear the sound of the heart monitor. Beep. Beep. I watch my little sister lying in her small hospital bed, the tubes running from every part of her small body. The heart monitor beeps steadily, as her heartbeat is stable. Then, all of the sudden, the monitor goes crazy. Her heartbeats become irregular and the beeps stop. The last breath is taken, and suddenly, I sit up in my bed. I shake my head as I clear the nightmare away and rattle the haze from my brain. The tears stream from my eyes and down my cheeks as I stumble from my bed. I run downstairs and I fling open my older sister Katie's door. I hear her protests as I climb into her bed. She takes a look at my tearing eyes and she scoots over, allowing me to snuggle into her warm side.

A hero is usually thought of as someone who is strong. They save thousands of lives, are totally selfless in everything they do. They are beautiful people who are physically robust and mentally unbreakable. In my eyes though, I see something totally different. My hero is not amazingly strong. She's not perfect. She may be emotionally strong but she can break. She may not have saved thousands of lives, but Katie saved me. My hero is my older sister.

Ever since I was little, my older sister and I have shared a special bond. Tragedy struck our family from the earliest age that I can remember. I was only five years old when my grandmother died, and my family adopted Elizabeth, a sickly baby with Down syndrome and many special needs. Katie became my rock as we watched Elizabeth's health deteriorate.

I remember when I was five and Elizabeth had to go to the hospital again. I struggled as Katie got me dressed and attempted to persuade me to brush my teeth. I hit her and screeched hateful words at her. At the time, it seemed rational. I didn't want to brush my teeth. I was five years old, and she was not my mother. My little sister was going into the hospital and I was upset. However, now that I look back, I see something totally different. Instead of seeing the big, annoying force of Katie, I see my older sister, trying desperately to help my family. I see an eleven-year-old, just entering middle school, dealing with a sickly little sister, and a brat who made her life difficult with every turn.

Katie was still a child, just barely entering a world that was all new to her. She was entering middle school, one of the first real steps to becoming an adult. Elizabeth soon got sicker, and had to go to a faraway hospital in Delaware with my mother. Dad worked long hours every day and was barely home at all. My older sister struggled to become a mother to me, working hard at her schoolwork and still saving energy from me. She would dress me in the morning, make sure I had food for lunch, ensure we left on time, brush my hair and teeth when I wasn't willing, wash my clothes, discipline me, and most other things that parents do for their kids. My sister became my mother.

One morning, I woke up to my parents gone. It wasn't unusual. Elizabeth had been in and out of the hospital ever since she had gotten back from Delaware many months before. It wasn't unusual to have Elizabeth be brought back to the hospital because of some major problem during the night. I could wake up and find no one in the house besides Katie. That morning was no different.

I woke up to absolutely no one around. I searched for my parents in vain, as I rushed to my sister's room, sighing in relief when I saw she was there and I wasn't alone. As usual, she did something small to keep me occupied while we waited for our parents' arrival. We knew it wouldn't be too long, but I worried again about what had caused yet another trip to the hospital. We waited and waited, and no one came home. Until finally, my parents came in the front door, my mom at my father's side. There was no baby Elizabeth. My mother cried upon my father's shoulder and Katie and I realized that our lives were forever changed. And that was the moment that we all broke. Even Katie.

I don't remember much after that. I barely remember the next few days or the funeral. My parents walked through life for the next few years in a haze. Katie made Christmas that year, as we walked up the creaky stairs to the bee-filled attic of our garage to search for the Christmas decorations. She was only thirteen. She still did things for me, washing my clothes and making sure I had food. I don't think the mother instinct ever left her after that. To this day, I still treat her like a mom occasionally even though my mother is home. To this day, Katie still lets me cry on her shoulder when I'm upset with my parents. She let me call when I was nervous about my first kiss, and she let me whine when I was needy for attention.

Katie is moving away next year, and I am heartbroken. My hero is moving farther away from me. Though she may be far away, I'm certain that she will always be my hero. I cannot forget what she has done for me in the past and continues to do today.

So while many see heroes as strong people who save thousands of lives, Katie is different. She saved one simple life and she was brave in the face of death. Katie is one of the most heroic people I know and I don't know how to thank her enough.

~Erin Eggleston

75

The Substitute

The mediocre teacher tells. The good teacher explains.
The superior teacher demonstrates. The great teacher inspires.
~William Arthur Ward

I'll never forget the day I met Mrs. Ferguson. She walked into our tenth-grade biology class wearing a pastel-pink blouse with puffy sleeves and a denim jumper—and dingy white tennis shoes. Thick glasses made her eyes look enormous.

"Mrs. Peterson has had her baby," she announced, brushing a strand of stringy hair behind her ear. "She's decided not to return to teaching this year—so I'll be taking over the class."

I groaned. Everyone loved Mrs. Peterson. A pretty woman in her late twenties, she had a wonderful way of making the most boring lessons fun. She was about as cool as a teacher could be.

Mrs. Ferguson was anything but cool.

Right away, the popular kids started making fun of her. I'm not proud of it, but I joined in. We usually made fun of Mrs. Ferguson behind her back, commenting on her lack of style and greasy hair. We whispered mean jokes about her and snickered as she did experiments for the class.

I felt bad about how I treated Mrs. Ferguson. But I was a cheerleader, and I felt I had to go along with the popular crowd.

Then one day after school and a long cheerleading practice, my friend Jenna and I were looking for a place to freshen up before the football game. We walked past Mrs. Ferguson's room and were surprised to see her at her desk, grading papers.

"Girls, can I help you?"

Our shoes squeaked as we stopped in our tracks. "We're just looking for a place to plug in our curling irons," I said. My face felt hot. She probably thinks we're vain, stupid cheerleaders.

"You're welcome to use the plug in here," she said, motioning to the sink, mirror, and outlet at the back. I didn't know what to say. I couldn't imagine fixing my hair in Mrs. Ferguson's room.

"Sure, that's really nice of you," said Jenna, elbowing me.

"Yeah, thanks," I said.

We set up our stuff by the mirrors and started primping. Mrs. Ferguson was silent as she finished grading papers. Then she pulled a chair over near us. What's she doing? I wondered. Is she going to lecture us?

"So how do you keep your hair from falling out of that style while you're cheering?" she asked Jenna.

Then the strangest thing happened. Jenna and Mrs. Ferguson started talking hair products. That led to a discussion about make-up, and cheerleading, and guys… stuff you'd talk to your best girlfriend about. By the time we left her room, the three of us had covered everything from lipstick to curfews.

After that, I started to see Mrs. Ferguson differently. So what if she was nerdy? She seemed to genuinely care about her students. I stopped joining in when people talked behind her back. I didn't care if it made me unpopular.

One day after class Mrs. Ferguson asked me if I was going to try out for cheerleading again. Spring tryouts for next year's squad were only a week away. "I just can't do it," I told her. "My heart isn't in it. I need to make my grades my priority."

"I bet that was a hard decision for you," she said.

"But I know it's the right one," I said, my voice shaking.

"Is Jenna going to try out?" she asked.

"Yeah, and she's really nervous," I said, hoping Mrs. Ferguson didn't notice I was getting emotional. "It's a tradition to take flowers to the girls trying out, so I plan to get some for her."

"What a neat idea," she said. "You hang in there, Kim."

The week of tryouts was hard. I'd been cheering since the eighth grade, and I was going to miss it—the pep rallies, making posters, performing at games with my friends. I kept wondering if I'd made the wrong decision.

On tryout day, I decided to go and watch, to support Jenna. As I waited in the bleachers for things to begin, I glanced over at the gym door. Mrs. Ferguson was walking toward me.

"Mrs. Ferguson, what are you doing here?" I asked.

"I wouldn't miss it for the world!" With that, she handed me a small bouquet of pale blue flowers.

"What are these for?"

"I knew today would be tough for you, not trying out and all. It was the least I could do," she said, squeezing my arm.

I gave Mrs. Ferguson a huge hug. And as we watched the tryouts together, I realized how blessed I was to have a teacher who took the time to care about me so much. Sure, Mrs. Ferguson may not have been the most fashionable person in the school. But looks really don't mean a thing. Take it from me—and my favorite teacher, Mrs. Ferguson.

~Kim Rogers

76

The Man with the Cassette Player

Good things happen when you meet strangers.
~Yo-Yo Ma

"**C**an I please have a strawberry Coolatta and a lightly-toasted cream cheese bagel?" I asked the Dunkin' Donuts cashier. He handed me my food and I strolled over to my usual seat at the corner table by the window where I could watch the people strolling by. Every day for the past four days, I had ordered the same food, sat in the same place, saw the same things and thought the same thoughts.

It was my fourth day working at the zoo, and like the previous three days, I finished my work with the farm animals, signed out, made my way to the zoo exit, and crossed the street to reach the Dunkin' Donuts. It was the summer after my sophomore year, and I had not become particularly close with any of my co-workers as they were much older than me, so I spent most of my lunches sitting alone in Dunkin' Donuts.

Every day I sat in Dunkin' Donuts and saw the same disgruntled-looking man. He appeared to be around sixty years old, and he sat just two tables away from me. His eyes were always squinted, and his eyelids were squeezed together so tight that I imagined his vision must have been constantly blurry. He wore baggy pants and the same puffy raincoat every day, rain or shine. I could not tell you if he was short or tall because he never got up. In fact, he rarely moved at all.

He never ordered any food and he just sat hunched over his little table, pressing his ear to an old cassette player. He was always alone, and he rarely made eye contact with passersby—it was as if he was enveloped in his own little world, just him and his cassette player.

As I watched this man with his cassette player each day, my mind filled with questions. What was he listening to? Was he waiting for someone? If so, who? Did he have someone to wait for? I had so many questions burning to be answered! My mother always taught me never to talk to strangers and even though I rarely listened to this rule, because of this man's dubious appearance, I thought it might be wise to take it to heart at least this once.

However, being the curious person I am, it is no surprise that in the end I failed (yet again) to listen to my mother's advice. It was my fourth day of sitting just two seats away from this mysterious man when I finally made the decision to sit with him. After all, I justified to myself, if the man sits here every day, just as I do, what could possibly happen? Who am I to think that just because he looks a certain way, he might be dangerous? Is it fair to judge a person by his looks?

I walked slowly to his table. I stood right in front of him, bent my head slightly, and said hello. I saw the man's head lift up slowly. Feeling anxious about what he might say or do, my hands began to shake. Before I could apologize for disturbing him, he looked up at me and I saw a scrunched-up face beginning to de-scrunch. As his eyes opened wider, there was suddenly a big smile looking back at me.

I was taken aback by the warm smile, and I was filled with a sudden sense of relief. Confident now that I had made the right decision, I put out my hand to shake his and said, "Hello there, my name is Adina and I see we both seem to enjoy Dunkin' Donuts. I was wondering if you would allow me to sit with you today?" With a thick Hispanic accent the man said in a very raspy voice, "It would be my pleasure if you would sit with me today." And so I sat down at the table with this man I had just met.

He told me his name was Carlos and that he was from Argentina.

I learned that he liked to listen to music from Argentina on his cassette player. For the next two weeks that I worked at the zoo, I would sit with Carlos every day during my lunch breaks, and although it was hard to understand him through his accent sometimes, we still managed to learn a lot about each other. Carlos worked as a crossing guard for little kids in front of the school; he always told me how concerned he got when the older children would neglect to take the younger children's hands—he was a kind man. Carlos never got married and didn't have much of a family here in America, but he hoped to go back to Argentina one day. He told me all about his dreams of becoming a big movie producer and his eyes always lit up and sparkled when he spoke about his ideas for movies. He shared his dreams with me and I found myself sharing mine with him.

It was my last day working at the zoo, so I wouldn't be going to the Dunkin' Donuts nearby anymore. This upset me because it meant losing my lunch dates with Carlos. He had taught me so much. By spending time with him, I had learned never to judge people by the way they look. I said goodbye to him on that last day, and wished him luck. As I turned to walk away, right before I reached the door, I turned to him and asked, "Carlos, why do you listen to that cassette tape every day?" He looked up at me and said, "It keeps me company so I'm not so lonely." And at that moment, I was glad I had kept him company, if only for a few insignificant weeks.

~Adina Lichtman

77

Lessons Learned Outside the Classroom

A teacher affects eternity.
~Henry Adams

Mr. Bley was my history teacher my sophomore year of high school. I couldn't tell you what kind of history he taught for two reasons: one, I never liked history, and two, my body was in class, but my mind wasn't. Mr. Bley wasn't the teacher who offered extra help or retakes on tests; he did so much more for me than that. He offered me a pair of ears and a shoulder to cry on.

Before Mr. Bley came along, before I started the tenth grade, two major events were taking place in my life. I was dating my first boyfriend, and my mom told me she wanted to divorce my dad. Talk about a high and a low... I was in love and I was angry. I was so angry with both my parents. Why then? Why after twenty-plus years? I didn't understand. A big part of me had known, since I was little, that they were never happy together, but I guess I got used to it and it became how we lived.

We continued to live that way for a while. Dad worked nights and slept in the second bedroom during the day, Mom worked days and started going out with friends at night, and I barricaded myself in my basement bedroom, listening to angry music and sleeping.

I fell into a depression and my first relationship ended shortly after our one-month anniversary. I listened to more angry music, and slept even more. My mom was concerned and alerted my guidance counselor and some teachers about what was going on at home. I vaguely remember my science teacher ask if I was okay after seeing my falling grades. Then there was Mr. Bley.

I sat against a brick wall outside the library, knees pulled into my chest, hood up, head down, surrounded by the chatter of my group of friends that I was slowly alienating myself from, when I heard his voice: "Ever feel like you're a fire hydrant and every dog in the neighborhood is stopping by to visit you?" I picked my head up and Mr. Bley's shoes were the first things I saw from underneath my gray hoodie.

I had heard him use this line in the classroom a few times before, when it looked like a kid was having a bad day. It usually aroused a smirk from both student and teacher and ended there. This time was different though. Mr. Bley wasn't going anywhere and it wasn't a rhetorical question; he was waiting for an answer. Next thing I knew I was on my feet and following him into the library.

We sat amongst the stacks of the mostly empty library for the remainder of lunch. I don't remember much about that first conversation other than the unconditional promise he made me of lending a pair of ears and a shoulder to cry on. To this day, I can't remember the exact content of our conversations. But I know they made a lasting impression.

A bond wasn't formed between Mr. Bley and me in the classroom. What made him such a special teacher was that he saw that I was struggling and reached out to me outside of the classroom. That didn't change our classroom relationship—he still called on me and I still didn't know the answers more than half the time. But I think he knew that I was at a crossroads in my life and that my history grade sophomore year didn't matter much compared to everything else that was going on.

Many lunchtime library conversations followed throughout the school year. They always made me feel freer and although I still struggled, I didn't feel trapped like I had before. Mr. Bley had presented me with an outlet for my pain and frustration; he was always there unconditionally and in a non-threatening way. One day he gave me a newspaper clipping on how to argue fairly, because I often talked about how every conversation I had turned into an argument. He helped me get to the root of the problem, which was that I was being defensive. The article talked about making the discussion about yourself and how you are feeling, rather than pointing fingers and accusing people of what they are doing. I held onto it for years and when I lost it I was devastated, probably because it felt like the last link I had to my mentor.

Mr. Bley retired after that year and we lost touch. I never found a way to contact him and I can only hope and pray that one day I can thank him for helping me through one of the toughest struggles in my life. And if I can't, then this story is a tribute to him.

~Cari Resnick

The Prom King

Be kind, for everyone you meet is fighting a hard battle.

~Plato

My hands gripped Tyler's heavy wheelchair as I guided it down the hallway. We reached the commons and I turned onto the ramp that wrapped around the seating area and down to the entryway. A few straggling students sat on the sofas even though the bell had already rung.

"Hey Tyler," one of the students called. "Pump it up!"

Tyler threw himself back in his chair and flung his arms into the air. "Woo! Woo!" he yelled.

I smiled and struggled to keep the wheelchair under control as it rolled down the ramp, rocking with Tyler's movements. I had seen Tyler do that so many times I'd lost count. We entered a large hallway and I pushed the wheelchair into the drama room. After getting Tyler set up near a desk, I sat down by him.

"Hey," Tyler whispered, leaning towards me. "You're Lena's cousin, right?"

Lena coached his Special Olympics team. "Yeah," I whispered, smiling again. He asked me this every time I took him to drama.

"Can I keep your cousin?" he asked.

"Yes," I said. "Tyler, we need to be quiet."

Tyler lifted his head up and moved it in an arc to look around the room. He leaned back towards me. "Can I keep her until May? That's when I graduate."

"Shh," I said. I glanced at the teacher, but he didn't seem bothered by Tyler's talking.

"Are we friends?" Tyler rocked his chair a little and waved his arm towards me.

"Yes," I said.

"Can I hold you?"

I blinked. He hadn't asked that before. I floundered for a response for a few seconds and settled on trying to distract him. "We need to be quiet, Tyler; the other students are trying to listen."

Tyler grinned. "Do you want to blow raspberries?"

Heat spread from my nose to my ears. Where did that come from? I said the first thing that came to my mind. "I'll play 'Go Fish' with you. You can do those other things with your mom."

"My mom?" Tyler looked thoughtful and then smiled. He started the conversation over. "We're friends, right?"

"Yes," I said again.

"Will you hold me?"

"Tyler," I said. "Who will hold you?"

"My mom," he laughed.

After I helped Tyler back to his class, it was time to go home. As I walked through the halls to my locker, I noticed posters advertising prom on nearly every wall. I sighed. With my senior prom only a few weeks away, my chances of going were starting to look poor. My memory of the awkward conversation with Tyler faded as I thought about missing the dance. By the time I got home my discouragement showed.

Mom tried to reassure me that things would be okay if I didn't get asked. She reminded me that anything could happen. A few days later my friend Justin asked me out.

The Friday before prom, the student body voted for Tyler as Senior Prom King. They crowned him in a school assembly and he wore his crown all day. When I saw him, he waved his arms from side to side as he rolled down the hall. His normal yell of "Senior Boy, coming through!" had changed to "Senior King, coming through!" Crowds of students parted to let him pass.

On prom night Justin arrived in an old beat-up car driven by a kid named Drew. I hoped the night would be perfect, but we got off to a weird start. Drew had asked two girls out.

"How could I pick? They're best friends! How would they have felt if one of them didn't get to go to their senior prom?" he said. I understood his reasoning, but that didn't make it less strange.

Since the car belonged to Drew, he drove. I sat sandwiched in the back between Justin and one of Drew's dates. Justin looked glad to have the window seat.

They hadn't made reservations for dinner. After trying several fancier restaurants, we ended up at a place that served hamburgers. We made quite a scene when we walked in, Drew with a redheaded girl on each arm. The people in jeans and T-shirts who had expected an uneventful dinner watched us slide into the springy tan seats and order our meal on the phone in the booth. We ate carefully so we wouldn't get ketchup on our formal wear.

We drove to the local college where the high school had rented a room for the dance. The ballroom walls were covered in blue-gray carpeting and the ceiling seemed very low. It could hardly be called a ballroom. As Justin and I started to dance, I noticed Drew and his dates devised a way to slow dance with three.

The time for the Royal Dance came and Justin and I found a spot where we could see. For the first time that night, I wondered who Tyler's date would be and how he would dance. Tyler's mother wheeled him to the front of the room and everyone cheered. I smiled. It looked like Tyler's mom would be his date.

The DJ started our theme song. The other royalty began dancing in the standard slow moving rock that we learned so well in middle school. Several of the special education teachers came up to the side of Tyler's wheelchair and Tyler's mother walked in front of him. I wondered what they were doing.

To my surprise, they began helping Tyler out of the wheelchair. His tight muscles seemed to have a mind of their own and his arms moved with jerking motions as he struggled to stand. When they got him to his feet he hunched over and leaned against his mother. His legs weren't quite straight but he could stand with her support. She held him up as they rocked through the rest of the song. When he stumbled, she tightened her arms and helped him regain his balance. Tyler's smile covered his entire face.

Tears blurred my sight. I had never seen Tyler stand. In my mind I heard him saying to me, "Who will hold me?" and then the answer, so sure, "My mom will hold me."

Prom had been about the dress, the magic of dancing with a cute boy, everything that made the night feel like a scene from *Cinderella*. The night had been different from what I expected and, admittedly, disappointing so far. A strange homesickness for my own parents spread through me.

I watched silently as other couples started to dance around me, afraid that someone would see my tears. I glanced toward Justin, and he wiped his eyes with his hand. Worry faded and I smiled, letting myself join the dance. From the corner of my eye, the prom king, held up by his mother, seemed the pivotal point in the room. I could finally see what really mattered, and it had nothing to do with a formal dress and fancy dinner.

~JoLyn Brown

79

Fear of Frogs

A good teacher is like a candle —
it consumes itself to light the way for others.
~Author Unknown

All summer long I fretted over the frog dissection that awaited me in the upcoming school year. What many kids considered a rite of passage, to me was a fate worse than... well, I suppose the frog wasn't looking forward to it either. With my anxiety in tow I trudged down the hall toward the biology lab where I first set eyes on Sister Frances De Chantal as she stood in the doorway ushering us inside.

Her petite frame struggled under the weight of the voluminous religious habit that swallowed all of her except the frail and gentle smile she offered as we filed into her classroom. Clearly, she didn't have a single imposing bone in her body, so I breathed a sigh of relief. If forced to examine the innards of a frog, one good sneeze in Sister's direction would surely blow her right out of the classroom and allow me time to flee the scene before she could ever collect herself to catch me.

Initially I attended class every day, determined that neither Sister Frances De Chantal, nor all the saints in heaven could motivate me to see what lay beneath the slimy skin of an amphibian. The good news was that according to my calculations, the day of doom wouldn't take place until some time in April. At least it seemed that way based on the placement in the textbook of that multi-page spread of Kermit with every anatomic detail displayed in living color.

After the first week I realized that Sister Frances had the uncanny knack of presenting every lesson like a full-length feature film. She spiced each topic with humorous tales of her childhood growing up with eight brothers and sisters on a farm in Oklahoma. It was never just dry fact with Sister Frances. If she set out to teach the life cycle of a blueberry, by the end of class you'd have the facts committed to memory and the recipe for her mother's blueberry pie in your notebook. Much to my surprise, I began looking forward to class every day.

Soon the warm September breezes we enjoyed at the start of the semester turned brisk and chilly. By October swirls of autumn leaves in shades of russet and orange rushed past the windows as Sister Frances waltzed across the front of the classroom with a full size human skeleton on wheels that she had named Skelly. To this day I remember that the femur, fibula, and the tibia are the major bones of the human leg, thanks to Skelly.

Then, right before Thanksgiving, Sister Frances was out sick for a whole week, but she returned after the holiday, assuring us that she was on the mend. Though her health seemed fragile she still overflowed with pep and plenty of stories for us every day.

As the calendar pushed toward Christmas we decorated a tree in class with dried specimens of all the flowers and plants we had learned about throughout the year. Sister Frances made little tags for each bearing their Latin names in gold lettering. It was quite a sight to see. On the last day of class before Christmas vacation Sister Frances reminisced about her dad and how he loved playing Santa on Christmas Eve. Santa's knowledge of her and her siblings, what their favorite subjects were in school, and the all important—who ate all their vegetables and who didn't, astounded her back then. How she cherished those memories.

When Sister Frances was in the convent, before she began teaching, the song "I Saw Mommy Kissing Santa Claus" became popular. Whenever she heard it she reveled in the memory of her dear dad in his Santa suit. Toward the end of class she asked if any of us knew that song. Only one other girl raised her hand aside from me and instantly I regretted it because just as I suspected, Sister Frances asked if we would sing it for her.

My reputation was clearly at stake here. Standing up in class and belting out "I Saw Mommy Kissing Santa Claus" is a big fat invitation to a ridicule party when you are a sophomore in high school. But I knew that the only thing worse would be the disappointment on Sister Frances De Chantal's face should I refuse. Satan himself could not have endured that. She was just that sweet. So Bridget O'Hanlon and I stood up and sang it for her. Just as we finished, the bell rang and we all cheered the start of Christmas vacation as Sister Frances stood in the doorway and waved goodbye.

When we returned from the holidays a substitute teacher awaited us in biology class. Sister Frances had fallen ill again and would be out for some time. Mrs. Warner, the substitute, was pleasant enough and a good teacher too, but class just wasn't the same without Sister Frances. We often sent her get-well cards to cheer her as the frigid months dragged on.

In early spring, right before Easter, just as the purple and yellow crocuses started blooming around the flagpole in front of school, we learned that Sister Frances De Chantal had passed away. Mrs. Warner explained to us that she had been diagnosed with lung cancer in November. This heartbreaking news arrived on the very day we were scheduled to dissect frogs.

We never did go to the lab that day. Instead Mrs. Warner encouraged us to recall our favorite memories of Sister Frances. At the end of class we said a prayer for her and thanked God for having blessed us with the privilege of knowing such a warm and wonderful teacher.

I imagine dissecting a frog in biology class is a milestone moment for most high school students, and one that is remembered for a long time. For me, encountering Sister Frances De Chantal and observing her unyielding respect for all living things impressed me in an unforgettable way. I don't recall much of the science behind blueberries or a lovely rose in bloom, but thanks to Sister Frances I appreciate the splendor of each and the imprint of God's great hand in their creation.

~Annmarie B. Tait

80

The Troubled Teen

A successful person is one who can lay a firm foundation
with the bricks that others throw at him or her.
~David Brinkley

He had these eyes. Dark pools of pain and energy and intelligence shimmered regularly to the surface during his days at Cabrillo High School. Like the rest of us, Brian was a walking vault of life experiences, but unlike many of us, his initial foray into the living world was a bit more traumatic than most.

Brian's high school career started out shaky. His freshman year, he got into a fight with an older boy, and the fight was serious. For this infraction of the rules, he was expelled, and spent a year attending classes at a nearby school district. There, he met a teacher who figured out that underneath all that anger, a fine intellect and sense of humor existed.

All that year, Brian and Mr. James worked together to get caught up with high school credits. By the end of his freshman year, Brian had successfully completed the necessary forty units to be classified a sophomore. Maybe even more important than the credits, with Mr. James mentoring and counseling, Brian began to slowly let go of some of the anger that so readily bubbled to the surface during each school day. I guess the best way you could describe Brian's transformation was miraculous, but at the time, nobody could have predicted just what a miracle his recovery actually was. We just didn't know enough about his past.

That changed in August before Brian's sophomore year.

As chair of the English department, Brian's paperwork arrived in my hands a few weeks before school started. On top of his folder, an impassioned letter written by Mr. James pleaded with us to allow Brian to return to Cabrillo High School. Examining his grades and behavior plan, it was clear to us that Brian had indeed made a sharp U-turn in his life... and was now headed in the right direction. However, we still had lingering doubts as to whether this young man could emotionally hold it together at a large, public high school. We also wondered what would happen if Mr. James wasn't around for support. I decided to dig a little deeper to find out more about Brian's past.

What I discovered was painful to read. That said, more importantly, it must have been an excruciating life for Brian to survive.

Brian was the oldest of five children. He never knew his father, and his mother was a meth addict. Brian's earliest memories involved digging in trash cans to find food, violent men who showed up at all hours of the night, and a mother who would disappear for days at a time. I spoke with Brian's third grade teacher, and he told me that Brian's case was one of the worst he'd ever seen. His eyes watered as he described the situation. "I called Child Protective Services at least four times that year—they'd take Brian for a couple of days, and then a relative would come and pick him up. A few days later, that relative would hand the kids back to Brian's mother. It was a vicious cycle."

Throughout the chaos of his childhood, Brian's report cards were fairly consistent in their comments: Brian is very bright and inquisitive in class; Brian is a fast learner; Brian is a gifted writer; Brian is very responsible and a good friend to others. It wasn't until Brian reached middle school that the grades and comments on his report card changed. Instead, the comments began to include statements such as: Brian needs to focus in class; Brian has missing assignments and is in danger of failing; Brian loses his temper in class when confronted with his grades; Brian seems to be a bright boy but lacks motivation.

By eighth grade, Brian was losing hope.

During his last year of middle school, Brian racked up a serious array of discipline offenses. From fights to alcohol possession to defiance, Brian earned over thirty discipline referrals, was suspended twenty-eight days, and spent a whopping thirty-eight days in in-school suspension. His grades dropped to a 1.2 GPA and he had stopped making any effort to complete homework. Most of the time when Brian was in class, he slept.

That was on a good day.

So it was with some trepidation that I allowed Brian to return to CHS. I'm glad I did. For whatever reason, Brian felt obligated to me for making that decision, and we built a relationship that still exists today. Brian worked hard during his high school years, amassing a 3.1 GPA, he played sports, and was even elected to the homecoming court his senior year. His anger was still there, but it simmered gently, and with continuous support of his teachers and friends, Brian found his hope again. A popular boy with a great sense of humor, he worked his way into the hearts of his teachers, his coaches, and his peers.

Because Mr. James gave him a chance, because we gave him a chance, but more importantly because Brian gave himself a chance, he overcame the odds, and graduated from high school. At the school's baccalaureate services, the senior class always voted for one senior to give an inspirational speech. That year, Brian was the unanimous choice. I worked with him on that speech, and as Brian relived some of the painful details of his past, I started to choke up. He walked over to me, wrapped his 6'2" frame around my shoulders and said, "I'm okay that all this stuff happened to me. It made me stronger. I wouldn't be who I am today if I hadn't lived through it."

At that moment, Brian gifted me with the realization that it's through our struggles (not our successes) that we experience the most emotional and spiritual growth. Brian had learned to embrace his past, learn from it, make his peace with it, and move on.

He took those lessons and decided to help others. I was at his college graduation the day he told me he'd decided to become a teacher.

It was, maybe, the best day of my educational career.

~Suzanne Nicastro

My Reflection

*A man needs self-acceptance or he can't live with himself;
he needs self-criticism or others can't live with him.*
~James A. Pike

"Ewww. I can't believe I touched her. Now I'm going to catch a disease."

I didn't hear comments like this often, but when I did, it would stop me in my tracks. It would take me a minute to realize that whoever said it was talking about me; not the me I knew myself—daughter, sister, and friend—but the me with mild cerebral palsy, the me I tried desperately to ignore.

Adolescence is supposed to be a time of great self-discovery. Unlike most kids my age, I was all too aware of who I was and what people thought about me. I wasn't the most popular or the most athletic student in the school. I was the girl with the disability. The girl no one wanted to accidentally bump into in the halls, for fear they would catch my non-contagious condition. Mild cerebral palsy is a neurological condition that affects my motor and developmental skills; it also causes my knees to turn inward when I walk. Needless to say, it was difficult not to notice me walking down the seventh grade hallway.

While everyone else could cover up their insecurities with make-up or cool clothes, I wore mine for the whole world to see. At the time, I thought everyone saw me as the girl with the weird name, Deandrea, and the even weirder walk. And while I did have a disability, I was determined to make sure it did not define me. In a effort to make sure people noticed me for what I perceived to be the right reasons, I refused to acknowledge I had CP by not talking about it, even with friends.

One girl asked me while walking home from the bus stop, "I'm not trying to be mean or anything, but why do you walk like that?"

I knew she wasn't teasing me like the other kids who'd asked if I was crippled or bowlegged, but her question irritated me because she wasn't supposed to notice. After all, I was normal just like her. Why did it matter?

"Because I do," I told her quickly, with much attitude, and switched the subject. The more I tried to hide the fact that I had a disability by blending into the background, the more attention I received. For instance, in woodshop, instead of admitting my hands were a bit unsteady, a result of the CP, I cut my finger with an electric saw and hid it in my jeans pocket. It didn't remain a secret for long. When I finally showed the teacher my injured finger, I flung it out, causing blood to splatter everywhere like in a horror movie. It landed on a basketball player's jersey right before the big pep rally. Two days later, I was transferred to a different class down the hall. Another time, while trying to carry two-inch binders and books to class I walked right into a small trashcan, spilling the trash and all my things on the floor.

My teachers finally suggested I have a teaching aide come in to help me. The way they explained it, she would help me carry my books and avoid any further incidents. I agreed, since most of my classes had two teachers in them anyway; I was sure no one would notice. I figured as long as she stayed out of my way, we wouldn't have a problem. Things didn't work out the way I hoped they would.

My aide's name was Ms. Dawn, and she took her job very seriously. It was her job to help me, and she made it her mission never to leave my side. I immediately hated everything she represented, including the fact that I had a disability and needed extra help. I took all of my anger out on her, ditching her whenever I could. How was I supposed to maintain my independence with a shadow following me around, six hours a day? It was like having my mom or dad with me at school. She would ask me about my friends and how I was feeling, trying to form a friendship, but I would just give her the cold shoulder.

"Deandrea," my friend asked me one day, "who's that lady always walking with you in the hallway?" I looked behind me at Ms. Dawn, who waved, hoping I'd introduce her.

"I don't know her. Maybe she's new."

I could tell by her face she clearly didn't believe me. I hurried my friend along and dropped my books on the floor, hoping it would slow Ms. Dawn down, but inevitably she would meet me in class with my books in her hands.

"Deion, you dropped your books," she said with a smile, even though she and I both knew I did it on purpose.

"My name is Deandrea, not Deion," I said through gritted teeth, taking my books and walking to my desk, making sure everyone knew how unhappy I was. I had told her countless times not to shorten my name, but she claimed my name was too long for her to remember. Sometimes I refused to answer her at all. No matter how bad my attitude was, she always tried to get on my good side.

When I look back, I realize the embarrassment I felt had less to do with the average teenage angst of not wanting to be seen with a parental figure, than it did with my lack of self-acceptance. At thirteen years old, I thought I had it all figured out. I thought that being comfortable in my own skin meant accepting that I had mild cerebral palsy, and then doing everything in my power to prove everyone wrong about me.

By trying to empower myself, I did the exact opposite. Because I didn't fully embrace it, my CP had become this diseased, damaged thing that I didn't want to associate with, much like the kids who teased me at school didn't want to associate with me. I credit Ms. Dawn with helping me to embrace a part of myself I had ignored for a long time. It all started with picture day.

After Christmas, my school had picture day for all students involved in any club or sport activities. I was more than happy to stand in the choir picture with my friends, but when Ms. Dawn asked me to take a picture with her and the other aides, I told her I couldn't do it. I looked around the room at the students in wheelchairs and thought, "I'm not like them; there's nothing wrong with me." But there was, and my self-image was completely distorted.

I was going to walk out, but then I saw her face. She looked rejected, like I had just told her she had a disease I didn't want to catch. Sometimes, all it takes is one moment to change your perspective on life. And in that single moment, on picture day, with her eyes full of hurt, it seemed that I was looking at a reflection of myself. It was the first time in my young life I chose not to ignore the face staring back at me.

As I smiled for the camera, my body slowly began to relax. It was okay, I realized, to embrace myself and this woman, who had been nothing but kind to me. I finally embraced my true reflection, and for that, I will always be thankful for Ms. Dawn and her presence in my life.

~D.D. Myrick

Into Her Arms

There is no psychiatrist in the world like a puppy licking your face.
~Ben Williams

"**H**ey, Bonnie! Your leg any better?" I asked my Aussie/ chocolate Lab mix when we came in the door. Her bobbed tail wiggled and her long brown body squirmed closer. She looked at me with her one green eye. The other was blind and a nasty purple.

"Oh, you're still limping. I don't know how you manage to get yourself so banged up—first your eye all those years ago, and now your leg."

"Would you all come into the kitchen?" Dad asked. His voice was choked.

"I've just gotten word," he said. "Your Uncle Alan passed away a few hours ago."

The words hung in the air like daggers. They could only hurt me if I believed them—but the truth slowly sunk its cruel blade into my heart.

The next few days were endless in their tears, heartache, and worry. Always in my thoughts was Paige, my sixteen-year-old cousin whose father was now dead.

When I saw her, she said nothing. When I visited her home, she said nothing. Her face was pale, her blue eyes expressionless, and her blond hair pulled back. Saying nothing.

On my way out their door, I froze when I saw a picture of Alan's dog, Annie, hung on the wall. The beautiful chocolate Lab had died four years before, but suddenly memories flooded my vision.

My bearded Uncle Alan, middle-aged, slim, average height... his calm voice growing excited as he rewarded Annie.

"Sit, Annie. Stay." He placed a treat on her velvety muzzle.

"Catch! Good girl, Annie! Shake... good. Roll over...."

They nuzzled each other, Alan caressing her soft brown fur, her long tail wagging. I imagined I saw them together again—together, happy. I knew Alan was in heaven. I knew that he and Annie were reunited.

"You know, I never liked that dog," Paige said. I turned, wiping the tears from my eyes.

"Dad sure did love her," she went on. "It was awful when she died, after he rescued her, trained her, and kept her all those years."

"Yeah, I know," I managed.

"You remember how he buried her on the hill? He'd always told Mom to bury him on that hill. So we're going to, right alongside Annie."

The day of the funeral dragged painfully by. Paige's friends surrounded her the whole time. She spoke to them, and they received her hugs and tears. I gave her one hug and drew away, realizing I wasn't needed and longing to do anything for her. If I could ease her pain, then somehow my own would shrink.

But she got through fine without me.

Days afterward, I paced, cursed myself, racked my brain for a way to cheer up my cousin, to say I was there. Not that she needed me—she had her other friends.

But things came to a head when Bonnie's blind eye got worse.

"Come here, Bonnie. Come here!" I chirped.

She came eagerly, still limping. I rubbed the white hourglass on her chest and scratched her brown ears, silky as rabbit fur. Her eye was oozing. I reached for the phone.

"Bonnie, you're going to hate this, but we've got to get this taken care of, even if you're going to fight the vet like a demon."

We dragged her to the vet, snapping and growling, but finally the sedatives kicked in and the vet removed Bonnie's blind eye.

"It was ruptured," the vet told us. "And causing a lot of irritability and pain. We've sewn the socket up, but it's swollen."

The medicines knocked Bonnie out and made her act drunk. She stumbled and fell, couldn't eat, couldn't drink. She couldn't bear for us to leave her. She looked scared, her heart rate was high, and her legs shook uncontrollably.

Thanksgiving came amidst all the confusion.

"It's important for us to be together—especially now," Mom said. "So we invited the family over. We'll move Bonnie to the bathroom and let her sleep."

"When do you think she'll come out of it?" I asked.

Mom sighed. "It won't be for a while yet."

Thanksgiving filled our home with vines of orange and yellow leaves twisting around the banisters, maroon cloths draped over tables, wood and glass polished, stone hearth swept, burgundy curtains drawn back to let in the light of the November sun. The smells of pumpkin, potatoes, turkey, and apple pie perfumed the air.

Everything was ready, including Bonnie, who we carried away to the bathroom. She was so weak she couldn't stand, and it was painful to watch her—barely able to open her eye halfway.

I dreaded seeing Paige. Much as I longed to, it would be so awkward not knowing what to say.

All the family tromped in. They piled their muddy boots and designer clogs in a corner and got in line for food.

The entire time, something was missing. Alan was gone. I missed the heated political discussions where we all agreed with each other, but pretended we didn't. I missed him competing with Dad in *Guesstures*, pulling Paige's hair, hugging my aunt, laughing at Grandpa's jokes.

We sat in the living room, the adults on the plush couches, wicker chairs in an uneven circle. Paige sat with her back against the hearth, her knees drawn up to her chest, blocking out those around her, her face mournful. Why was there nothing I could do? If only I could help...

I couldn't stand it any longer and went to check on Bonnie.

"Hey, you're awake!" I laughed. She was alert and standing at the door, triangular ears perked up, looking as well as ever.

"You must've smelled that food! Let's get some exercise."

Instead of going to the kitchen like I expected her to, she bounded into the living room, straight to Paige, to whom she'd never shown personal preference before.

Bonnie's stump of a tail bobbed furiously, her nose cuddled into Paige's neck. Paige looked surprised as her hands went up to Bonnie's sides.

"Go lie down, Bonnie," Mom commanded.

"No, no! She's fine, really," Paige said.

And something happened that warmed me all over.

Paige smiled. Really smiled. That sweet, happy grin that Alan said he loved to see. For the first time since his death, I saw joy in my cousin's face, and quick tears came to my eyes when Bonnie plopped into her lap like it was the most natural thing to do.

Thank you God, I prayed. Even though I couldn't help her, Bonnie could. She knew Paige was hurting. I guess wise words and glorious deeds aren't needed—just being there is all that matters.

Bonnie wouldn't be lured away from Paige for food or toys, and that in itself was a miracle. The sight of an old, torn-up, bob-tailed, one-eyed, limping dog comforting a mourning girl who didn't even like the animal reached into my very core—that was the miracle.

For a moment in the history of this hurting world, two creatures came together and offered each other comfort, the solace of a kind touch and having someone to hold. Those few moments made a world of difference in the lives of all who witnessed it.

As the hum of afternoon voices drifted around us, Paige sat there with one arm encircling Bonnie's chest. Maybe she was thinking of the love her father had shown his own dog. I don't know. All I know is that the smile never left her face the rest of the day.

~Alandra Blume

Just for Teenagers

101 Stories of Inspiration and Support for Teens

Chapter
9

Funny Moments

*Above all else: go out with a sense of humor. It is needed armor.
Joy in one's heart and some laughter on one's lips is a sign
that the person down deep has a pretty good grasp of life.*

~Hugh Sidey

Good Tread

You will find that you survive humiliation
And that's an experience of incalculable value.
~T.S. Eliot

Humiliation abounds during the high school years. In high school, you learn that embarrassment is just a fact of life. Unfortunately, it doesn't stop once the glorious day of graduation ends.

I had one major humiliating moment. Okay, probably more than one... but I'd like to stick with that.

My junior year I got the chance to start a junior varsity basketball game. I wasn't a very good player, but we weren't playing the best opponent either. Nervous? Naturally. Excited? Of course. As we warmed up, tossing baskets and doing drills, I felt pretty good. My determination to prove to the coach that I should start more often fueled my fire.

We gathered on the red and gray bench, waiting with little patience while the announcer called out each Tiger. We clapped politely. Then it was our turn. I would be called fourth. One by one, my teammates ran out, slapping the other girls' hands. I waited.

"Number 52, Murphy."

I pushed off with my foot and jogged out as nonchalantly as I could in my cheap sneakers. When I got to the end of the Tiger line, I stuck my hand out to high-five the orange and black mascot.

And fell on my face.

The gym erupted. My own team rolled on the floor in fits of hysteria. To add to my humiliation, the Tiger offered me a hand.

I took it. The Tiger pulled me to my feet and I threw my hands high in the air like a gymnast that just landed an impossible vault.

What else could I do?

For the rest of the year, I heard about my spectacular tumble. I laughed it off but it burned me. I cried for about a week in my room, alone. The moment replayed over and over in my head. Worse yet, it replayed in slow motion. I wasn't tripped on purpose or on accident. My jogging was more like shuffling my feet. Then one foot didn't shuffle and my shoe stuck to the floor. I kissed the blond hardwood of the court.

Today, whenever I see one of my old classmates, they always bring it up. Always. It doesn't hurt now. In reality, the moment hurt more then because I didn't want to be remembered for something so stupid. Now, I'm glad it happened. It's funny. And it still makes people smile.

One moment does not define a person. It can just make for a good story later in life.

~L.S. Murphy

My First Dinner Date Disaster

Cooking is like love. It should be entered into with abandon or not at all.
~Harriet Van Horne

As a child, I'd always heard the way to a man's heart was through his stomach. I believed it. What I didn't realize at the time was that the food had to taste good to get there.

When I started dating my boyfriend Tony, I made the mistake of bragging about how great a cook I was. I failed to mention that most of my gourmet meals consisted of peanut butter and pickle sandwiches and toast. I could go through half a loaf of bread before making edible toast.

I should have known it wasn't in my genetic makeup to be a great cook. My mother's favorite meal was boiled ground beef, pasta and cheese slices melted into the concoction. I don't know what I was thinking, offering to make lasagna for my Tony. Anyone else would have known better but I was determined to get into Tony's heart and stay there. Did I mention he was Italian and he loved his mother's cooking?

I shopped at the grocery store for everything I was going to need. I bought everything the recipe called for. I even bought garlic bread—the kind you just throw in the oven and heat up. I got home with several hours to spare before Tony was supposed to arrive.

I prepared everything perfectly and popped my tray of lasagna into the oven. I figured I'd wait and heat up the garlic bread just before we ate so it would be hot and fresh.

I ran upstairs to get ready. It took me almost an hour to do my hair and make-up and choose the perfect outfit. Just as I sprayed the final touches on my hair, the oven bell rang and I knew the lasagna was finished. The box had said to bake for an hour. How could I go wrong?

I pulled the lasagna from the oven. It smelled delicious. I popped the garlic bread into the oven and set the table.

The sound of the doorbell set my heart racing. Would Tony love my cooking? Would he compare it to his mother's and declare mine the winner?

I opened the front door and for a second I couldn't breathe. He stood there, gorgeous as ever, holding a bouquet of flowers and a bottle of sparkling grape juice. It was so romantic.

"I'm really looking forward to this," he said as he stepped toward me and kissed me on the lips.

"Me too," I said, or squealed. I'm not sure.

He followed me into the kitchen and helped me put the flowers in some water. I watched him carry the vase into the dining room. I felt so proud of myself. My very first romantic dinner. It couldn't be any more perfect.

Tony walked back into the kitchen and gave me a soft lingering kiss. The sound of the oven bell rang. "It's ready!" I said.

I pulled the garlic bread from the oven, cut it into pieces and carried it into the dining room. Then I brought the lasagna in. Just as I was about to start cutting the lasagna into pieces, Tony walked over and took the knife gently from me.

"You worked so hard, let me serve it at least," he said sweetly.

It was too good to be true. No, seriously, it was too good to be true. He tried to cut through the beautiful tray of lasagna, and all we heard was the sound of knife hitting hard pasta. I was horrified. Okay, maybe it was just that noodle. He moved the knife to another spot, and again tried to cut through.

After several unsuccessful attempts, he set the knife down and turned to me. "I think maybe you forgot to cook the noodles."

My eyes must have grown so wide at that moment I probably scared him half to death. Then the tears. Those terrible tears that erupt whenever I don't know what to say or do.

He grinned. "It's okay."

"No it's not! I wanted this to be perfect," I said as I tried not to break into a full-out cry.

He sat me down in my chair and poured a glass of sparkling grape juice for us both. He sat down beside me and told me a joke that finally got me to stop being sad. We ate garlic bread and laughed and ended up having a super date despite the ruined lasagna.

A week later he invited me to his parents' house for dinner. His mother cooked up a delicious Italian meal. I felt silly for thinking that I could have made a better lasagna than her.

As we sat down to eat, she motioned for me to sit next to her. "Tony told me what happened with the lasagna," she said.

I was embarrassed all over again. Why did he tell her?

She smiled at me. "That's nothing. The first time I cooked a meal for my Anthony, I burned everything. I was so nervous, I set the temperature too high and nearly burned down the kitchen."

We laughed about our cooking fiascos and then his mother and father told us a whole bunch of stories about all the crazy things that happened to them over the years. The way they smiled at each other with each memory made me realize something—the way to a man's heart may be through his stomach, but you'll only stay there if you can laugh together.

~Christine Dixon

85

The Greatest Monday

If you want others to be happy, practice compassion.
If you want to be happy, practice compassion.
~Dalai Lama

onday started out great. I woke up on time, got dressed, ate breakfast and did some last-minute studying for my first hour pre-algebra test. I sat by my friends on the bus. We were busily chatting about how we spent our weekend when, THUMP! Ryan tripped over someone's foot and landed flat on his face in the aisle between the two rows of seats.

Everyone on the bus laughed hysterically. Ryan picked himself up and made his way to an empty seat. He tried to laugh with us, but his face was bright red with embarrassment. Unfortunately, Ryan's Monday wasn't going nearly as well as mine.

The rest of the morning flew by. I aced my pre-algebra test. I read two more chapters of *To Kill a Mockingbird* in English class. Even gym class rocked because we got to play volleyball. It wasn't long before the lunch bell sounded. I met my friends from the cheerleading squad at our regular table. As we picked at our salads, I couldn't help but notice Ryan sitting alone a few tables over. He caught me looking. I smiled quickly and turned away.

When we finished eating, we headed out to the courtyard to practice a cheer we wanted to do at that night's football game. After a little practice, we nailed the cheer, so we decided we only needed to run through it one last time. Again, just like the rest of my day thus far, the cheer was going great. I raised my leg for one last toe touch.

Riiippp! I felt my jeans split down the middle of my backside.

I froze. I didn't know what to do. Then I heard people laughing, and I saw them pointing. Trying to cover myself with my hands, I tried to laugh too, but I felt tears begin to escape from my eyes. Through blurred vision, I saw Ryan walking toward me. I remembered earlier that morning when he had fallen and I had been one of the many who laughed at him. This would be his opportunity to return the favor.

But he didn't. Instead, Ryan offered me his jacket to cover up my torn pants. He also offered me his phone so that I could call my mom to ask her to bring me some jeans. I could feel my tears drying up. I thanked Ryan for his help, and a few days later when I saw him again, I apologized for laughing at him on the bus. Ryan shrugged it off as no big deal, but my own humiliating experience and Ryan's kind response taught me about empathy and compassion for others. Thanks to Ryan, I can honestly say that Monday was still a great day!

~Kimberly M. Hutmacher

86

Comedy for Dummies

Nothing in life is to be feared. It is only to be understood.
~Marie Curie

s a dedicated theatre student, I've received my fair share of questions from curious audience members: "Don't you get stage fright?" "Who makes the lights change between scenes?" "How long do you have to rehearse?" And, most frequently, "How do you remember all those lines?"

What always strikes me about these questions is that these are the things I rarely give a second thought. Learning lines, for instance, is just something you have to do in order to perform a play; it is mandatory, and thus, unremarkable. However, there are other things about theatre that people never ask about — things that I find difficult, but which never seem to occur to the average audience member.

The biggest one? Comedy.

When you stop to think about it, I guess it's not surprising that people don't ask, "How are you guys so funny?" Most of us accept that the gift of comedy is just that: a gift. People are simply born funny or not funny, in the same way you could be born with attached or unattached earlobes. A genetic fluke, the right combination of chromosomes, and hey presto! A funny baby! God takes a bow as the curtain falls.

For better or for worse, I missed out when the Gift of Comedy was bestowed upon a select, fortunate few; instead, I got Brains, with a capital B. For most of my childhood, I was Hermione Granger incarnate, with a mind like a steel trap and a hand that seemed magnetically drawn towards the classroom ceiling. Fortunately for everyone involved, my know-it-all tendencies subsided near the end of middle school, but I still cruised through my class work with ease and confidence.

I was smart, so who cared if I wasn't funny? Well, I cared, actually. I cared a great deal, particularly once my junior year of high school rolled around. Over the past two years, I had become deeply involved with my high school's theatre department, and that fall, I was cast in our production of *Rumors*, a farce by Neil Simon. On one level, I was delighted—it was an excellent cast, and the script was hilarious. On an altogether different level, however, I was terrified. How the hell had I, a girl with no talent for making people laugh, ended up being cast in a farce? How could I possibly disguise my ineptitude from my director, my cast-mates, and most importantly, the audience?

I read through my script every day, looking for clues. My character, Claire, had a lot of acerbic, snarky lines, and my eventual strategy was to rely on the text of the play for the humor. It seemed like a good plan, and initially, it did work. But my cover didn't last long. Unfortunately for me, there were moments in the play that required comedic timing, something I lacked in abundance. One particularly humiliating incident was a scene where the humor depended on a pause before I delivered my next line, a pause that had to be just the right length. After several failed attempts, Owen (our director) decided to stop and work just this section of text, over and over and over. It didn't help. Each time I got it wrong, Owen and my scene partners would offer advice: "I'd say it's about three beats long," or, "Just let the awkward silence settle before you speak." Each time, I nodded, flustered, and tried again... to no avail. Out of the dozens of times we ran this section of text, I only nailed the moment once.

I'd always known I wasn't an inherently funny person, but this incident took my belief a step further: I was the least funny person on the face of the Earth. My embarrassment, while painful, might have been manageable had one of my scene partners not been a friend of mine who was without doubt the funniest person I had ever met.

Tom was our class clown, the sort of guy who could crack up an entire room with a mere flick of his wrist—and to be honest, it certainly didn't help that I had recently developed an enormous crush on him. With him present for the entire rehearsal, the incident was downright mortifying; I suppressed a strong desire to crawl into the orchestra pit and die.

My troubles were not over yet, though. About two months into rehearsals, my drama teacher announced that our theatre class was going to have a special guest teacher! A talented young actor from the local Shakespeare festival was going to be doing a clowning workshop with us for a few months.

Clowning? I thought. Wait, you mean, like... being funny?

Suffice it to say that, with *Rumors* rehearsals as an everyday reminder of my struggle with comedy, the workshop was a terrifying prospect, and I looked forward to it with all the enthusiasm of a French nobleman bound for the guillotine. In fact, I took it as a sure sign that the Theatre Gods had decided to torture me with my own lack of comedic skill. Who knows? Perhaps it was their idea of a good joke.

The workshop began with a long discussion about what makes a clown, and more generally, what makes something funny. The almost-scientific approach that we took, breaking down comedy into its basic elements, was something of a revelation, but I still didn't see how it could work for me. Eric, our teacher, made humor sound so easy, but experience told me that this was far from true.

Then we began work on our clowns.

"To start off, you're each going to pick one physical trait that you don't like about yourself, and you're going to exaggerate and magnify it," Eric explained. It was a bit uncomfortable, acknowledging out loud what it was that we didn't like about ourselves, but everyone did it. I picked my bow-legged-ness, and highlighted that quality with baggy pajama pants that were too big for me. I also walked with my legs splayed out, as though I'd just spent a month on horseback.

Thus it was that, bit by bit, I began to understand how humor worked. It was a painfully slow process. In all honesty, there were a couple of moments during the class that leaned dangerously towards the nightmares I had suffered before the workshop began. However, there were also times when my audience of friends giggled at my antics and applauded with enthusiasm at the end of my sketches. For our final presentation, I worked to incorporate everything I'd learned into my sketch, and the result was a success! The audience laughed heartily as my clown, a five-year-old Harry Potter fanatic, tried to cast spells on her stuffed animals.

I wish I could say that, following these experiences, I become riotously funny and went on to win several Emmys for my hit CBS comedy show. The truth of the matter is that, little by little, I just got a bit better at being amusing. And at some point along the road, those pesky Theatre Gods must have had a change of heart, because Tom asked me out just a week before *Rumors* closed. Who knows? Maybe that was part of their master plan all along. Life is funny like that.

~Ari Susu-Mago

The Tin Boy's Lament

Be nice to nerds. Chances are you'll end up working for one.
~Bill Gates

Looking back, I was the king of geeks in tenth grade. I finished all of my homework, followed all of the rules, studied for all subjects, and tried to please everyone. At the time, maintaining straight A's was the most important goal I had. I was ready to give up club activities and tennis (the only sport I played in high school) for my grades. When people asked me about my free time, I was possibly the only tenth grader who said, "What free time?" Usually I would go home, eat dinner and then study until I fell asleep.

A typical day in chemistry consisted of a lecture, note taking, and bookwork in a room where the only lights were the tubes of florescent gas. I liked the structure of the class; it made it so systematic. A rigid structure was also my ideal way to live life. However, with many other things, I found rigid structures hardly worked—except for solids, but even they move around at the atomic level. One day, after being deprived of sleep, I was surprised to find myself struggling with a concept. This was highly irregular because I usually figured out everything on my own. Several minutes of arduous calculations made me resort to asking my classmates. This story would not have occurred if no one in my class knew the concept well. But as it would happen, someone did know. She was one of those popular girls: social, participated in ridiculous school activities, and beautiful. Unlike the other popular girls at my school, she was considerate to everyone, modest, and smart, something I never expected to come from that type of girl. While she explained everything to me, something in my head went "click," like the universe stopped, took a breath, and then everything made sense. I rushed back to my desk slightly embarrassed that I had to ask somebody else for help. But there was definitely some weird chemistry messing around with my head.

From that day forth, I had a strange yet powerful attraction to her, like an electron whizzing around a nucleus. Except I never got too close to her. The most upsetting part was that I couldn't do anything with my emotions. Normally I was distant from people. However, at this point, my "normal" life was lost. Usually in my life I could deal with problems systematically: first, control it, if not, contain it, and if nothing else could be done, delete it. However, I couldn't do that with this particular interference. I had never felt that close to anyone, or anything for that matter.

Months passed by as fast as a speeding bullet train. I talked to her more and became good friends with her. She was on my mind so much that even when I studied history I thought of her. I got used to walking over to her table and conversing with her for a few minutes. We did labs together even though we weren't part of the same group. To me, it seemed we were heading in a good direction. Then came the day that completely changed everything I tried so hard to achieve. Somebody asked her out on a date and she accepted the invitation. I don't even remember the name of the boy who asked her, but I do remember what my reaction was—I just absorbed the news and sat there like a rock. For the rest of the week, I was completely off. I couldn't concentrate properly and even my grades suffered. Instead of smiling when I thought of her, I subtly clenched my fist in anger. I didn't know where my anger was directed: her, the boy, or myself? Eventually I decided I needed some help from a third party.

A friend of mine helped me discover what I was feeling and set me on a better path. The advice he gave me seemed like common sense, but in reality, I needed to hear it. He told me the problem was me—more specifically, my personality. I didn't have the guts to ask her out like the guy who did, nor was I able to show her that she was special to me. In my whole life, I never loved a person the way I loved her, but I was unable to show her.

Still, I was determined not to let my problems weigh me down. When something breaks, it is always possible to pick it up and fix it. So that was what I did; I picked up my heart, mended it, and looked forward to a better day.

Although I was never more than friends with that girl, my experience with her taught me a lot about love. I still don't have a girlfriend, but I know that someday there will be someone I can share my feelings with. Next time, I will know what to do because of my mistake.

~Ryan Eng

A Nighttime Adventure

Mistakes are part of the dues one pays for a full life.
~Sophia Loren

I'd always wanted to know what it was like to sneak out at night. I slowly peeled back the covers on my bed and gingerly placed a trembling foot on the floor. It was past midnight and the house had finally settled down. My brother and sister had long since said goodnight and gone to their separate rooms. My parents had turned out their lights. The only sound was my dad's snore drifting down the hallway.

Placing both feet on the floor I slowly curled into a standing position and tiptoed around my bed, towards the window. My body was coursing with adrenaline and excitement. I had inconspicuously left the blinds open before going to bed, so that I wouldn't wake anyone by pulling them up. Sweat beaded on my forehead and a knot of apprehension sat like a rock in my stomach. When the floor creaked a minuscule amount I froze, waiting to hear my parents getting out of bed to check on me... but nothing happened.

I began to slowly push the window open, feeling the cool summer breeze on my face. Outside, the trees cast eerie shadows on the backyard and crickets sang at the top of their lungs. Fear filled my stomach as I realized all the noise the darn crickets were making. Taking one last look at my bedroom, I pulled myself over my window ledge and onto the not-so-firm ledge of roof. My legs wobbled with fear and excitement as I stared triumphantly around at my surroundings. Suddenly I heard a "snap!" behind me. Turning my head I realized I had just made a deadly mistake... I had pushed the window closed.

I realized I was locked outside, in my pajamas, wearing only socks, on a school night. Dread filled my stomach as I looked down on the silent, shadowy backyard. Not only that, I was high on the roof. The second floor to be exact. I became dizzy as I realized that I had not planned ahead enough to figure out a way down from the roof... and I was scared of heights. I made a mental note not to try this stunt again.

I inched along the four-inch ledge on the roof until I came to a slope leading up to my brother's room. Should I go up there and knock? No, of course not. He would tattle immediately. Should I sit here until morning? Definitely not. I had no idea how I would be able to explain my predicament. I mean, the whole reason I'd come up here was to have an adventure. Writers need to have experiences to write about, so I needed to create my own. How many books have you read where the main character has to sneak out of their house? Lots. In basically every romance novel the girl sneaks out to meet some boy.

I edged over to the ledge of the roof and peered down at the ground beneath me. I could just barely make out a bush in the darkness. Could I, just maybe, land softly enough if I jumped on it? I thought back to all the times my brother and sister had told me I was an idiot. Maybe they were right.... Oh well, best not to think of that. I took a deep breath and leapt off the roof. For a minute I was flying... flying... flying... oof! I landed with a splintering crash that seemed loud enough to wake up the entire neighborhood. My ankle twisted awkwardly, my arms and face became scratched and tangled in the branches, but hey, I was alive! I crashed through the branches and emerged from the bush, just in time to trip over a gnarled root and crash to the ground. I lay there panting, aching, and holding a strong grudge against gravity.

Clawing at the ground and pushing myself to my stocking feet,

I looked around. Suddenly, I heard a growl. I was freaked out, I almost screamed. In the darkness behind a fence was my neighbor's dog—a big, black friendly mutt, who obviously didn't recognize me. His growl switched into a cacophony of loud barking. He sounded absolutely hysterical, if dogs could. I decided that now would be a good time to make a run for it. I ran from the backyard, narrowly missing colliding with a tree, and raced into the front yard, leaving the neighbor's dog yelping far behind me. I'd asked for an adventure. What did I expect? Did I think I could just climb out the window, go on a little stroll (in my stocking feet, mind you), and then climb back into my room and go back to sleep (and be fully rested for the test at school tomorrow)? I guess my planning ahead needed some work.

I wandered through the dark and foreign front yard and stared longingly at the locked door, before meandering to a nearby pine tree and curling up under its long, hanging branches. I drifted in and out of sleep on the hard, pine cone-covered earth as the crickets and birds sang at the top of their lungs. The sun was starting to rise when I suddenly came to and remembered that, oh yeah, I was still locked outside in my pajamas. I just prayed my mom wouldn't open my room door to find the bed empty. What would she do? Call the cops?

Suddenly I heard the familiar rumble of the garage door opening. I couldn't believe my ears. Why was the garage door opening at 5:30 in the morning? Was it a miracle? I peered out from the long, bushy pine branches to see my mom slowly trudging out into the driveway, pushing our large black trashcan ahead of her. Could it be? Could it really be? It was Tuesday—trash day! This was my chance. As soon as my mom had passed on her way to the end of the driveway I ducked out from under the branches and sprinted as fast as I could into the garage. I quietly opened the door to the house and tiptoed inside and down the hall. Everyone else was still asleep. Cautiously climbing up the stairs two-by-two (and avoiding the creaky ones), I ducked into my bedroom and let out a sigh of relief. It was almost time to go to school anyway, so I opened my closet and grabbed my clothes for the day.

When I headed downstairs at 6:00 for breakfast my mom looked like nothing had happened. All she said was a simple, "You look like you've had a hard night," and grabbed me a box of cereal.

When my sister came down a few minutes after me she gave me a strange look and pulled a leaf out of my hair. None of them seemed to notice my bruised, swollen ankle or the scratches across my face and arms that I had tried so hard to cover up.

To this day they haven't found out about my little nighttime adventure. After all, every girl needs her share of experiences, and I just went to find mine on my own.

~Christine Catlin

First Kiss Disaster

Honesty is the first chapter of the book of wisdom.
~Thomas Jefferson

Everyone knows that your first kiss is supposed to be mind-blowing and life changing. At least, this is what fairytales and Hollywood like to promise young girls who are seeking their own Prince Charming. I have to admit that before last night, I—like many girls—was suckered into the belief that my first kiss was going to be the best thing that ever happened to me. I assumed it would be magical. I was convinced that at the moment my lips made contact with the love of my life, the starry skies would explode with color and a choir would immediately start singing "Hallelujah!"

Well, I sort of feel like an idiot now because my first kiss was definitely not the best thing that's ever happened to me. In fact, it was quite the opposite.

•••

The instant I hung up the phone I began bouncing up and down, squealing immaturely with sheer delight.

"Oh my gosh! No way! The movies?" my younger sister Jane asked excitedly. My cousin Clare walked in with a towel wrapped around her head. "Roxy is going on a date with Derek Corey!" Jane said.

"Shh," I said angrily. "Mom is in the other room."

"You aren't telling Aunt Sharon about this?" Clare asked, smiling mischievously.

My mother is, well, a very uptight kind of person. Jane and I have concluded that she was a drill sergeant in a previous life. We were only allowed to group date until we turned eighteen, which was a huge problem because I had just agreed to go out on a date with Derek Corey... alone.

My mother was going to kill me.

I walked into the living room and there my mother sat on the couch, talking on the phone, and watching *Oprah*. I plopped down on the leather chair next to her.

"Oh no!" she said angrily into the phone. "This is terrible!"

My eyes widened in fear at her tone.

"Kids these days." She shook her head in disgust. "At least my Roxanne is still safely group dating."

I gulped.

My mother hung up the phone, shaking her head disapprovingly. "Penny is pregnant," she fumed. Penny is a girl my age from church. "Stupid, stupid, stupid."

"Uh, hey Mom?" I began nervously. "I'm going out on a date with Derek Corey to the movies tonight," I said, rushed. "That's okay... right?"

"A group date, right?"

I heard two sets of giggles erupting from my bedroom.

"Yes, of course," I lied to her, something I rarely do.

She waited before answering. I felt moisture quickly developing on my forehead.

"Okay," she said. "Is he picking you up?"

"Yep," I answered. "And then we'll meet up with everyone at the movies."

"Alright," she said nonchalantly.

When I entered my room I let out a huge sigh of relief. My legs were shaking. Suddenly, I was overwhelmed with guilt. I hoped my lie wouldn't come back to haunt me.

Five o'clock rolled around slowly. When I saw Derek's car I

quickly told everyone goodbye, grabbed my purse, and raced to the front door. My hands were dripping with sweat. At first, the car door handle slipped between my fingers. Frantic, I wiped my hands against the side of my sweater before entering the car.

After I took my seat, I gazed up at Derek, who is simply gorgeous—dark wavy black hair and striking indigo blue eyes. I was the luckiest girl in the universe.

"You look nice," he said and his breath smelled like wintermint. "Ready?"

I nodded.

I glance up at my house, noticing Jane and Clare staring at me through my window, laughing. I didn't really care because I was with Derek.

The entire drive to the movie theater I kept thinking of how lovely my new name would sound. Roxanne Corey. I loved it.

We pulled up to the movie theater and hopped out of the car. He quickly started walking off. I raced up to him, wiping the sweat off my hand onto my sweater once again and took a risk by holding his hand. My face heated up. He looked down at me, smiling.

Yes!

We walked up to buy our tickets. I couldn't wait to see *27 Dresses*. "Two for *There Will Be Blood*," Derek said.

"What?" I asked. "I thought we were seeing *27 Dresses*?"

"Don't worry," he told me. "If you get scared you can hide behind my arm."

I was starting to have a bad feeling about this.

Before going into the theater, Derek bought us a bag of popcorn along with two sodas. Then he asked for one more thing... a chilidog with extra onions.

Just when I thought I was going to get my first kiss he bought a chilidog with extra onions!

We took our seats. Derek watched the movie with his entire left arm wrapped around the bag of popcorn, holding the chilidog in his right hand and taking huge carnivorous bites out of it like he hadn't eaten in years.

Disgusting.

All I could hear were his teeth tearing away at the meat, obnoxious chewing noises, followed by several delighted moans. "Mmm, this is so good," he said with a mouth full of chilidog. I almost gagged.

I reached my hand inside the bag of popcorn and it was empty! He ate it all. What a pig!

The entire movie was nothing but blood and guts. I had to stare down at my feet for the majority of the film, but what I heard made my stomach churn and at times I felt as though I was going to barf.

When the movie finally ended I let out a huge sigh of relief. "Well," Derek commented, "that was great!"

"Yeah," I muttered sarcastically, rolling my eyes. "Fantastic."

"Alright, let's get out of here," he said.

We walked out to the car. He didn't even bother to open the door for me! When I got into the car I almost gagged because Derek's breath was beyond revolting and he wouldn't stop burping.

"Whoops," he laughed, after belching yet another time.

The whole drive to my house Derek went on about how amazing the movie was.

Soon we are approaching my sister's middle school, which is only a few blocks away from my house. However, instead of passing the school, Derek pulled directly into the parking lot and cut the engine.

Before I could say anything, Derek lunged for me with his hands, one at my shoulder, turning me to him and one behind my head, pulling my face into his. He kissed me violently. I pressed my hands against his chest in protest. This only caused him to pull me closer. Then without warning he slipped his fat, slimy, disgusting tongue into my mouth. It tasted like chilidog and I swear it touched the back of my throat, gagging me. I immediately clamped my teeth down.

He jerked back, wailing, "Ouch! You bit me!"

"Derek," I shrieked at the top of my lungs. "You drive me straight home this instant!"

He shoved his keys into the ignition and drove me home. I exited the car the second it came to a stop, slamming the door behind me. I leapt up the steps to my house.

Inside, I greeted my family.

They were all seated on the couch, watching a biblical film. Clare looked up at me with a smirk on her face. I walked briskly to the bathroom and pulled out my mouthwash and toothbrush, removing all traces of chilidog and Derek.

Jane and Clare sat on my bed, eagerly waiting to hear what happened.

"Everything that could possibly go wrong did," I cried, and then explained the rest of the story. They were supportive and tried to reassure me, but once I said, "Derek has no idea how lucky he is. I was just about to grab Dad's shotgun," they burst into laughter, so hard they began crying and suddenly I was laughing too because of the sheer ridiculousness of the whole event.

• • •

After that, I didn't want to kiss a boy ever again. I was through. But looking back, I couldn't help but smile and think that karma played a part in my chilidog-flavored first kiss, because honestly, what good can come from lying to your parents?

~Amanda Yancey

Just for
Teenagers

101 Stories of Inspiration
and Support for Teens

Chapter
10

Setting and Reaching
Your Goals

*Only those who will risk going too far
can possibly find out how far one can go.*

~T.S. Eliot

10,000 Hours
of Perseverance

The road to success is dotted with many tempting parking places.
~Author Unknown

M y dad always used to tell me that when I was two years old, I told everyone I met that I was going to be the next Michael Jordan. I told the clerk at the store, I told my aunt, and I told a stranger I met on the street. I'd never actually played basketball, but I'd seen Michael Jordan on the TV, and that was enough.

At first it was cute. My mom made me a bright orange basketball birthday cake and my uncle bought me my own small pair of Air Jordans. It was my dad alone, however, that took me seriously.

One day he sat my three-year-old body down at the table and looked me straight in the eye.

"You want to be the next Michael Jordan, huh?" he asked.

I nodded eagerly, squirming in my seat.

"And you're willing to do any amount of work in order to do this?"

I hesitated a moment, feeling the weight of his words, but then smiled brightly and nodded.

"All right," he sighed. Then he turned and produced a sleek, lined, business sheet of paper. He rubbed his brow and straightened his tie before handing the paper to me, warning, "This will be one serious, serious commitment."

He gave me a pen and gestured for me to sign my messy signature at the bottom of the page. Even without the ability to read what he'd written on the paper, I sensed the seriousness of the moment.

The next morning I had completely forgotten about the paper until, at the crack of dawn, my father shook me awake. I was shocked to see that for the first time in my three years of life, my father wasn't wearing a suit and tie. Instead he was dressed in a distasteful baggy T-shirt, shorts, and an old, ratty pair of gym shoes. I wrinkled my nose.

"What?" I asked.

"Get up," he ordered. "Basketball practice commences today."

I groaned, squirmed out from my warm alcove of stuffed animals, and followed my dad, still wearing my pink pajamas.

We headed out to the driveway and he revealed an old, beaten, orange basketball. He tossed it to me and I clumsily grabbed it with both hands, its bumps feeling foreign to me.

"First," he instructed in his firm, lawyer-practiced voice, "we will start with the art of dribbling."

I looked at him, unsure if he was serious, and threw the basketball with both hands back to him as he began to instruct me. I stood out in that driveway for three hours that morning, and never had I felt more exhausted in my three years of life. Every time my attention began to wander, my father would harshly drag me back to the present.

Although still unsteady on my own two feet, my father worked me until my pajamas were drenched in sweat and my wrists were aching from hitting the ball up and down. The neighbors out mowing their lawns had begun to stare at our strange scene — my father, a strict lawyer, standing in the driveway, domineering in ancient gym clothes, and me, a toddler perspiring in her pink pajamas.

Tired and voraciously hungry afterward, I went inside and devoured breakfast. My mother had brought out a feast of pancakes, sausages, muffins, and fruit, and simply pursed her lips and shook her head disbelievingly as I dragged myself in. Already, I was beginning to regret my decision to be the female version of Michael Jordan.

The next morning my dad dragged me out in the driveway at the crack of dawn, once again. This time I had come prepared. I was dressed in fresh shorts and a jersey, although, normally, I refused to wear anything but flouncy, flowery dresses.

Before I knew it, my dad was dragging me out for hours every morning. It was the same the next day, and the next day, and the next day. I began dreading the continuous lay ups, shooting, dribbling, and one-on-one. My only hope in my three-year-old brain was that soon, when winter came, I could take a break.

I couldn't have been more wrong.

Once the first flakes of snow started falling my dad started dragging me to the local gym to practice for four hours a day. I began complaining, sighing, and dreading each practice. My dad never gave up, though. Every time I screamed that I would never touch a basketball again he would take my signed piece of paper from his safe and wave it in my face, telling me that I couldn't take back my words now.

I wanted, in my dreams, to tear and burn that dreaded contract that bound me to four hours of practice seven days a week. I wanted to find his locked safe and burn it to the ground. Years passed and I began to accept basketball practice as just a fact of life. Even on days when I slept in, refusing to get up, guilt would soon overwhelm me, and I would head out to the driveway and find him waiting for me, knowing all along that I would come.

By the age of ten, after seven years of practicing (and approximately 7,350 hours) my dad predicted my skill was higher than any varsity player's in the state. He continued to coach me, day after day, from the sidelines of our driveway, pounding the knowledge into my brain about fakes, crossovers, and tactics. Our only days off in the year were work holidays and my birthday, which seemed way too far apart for my liking. But my dad kept a chart on the wall, measuring how much I practiced, and every 500 hours of practice time we would celebrate by heading to Dairy Queen.

My dad began telling me about his days as a star basketball player in college. He said that he had always dreamed of being the best basketball player in the world, but he had not had the perseverance to practice enough to become so. His theory was that in order to achieve the level of mastery associated with being a world-class expert, 10,000 hours of practice were required. Whether you were a writer, an ice skater, a guitarist, or a chess player. He said that one day, in basketball, I would become a true expert.

One fateful day, at the age of fourteen, I finally reached my goal. My 10,000 hours. The day was a Saturday, and from the morning I got up, I could feel something different as I met my dad out in the driveway before heading to school. A strange feeling of sorrow seemed to hang over me.

We practiced our usual four hours, and for once, I felt like I had learned everything there was to know about basketball. At the end of our practice session, my dad hugged me and said "Congratulations" before handing me that same old ratty basketball from eleven years back and saying, "It's yours now."

That evening we had more than forty of our friends and relatives over to a party, with a gigantic, basketball-shaped cake, and local newspaper journalists hugging the edge of the living room. On top of the cake sat five candles, with the numbers 1-0-0-0-0. I had never been so proud in my life. My dad made a speech about perseverance, and even his old coach from college came over to congratulate me. It was only when the cake's candles were lit that my dad finally handed me the forbidden contract I had signed on that fateful day at the age of three.

I felt tears well in my eyes as I traced the letters on that piece of paper, each word engraved in my heart. In my messy three-year-old handwriting I could still read my name signed in overly large backwards letters. "I hereby agree to practice basketball for as long as my father requires, until I have reached my goal of 10,000 hours." I read, for the last time.

"This is it," my father whispered, reaching for my hand. "10,000 hours of perseverance."

Those powerful words that had bound me for eleven years seemed so pointless now as together, we held the paper to the candle's flame and watched the paper slowly fold and crinkle into a brown paper mass. The crowd of family and friends cheered.

"So, are you going to quit now?" one of the journalists asked, speaking for the first time since the party had begun.

I looked around, staring at the many pictures of Michael Jordan, and of me playing basketball over the years. Then, without hesitation, I smiled and shook my head.

"Never," I whispered. "WNBA, here I come."

~Christine Catlin

91

Confessions of an Unlikely Chorale Member

Shoot for the moon. Even if you miss, you'll land among the stars.
~Les Brown

At my school, Select Chorale is a very big deal. Kids who make it into this class are an ultra-talented mix of musical theatre stars, piano prodigies, and soloists who have been taking voice lessons since grade school.

Then there's me. I'm the one who struggles with reading music, took three years to understand intervals, and enthusiastically performs choreography... in the wrong direction. Not exactly Select Chorale material.

Somehow, I made it into the group. I still swear it was some kind of paperwork error.

That's why I wasn't feeling too confident when our choir teacher, Mr. Avery, announced our first assignment. "By next Friday, you'll be singing one of our pieces in quartets," he said from his position at the piano. "This is an advanced class, so I expect you to work with it on your own time."

Quartets. I did the math. That meant one person on each part. Just me singing against a soprano, tenor, and bass. Chances were good that they would all sound better than me.

I gulped again when I saw what the piece was: "Sicut Cervus."

It was Latin. It was a cappella, so the piano wouldn't cover up any mistakes we made. And it was very, very complicated, with notes scattered all over the place, like someone had attacked the music with a machine gun.

The first day we worked on the song in class, I knew that the music was harder than anything I'd ever sung before, and I just wasn't getting it.

"By Friday, you'll be good enough to pass," one of my fellow altos advised me. "Just fake your way through. That's what we all do."

Something about that struck me as being very wrong. A lot of things in life came easily to me. Here was something that I had a hard time with, and I was supposed to just give up? "I don't think so," I remember muttering to myself as I put my music in my backpack to take home that night.

I did everything that I could to learn that song. I asked a friend to help me play my part and teach me some rhythms. As I did dishes and worked on homework, I listened to a recording of the song play over and over again until I literally heard it in my sleep. Every morning, I would stare at the list of solfeggio syllables attached to my mirror and sing my garbled "do, re, mi's" through toothpaste.

I even tried to play parts of the song on my own. This was harder than it sounds, since the only note I could recognize on the piano was middle C. The keys of our old, out-of-tune piano were soon covered with numbered masking tape so I could plunk out my part, note by note. Not exactly a typical Select Chorale strategy, I guess, but it worked for me. I got a little better at the piece every day, and in-class rehearsals helped too.

Then disaster struck. On Thursday, the day before quartets, Mr. Avery was absent. Our substitute teacher knew even less about music than I did, which was saying something. "I guess you're supposed to work on something called 'Sicut Cervus,'" she said, squinting at the note Mr. Avery had left.

I groaned. This could be interesting.

Everyone gathered around the piano, and one of the sopranos

gave all of the parts their starting note. We started to sing... and almost instantly fell into an off-key mess.

The only thing more painful than listening to our singing was listening to everyone argue about whose fault it was. "The guys need to come in stronger on the key change," the piano player insisted. "Mr. Avery's said that a dozen times, and you still mess it up."

"Hey, at least we weren't sharp," a tenor shot back.

"I think we need to go over the first section again," someone else suggested. "Our tempo is totally off, because some people," she gave another girl a pointed stare, "are trying to set their own pace."

It went on like that for several minutes. Too many people talking and not enough listening, especially the big, important seniors. We had been in the choir program the longest, and apparently that meant we had the right to order everyone else around. There were seniors glaring at sophomores, juniors, other seniors, the substitute teacher, posters on the wall—you name it, they were glaring at it.

Before I had a nervous breakdown, I glanced over at my friend Evan. He was serenely surveying the chaos with his hands in his pockets and a slight smile on his face. It was like he was secretly amused by all of us.

I hurried over to him. Clearly, he didn't understand the situation. "We have to sing in quartets tomorrow, and all of us sound awful!" I pointed out. "Plus, everyone is fighting and insulting each other! How can you be so calm?"

My little tirade did nothing to shake Evan. He shrugged. "I just stand where I'm supposed to and sing every song the best I've ever sung it."

Well. That was a new thought. Could it be that it my hustle and bustle to get every detail of the song down perfectly, I had forgotten that music is supposed to be fun?

Sure, it was a bad idea to fake it through the song and give a half-hearted performance. But stressing out about it wasn't going to help either. That was something I needed to be reminded of as performance day approached.

"All of you should have come prepared to sing in quartets," Mr. Avery said the minute the bell rang the next day.

We all nodded... or, at least, most of us did. A few people looked guiltily down at their music, trying to cram before they were called in front of the class. "Then you should be ready to sing the song by yourself." For a split second, everyone was silent, and even the rustling music stopped as we processed that thought.

No, it wouldn't be me against three other choir members. Not this time. It was just me against... me.

Maybe it always had been.

I waited to go until last, not necessarily because I wanted to, but because everyone else volunteered before I could force a word out of my dry mouth. I remember Mr. Avery calling my name, and then everything is a blurry mess of pitches and solfeggio.

I do remember the looks on my classmates' faces as I walked shakily back to my seat. Most of them seemed shocked, like they were thinking, "How did the shy, musically illiterate girl in the back row get up there and sing like that?"

Evan didn't look surprised. He just gave me a thumbs up.

I knew that, somehow, I had made that dreaded homework assignment into real music. When my "best," the vague, mysterious standard that I claimed to strive for, had actually required striving, I had risen to the challenge.

It ended up being easier than I thought. All I had to do was stand where I was supposed to and sing the song the best I had ever sung it.

~Amy Green

92

The End
of the Zombie Days

Education is not the filling of a pail, but the lighting of a fire.
~William Butler Yeats

I was a zombie in high school, shuffling from class to class barely even awake. I played video games into the wee hours of the morning nearly every night. Luckily there was one teacher out there who slammed his hands on my desk and shouted at me one day, and in doing so startled me out of my stupor.

Ray Seabeck wore the same simple clothes every single day. He stood before me on the first day of class my senior year, as I was slumped in my desk in an eighteen-year-old haze. I was not expecting much from this man, from his gray, feathered hair and glasses. I yawned, not even bothering to cover my mouth, and he leapt—he literally leapt—from the front of the room to my desk in the second row, and slammed his hands on my desk when he landed.

"Do you like Shakespeare?" he screamed at me.

My mouth was stuck in mid-yawn, wide open.

"Well, do you?" he hollered.

"Yes!" I lied. I had no idea what Shakespeare was. But I was going to find out. What's more, this man would fan some smoldering cinder of interest in me, a cinder only he could sense.

I had a 1.7 grade point average in high school. I had stayed back in the fourth grade. Often I didn't even go to bed; I let myself become a slave to video games, sadly satisfied with accomplishments in the virtual world, while I barely noticed significant events of my real life speeding past, like mile markers on a New Hampshire highway.

We read *Hamlet*, and bit by bit I found that I enjoyed the psychological complexity. Why did Hamlet keep hesitating? Why?

I had done a good job rationalizing my poor grades throughout school. My excuse was this: I'm joining the Army, so what does it matter? I'd already enlisted in January of my senior year, so what did it matter? I was set to ship out in August after I graduated. But as my high school career wound down, my anxiety increased. Suddenly I'd begun liking Shakespeare, and then Hemingway, and then Fitzgerald, Wordsworth and Blake. What if—and it was an "if" of epic proportions—what if I could become an English teacher like Mr. Seabeck? What if I could read and write and talk about it, and get paid for it?

But on the other side I had the Army to look forward to. I'd always dreamt of being a soldier; I coveted the prestige that came with defending our nation.

I stayed after school one day to ask Mr. Seabeck what he thought about my conundrum. I told him of my choices, and my ambivalence. Of my desire to become a teacher, and a soldier. Want to know what he said?

"Hamlet!" he said, pointing at me. "You're Hamlet! Here you have two paths laid open for you—to be or not to be. To become a teacher or a soldier."

I said, "The thing is, I've already signed my Army contract. But I could still get out of it if I wanted to."

"Well that's curious," he said.

"What is?"

"That's the third time I've heard you say that—that you could still get out of your contract."

"But do you think I could even get into a college with a 1.7 GPA?"

"No college in the U.S. will turn you down, Ron, from enrolling in one class. Get an A in that, and maybe one or two more part-time, and you'd have a pretty good shot."

I left school that day with college in my eyes and ears. Just thinking of joining the thousands of students matriculating that fall made me feel electric.

And Mr. Seabeck was right. I did have to take a class part-time to get accepted at Plymouth State University, but get accepted I did. I graduated cum laude, and went on to earn my Master's degree in English Literature from the University of New Hampshire. And now, as I sit writing this twelve years later, I'm sitting at Mr. Seabeck's old desk. I took over his old position, teaching English at Laconia High School in New Hampshire. I can still see that wry grin of his, and I can still hear him screaming, "Do you like Shakespeare?" I might never have known that I, in fact, love Shakespeare, if not for the spark he lit in me that caused me to examine my life, my habits, and my desires. I will forever bear his stamp, and the evidence is in my high school yearbook. My senior quote reads as follows:

"Tis now the very witching time of night,
When churchyards yawn and hell itself breathes out
contagion to this world. Now I could drink hot blood,
And do such bitter business as the day
Would quake to look on."
—*Hamlet*, Act three, Scene two, lines 349-353

~Ron Kaiser, Jr.

93

Sticking with It

"I must do something" always solves more problems than
"Something must be done."
~Author Unknown

I heaved the cardboard box out of the trunk of our rented van. The sun burned bright yellow overhead, the humidity so thick you could almost taste it. It took a moment for me to realize this is where I had dreamed of going, and finally, I was here.

"Help me lift this one," my mom said, gesturing toward a bulky package. My dad rushed forward and grabbed one end. Our Thai friend, Em, hoisted another out of the rental and followed us.

After we set down our burden, I looked at my surroundings for the first time. A few shabby houses stood near a clump of trees, and a thin metal roof was draped over six stone pillars, apparently used as a meeting area. Other than that, the scene was bare and lonely.

An engine roared behind us. All four of us turned to see a procession of motorcycles coming down the dirt road. I noticed that three, or even four people including children, squeezed onto one motorcycle. A couple of kids waved and smiled, but most just stared. A stab of sympathy shot through me like a lightning bolt before striking the pit of my stomach. These kids, these survivors had suffered through so much. Some had lost family members, best friends, and people they loved. Looking at some of their faces, I could tell the giant tsunami off the coast of Thailand damaged them internally, a wound that may someday heal for some, but stay a bleeding heart forever in others.

The children with mothers, fathers, aunts, uncles, grandmothers, or grandfathers assembled in the meeting area in front of us, looking excited. All chatting in Thai, as they cast interested looks at the three boxes sitting off to the side. My mom beckoned Em forward as people continued to file into the seating area.

"Could you translate?" she asked. Em nodded and smiled.

"Hello." My mom addressed the crowd, which fell silent almost at once.

Em translated in Thai, bowing politely with her hands pressed together in front of her.

"We have come to deliver art supplies and sports equipment," my mom said. "We have brought soccer balls, basketballs, pastels, colored pencils, watercolors, and of course, paper." Em translated again and then went to help my mom, dad and I carry the boxes to the front of the anxious crowd. One by one, we unloaded the supplies. My mom nudged me.

"Show them how to use the watercolor." With the crowd of kids closing in to get a good look, I unwrapped a watercolor paint set and painted a simple blue flower.

Once the children settled with their art supplies, my mom, dad, Em and I walked around, taking pictures of the kids as they talked, drew, and used watercolors. Some of the kids I noticed were talented. One girl painted a picture of a tree with a winding stream and mountains in the background. Other kids took time to blend shades and create shadows.

A couple of older boys started pointing to the second set of boxes. Apparently my dad noticed this too because he rushed over and unpacked the contents. Soccer balls and basketballs spilled out. The children grabbed them and quickly started a soccer game.

With the sun sinking behind the evening sky, we prepared to go. The children and their elders waved goodbye to us as we left down the dirt road. I leaned back in my seat, thinking about what just happened. When I started thinking about raising money to send art supplies and sports equipment to the tsunami victims, I told myself I would stick with it until the end. But deep down, I thought this was just another fantasy of mine. Never did I imagine I would actually be privileged enough to meet all these wonderful people who would change my life. But with all the support I received from my aunts, uncles, grandma, grandpa, and of course my parents, I knew that they would never let me give up. It is thanks to them I raised the hundreds of dollars to turn a dream into reality.

~Anna Thielen

94

Chasing a Dream

There are some defeats more triumphant than victories.
~Michel de Montaigne

I was 200 yards away from the finish line when my legs stopped working. In a moment faster than I could blink, I watched my dreams crash helplessly to the ground. Lifting my face from the dirt, I looked up and saw the horror in my dad's face. In his eyes I saw the sweat, the time, and the work we had put into our dream. The miles we had run together, all for this race, flashed across my mind. This race was the pinnacle of my hopes, the climax of my existence—the State cross-country race of my senior year of high school.

I was the fastest runner on my team, and I was supposed to make it into the top fifteen. We had been working towards this race for three years. It was everything to me, and it was everything to my dad. He was a runner and was exhilarated by my success in running. He made it to every race, even flying home early from business trips to see me run. I always listened for his voice, which rang above the crowd—telling me to relax my arms, calling out my time. He pushed me. He cheered for me. He believed in me. We spent countless hours on the sandy canals of Arizona. Breathing in the dust of the desert, the blossoms of the orange groves, and the stench of the dairy farm, we made our way across the city. We pounded miles and miles into our running shoes, marking with every step the path to greatness. It was a journey that was just ours. A dream passed on from one generation to the next.

I will never forget that November day. It was hotter than normal—too hot. My throat felt like a field of cotton, cracked with the summer heat, as I waited for the gun to fire. This was the day we had waited so long for. This was the day I was destined for. I gazed out at the crowd; dozens of familiar faces from church and school flickered across my view. They had come for me. They were counting on me. I saw my dad set his watch, worry and excitement etched across his face. Adrenaline pumped through my body, and the race began.

For the first two and a half miles, I felt great. I had never before been so ready for something. The weeks leading up to the race were filled with regimented practices and a strict diet. My friends hadn't seen me in weeks, but they understood the sacrifice required to make my dream a reality. The sizzling sun beat upon my back, blinding me with its brilliance. Nothing was going to stop me, though. Determination focused my mind, and perseverance guided my steps. As in all of my races, I didn't start out in the front. I loved the thrill of passing people as my endurance overtook their premature speed.

Without warning, my strength began to subside. My lungs fought to take in enough air, and my feet transformed into cement bricks. I still don't know what happened in those last few moments. Neck and neck with one of my greatest rivals, I could see the finish line. I had begun the final sprint into glory when my knees buckled and my legs gave way. Nothing I could do would make them hold my weight. They were as weak as Jell-O.

I watched with agony as runners rushed by me. Even though I knew my dreams of victory were destroyed, I had to finish the race. With all of the strength left in me, I got on my hands and knees and crawled, inch by inch, across the finish line. Voices, both foreign and familiar, cheered me on. They gave me the courage to keep going until the very end. The paramedics were there in seconds, sticking me with needles, covering my mouth with an oxygen mask.

My eyes scoured the crowd for him. Although my coach and teammates rushed to me, offering words of encouragement, there was only one person I wanted to talk to. Fear pulsed through my veins as he pushed his way to my side.

As the tears spilled over, I whispered, "I'm so sorry, Dad. I'm so sorry I disappointed you."

He looked at me with sadness and said, "You could never disappoint me. Sometimes these things just happen. All that matters is that you did your best."

"But we worked so hard. What about our dream?"

In that second, the world stood still. He reached over for my hand, holding back his own tears, and said, "Don't you know that you are my dream come true?

It wasn't long before my running shoes were back on, marking a new path for my journey. I learned something from that race — something I will never forget. All of the miles, the tears, the sweat, and the pain my dad and I experienced together were not for a race. When he pushed me to go faster, to work harder, or to breathe deeper, it wasn't for a dream that was unfulfilled. I thought my dad was running after a prize. What I realized, though, was that he was running after me. To him, I was the greatest prize he had ever won.

~Melissa Harding

95

Are the Golden Years Gone?

I believe the future is only the past again, entered through another gate.
~Arthur Wing Pinero

It's senior year, and life's a blur
People often ask me, "what's it like being her?"
With trophies and ribbons stacking my dresser with pride,
My accomplishments and hard work I'd rather not hide.

I feel no shame in what I've achieved
All I tell them is, "You just have to believe,
Believe you have the power and strength to do your best,
When everyone around you just expects less."

In high school I seem to have reached academic fame,
But all I can think is, "Have I actually lost the game?"
With college ahead and youth behind,
I rarely give myself some time to unwind.

And now I keep thinking, "Are the golden years gone?"
What if new achievements won't come with the dawn?
I don't want to be the girl who "used to" be great,
A slow, steady demise my only fate

Oh, how I hope that the best years of my life are still ahead
Instead of in the past, filling my life with constant dread
I still work with as much energy and passion as before
But maybe everybody else will expect something more

But I mustn't give up, I will survive
Just have to keep my head bobbing above the tide.
Take a deep breath, and the best will get better,
And maybe, just maybe, the golden years will last forever.

~Korina Chilcoat

96

Believe

Never underestimate the power of those who believe in you.
~Michael Phelps

When I look back on it now, all I can remember is a blur of pain—fatigue and pain that never seemed to end. One excruciating, long-lasting day followed another in which I could do nothing except lie motionless and will my body to stop hurting until I lost track of time.

The memory of CAT scans, doctors, nurses, and finally, the diagnosis of appendicitis made me cringe like I had just received a knife stab. Of all the events I had ever experienced, nothing had ever hurt more than three days with appendicitis, and one day with a fully ruptured appendix. This was followed by nothing less than emergency surgery, swine flu, a PICC line to administer antibiotics, and then despite the PICC line, getting CDIFF, an intestinal infection. After this, I abscessed in the area of my recent surgery, and had to get another PICC line that required the nurse to come in every six hours around the clock to administer the medicine.

I lost my appetite. I was simply not hungry, and was often not allowed to eat because of the possibility of more future surgery. Food, which I had always eaten more than enough of, became unappetizing. I lost twenty pounds in eleven days. It was like melting. All the muscle that had taken years of swimming to acquire was eaten away and my clothes started to hang off me. People who saw me during that time said I looked like a skeleton.

I missed school for a month, and I desperately wanted to see all of my friends again, but did not want them to see me in the condition I was in. Before my ruptured appendix, I could swim miles daily. Now it was an effort to sit up, and a huge accomplishment to get out of bed. When I finally did accomplish walking, it was only a few hunched over, excruciating steps leaning on my parents before I collapsed with the pain and effort.

Through all of this, the knowledge that I would not be able to swim again for almost three months mentally broke me down. You could call it a really bad start to my season.

After all that, no one was expecting me to have a great season—not even myself. Especially not myself. I didn't anticipate anything special or great, so I wasn't going to accomplish anything special or great. That's what I believed.

When I finally got back in the pool, I struggled with my newly limited ability, and the frustration that I couldn't push myself through the difficulties I was encountering. Race after race, I fell short of my goals. Every time I attempted to make Nationals, the biggest meet I could hope to make at my age, I failed by a miniscule amount. It was infuriating—to be so close, and yet so far.

Finally, I came to the last meet that could qualify me for Nationals. My last chance. Standing behind the blocks, I couldn't help but feel extremely angry about what I had been through. This time was my last shot; now or never. If I didn't do it today, all the work I had put in wouldn't matter.

Swimmers learn at an early age that to be able to swim well, you just have to gut it out and take everything in one blow, because eighty seconds of the hardest work and endurance you've ever encountered will be worth it later on. You learn to love every second of it, because otherwise, you'll never make it. You have to believe.

When I was called to the block, my fear melted away like a stick of hot butter. You can't be distracted during your race; the pool owns everything in you for that short while. Two minutes decide everything. So you can't mess up.

When I took my first stroke, I decided I wasn't going to mess up. In the next minute, I took all of the pain, the hours of training, the frustration, the doubt, and all the anger I had experienced in the last couple of months and threw it all into the pool. For that moment, emotions didn't exist, and neither did a limit on how far I believed I could push myself.

The closer I came to finishing, the closer I came to either coming out on top, or to just experiencing more disappointment. I couldn't face failing again—I had had enough of that. And with that thought, I slammed the touch pad with all the strength I had left.

When I saw my time, a wave of relief swept over me, and I felt silent tears of happiness rolling down my face, mixing with the water. Despite everything, I had done it. In a weird way, I felt that I had just stood up to myself. After six months, I had decided which emotion I would succumb to—doubt, or determination.

That day, I learned something about myself: that I can't let anything stand in my way, not even me. I've decided that doubting myself is just as bad as giving up. That even if others believe in me, it isn't worth anything until I believe in myself. I know now I can do anything if I want it badly enough.

Sometimes, you've just got to believe.

~Holland Anne Driscoll

Math

God does not care about our mathematical difficulties.
He integrates empirically.
~Albert Einstein

hen I was in seventh grade, my parents paid forty dollars
a week for a tutor to come to my house and help me with
math, which ended up raising my mark from a fifty to a...
fifty-five.

Okay, maybe it was partly my fault. Maybe I should have spent
less time worrying about that oh-so-important geography assignment
and more time plotting my y-intercepts. But math is a tricky thing.
And sitting down at a chair to work on confusing algebraic equations for two hours is a slow and painful process, usually involv-
ing unexplained fidgeting of the fingers and numerous trips to the
refrigerator in an attempt to get off that chair for at least five minutes.
Take it from me, you get used to teachers always leaning over your
desk during tests, and visits from past teachers always prompted the
million-dollar question: "How's math?"

So I became afraid of it. While normal people my age were
scared of spiders and that new ride at Wonderland, I became afraid
of anything to do with numbers. The thought of a teacher picking on
me in class was terrifying. The red marking—which might as well
have been a painting drawn by my math teacher for all the ink he
used on that stupid test—was like a component in a horror movie,
where I often felt like cutting that test up and then screaming my
head off, another component in horror movies. It only got worse in

ninth grade. Every report card I ever received was delivered with the comment: "Victoria needs to ask for assistance in class." But I couldn't tell my teachers the real reason why I didn't ask for help: I didn't want to be a dummy. Every question I had was, in my opinion at the time, something that the entire class got and I didn't understand. So instead, I resorted to the mindset of not caring about anything and concluding that everything would work out in the end.

It didn't.

After spending a semester not caring about homework and not trying on tests, still afraid of math and convinced I would never succeed, my math teacher called one summer morning to tell me I would spend the next three weeks at school, redoing the entire course so I could pass. As it turned out, I failed tenth grade math. With flying colours, I might add.

This news was met with sudden tears, a loud "this can't be happening to me!" and a refusal to do anything related to friends, family, fun, or life. I took to my books. English rules and math drools. I had morphed into some ridiculous failure, destined for a life of disappointment, because I would never graduate and never go to university and never, never, do anything good in my life.

That's when it hit me. Why was I scared of a bunch of numbers, anyway? Why was I so petrified of asking my teacher for help? Because I was afraid of looking like a moron? Why did I barely study for tests because I had convinced myself I would never do well? Who was this unconfident student and what happened to that determined, confident teenager I had once been?

I finally realized that I had let math take over my life. Sure, I still don't like numbers, and I probably never will. But if it's one thing I've learned, it's that math is just a subject. There was really no reason to be afraid of it—I just needed to take the bull by the horns. Face the music. Be the bigger person! Gradually, my attitude changed, and I became more positive once I let go of my mathematic fears.

So I'm off to three weeks of summer school, three hours of math each day. If there's any bright side, it's that at least I have some sort of self-esteem embedded in me, somewhere, and I'll be getting the help

I need. After all, maybe next year I'll be doing better because I studied more often in the summer than the other kids at school. Maybe failing wasn't the worst thing that could have happened.

So gone are my days of imagining numbers as something to be afraid of and thinking that algebra is out to get me. Substitution, elimination, factoring—here I come.

~Victoria Linhares

98

Embracing Life

Adventure is worthwhile.
~Amelia Earhart

Hungary?" I looked at my mom in confusion. "I never said anything about wanting to go to Hungary...." And with that, my adventure started.

My name is Hinako Takeuchi and I just finished an amazing exchange year in Hungary.

Going on an exchange had always been a dream. When my high school offered an all-year exchange program, I jumped at the opportunity. It would pay for almost everything and all I had to do was get a plane ticket. I knew where I wanted to go: Spain, the country of dancers wearing flowing red dresses. I was in love with their language, although maybe not for the reason you're all thinking. I wanted to go, only because I heard that Spanish is easy if you can speak both English and Japanese. My motto, of course, was always, "Take the easy way."

So when I heard that I was going to Hungary, I was pretty shocked. I won't lie; I didn't want to go at all. But I decided to make the best of it, since it was, after all, a once-in-a-lifetime opportunity. Before I knew it, I was on the airplane, bound for Ferihegy Airport, Budapest.

I had times when I almost gave up. Hungarian is the hardest language on the planet, or so I've heard. But I think it's beautiful. The change in the landscape was breathtaking, since it looked nothing like the tall skyscrapers, bullet trains, cars, and people in tiny houses that I was accustomed to. I fell in love with the relaxing lifestyle, the warm-hearted people, and getting home at 2:30 at the latest from school. And I was sad to leave on my very last day.

In Hungary, I learned how to give kisses as a greeting, to ballroom dance and jazz dance, and to use a knife and a fork the correct way. But these were only a few of the things I learned.

Having three host families who took me in as their own daughter/sister was the best thing I've ever experienced. From my little sisters, I learned how to embrace life to its fullest, to dance until you drop. From my big sister, I learned how to be yourself, to never care what others think about you. From my brothers, I learned that it's okay to be a kid, to run around the house, over couches. I also learned that locking people outside is actually quite fun. I learned to stay positive, to smile, and that when you pick the right person and take their hand, suddenly, you're friends.

I went to Hungary all alone, not knowing anyone. With fears and hopes all jumbled up, I boarded the airplane. But I don't regret it, not at all. I'm full with all my dreams, all the lessons that I've learned and the experiences that I had. They're all important, and each has earned a place in my heart.

~Hinako Takeuchi

99

Pain Is Only Temporary

Sports is human life in microcosm.
~Howard Cosell

Scared. That is all I'm feeling. Scared. I'm standing behind the starting blocks and the swimmers in the pool are finishing their race. As I gaze up at the clock at the far end of the pool, the yellow numbers looking faded through a pair of mirrored goggles, I realize these times are not going to be fast enough. I have to do better.

The concept of the race does not seem challenging: a 200-yard swim composed of two lengths of each stroke (butterfly, backstroke, breaststroke, and freestyle). Yet, I dread the event more than anything in the world at this moment. As swimmers from the previous heat struggle to exit the water, the official standing at the side of the pool blows his whistle, the shrill pitch reverberating off the high ceiling of the natatorium.

I jump up onto my block, give a thumbs up to Carter, who is seeded first in the event with a time five seconds better than mine, and proceed with my pre-race-on-the-block tradition: four lat slaps and two arm jiggles before reaching down to grab the edge of the sandpaper-like surface of the block.

"Quiet for the start, please. Quiet for the start," says the announcer, a young woman with a powerful voice. The silence that sweeps across the room amplifies my fear. Can we just get this over with? The official, dressed in his pure white uniform, grants my wish and says the four words all swimmers despise: "Swimmers, take your mark."

All eight of us tense up. Our bodies are rigid, knuckles turning white from grabbing the block. Beep!

My body uncoils and shoots off the block like a spring waiting to be released. Keep your head down, I think to myself. Entering the water is like diving into a bucket of ice, and I want to come up for air as my lungs start collapsing. No, stay under, you got this, keep kicking and surface in ten more yards, save your arms for later.

I finally come up and start butterflying my way down the pool. The first length is always the easiest; there are no aches or pains at the first turn. A quick breath and then back underwater for the second half of the butterfly. I surface and take a few strokes, when all of a sudden I feel my right shoulder move out of its socket. As I finish the stroke, the shoulder is shoved back in with a "POP" and I enter a world of pain. Maybe my physical therapist was right, maybe I should have stopped swimming. Oh well, too late now. This is my last race of the season and I'm not about to give up.

Five more strokes and I reach the wall, curl my knees into my chest, and shoot off the wall on my back. While underwater, I look around for Carter. Oh shoot, he's at least two body lengths ahead, there's no way I will win this race. I come up for air and begin the helicopter motion of backstroke. I can hear my coach's voice in my head saying, "Palmer, keep your head UP!" At this point my legs are starting to get sore from all the kicking. My shoulder feels like someone is driving a flaming knife straight into it. But I have to keep going.

I see the flags, take two strokes, and flip over to push off the third wall, staying underwater for as long as possible. A quick look to my side tells me Carter is still where he was twenty-five yards ago, four yards ahead. As I finish the first half of the race, my forearms are numb. I touch the wall with one hand, then back under for my favorite part of the race: breaststroke.

I make sure to push off the wall a little deeper than usual to maximize the underwater part of the length. Big mistake. My lungs are collapsing on me and my brain is punishing me for not giving it enough oxygen. My head pops up for just enough time to take a heavenly gulp of a mixture of chlorine gas and air. At this point, I can barely move my arms, but I know this is my best stroke, and I'm relying on these next fifty yards to get back into the race. Each kick drives me closer and closer to the wall, but also closer and closer to complete insanity. Resisting the urge to glide as far as possible has never been harder. Come on, man, this is what you've been waiting for, I think to myself as I rocket off the fifth wall. The lack of oxygen makes my fingertips numb and now each kick feels like someone is punching my thigh with brass knuckles. The burn is everywhere, but a surge of adrenaline persuades me to keep going when I look over and see that I'm now neck-and-neck with Carter, tied for first place.

Three more huge kicks take me to the final lap of the race. This is it. All or nothing. I clench my teeth and start the torture that is the freestyle section of the race. My entire body is numb. Each stroke feels like I'm moving a mountain and I can't even tell if I'm kicking or not. Get to the other end, flip at the wall, and start coming down the home stretch. I can't look at Carter. Any unnecessary movement will result in a swimmer's worst enemy: drag. Careening towards the wall, my shoulders can barely raise my arms out of the water. Just one more stroke until the end, I reach out as far as I possibly can and then reach even farther until my fingers slam into the wall. I look up and Carter is right there at the wall with me. I rip the goggles off my eyes and turn around to check the all-powerful Clock of Destiny.

Lane 4, Patterson, 2:15.70.

I can't tell if my heart is pounding out of my chest simply because my body wants to shut down or because I'm scared to read my time.

Lane 5, Palmer, 2:15.61.

I can't feel my arms, but I dropped a full seven seconds off my best time and won a seemingly impossible race. Reaching over to congratulate Carter, this is the most enjoyably painful hug I have ever experienced. The parents and siblings in the stands are cheering as I barely manage to hoist myself out of the pool. Ice packs and heat will help the pain go away, but how I feel at this moment will always remain. The blue ribbon will be hanging in my room long after the throbbing subsides.

~J.D. Palmer

100

Thirteen Years

There is a good reason they call these ceremonies
"commencement exercises."
Graduation is not the end; it's the beginning.
~Orrin Hatch

Thirteen years ago we met as children, small and hopeful,
Full of childish dreams.
Thirteen years ago we all were so small
And only glimmers of who we would become shone bright
    from our eyes.

We have grown together and grown apart,
Brought together by familiarity and separated by childish
    quarrels.
We were children together,
Young and naïve, happy and free.

Over the years our bodies have grown,
Our dreams have withered
And new dreams have been sown.
We have seen the worst and the best,
The highs and the lows.
We have changed, friendships destroyed and new relationships
    begun
Where before there were none.

And soon it will be over.
Soon we will be out of high school.
We will be adults, all of us who knew each other as children.
We will be in the real world, away from here,
But we can hold on to the memories.
We can remember childhood days of laughter and play,
Of when the world was not so hard, not so unforgiving.

Thirteen years ago we were strangers, entering a new world.
Thirteen years ago — a lifetime — we met, became, if not
    friends, something to each other.
We are a family; with each other we know where we stand.
Thirteen years ago we all were so young —
And now we are grown.

How quickly we have grown, how soon our final day looms.
Beyond that final walk lies what?
A future, bright and shining, beckons us.
Our hopes and dreams have shifted, grown.
We are adults; we are grown.
Thirteen years ago we could not have imagined this day.

We were children together,
And now we go our own ways.
We have our own lives to live.
We have spent thirteen years preparing for this day;
Thirteen years of dreaming, hoping, even of longing —
And here it is.
Our day has arrived.

Thirteen years ago we met;
We have grown together.
We have changed, become our own persons —
And still there are glimmers of who we were,
Faint and always fading.

Memories linger, old and fond memories, of childhood days
With those of us who were here
For those thirteen years.

Thirteen years ago we met.
Thirteen years have passed in a blink.
Thirteen years, full of pain and tears, full of hope and laughter,
Full of play and rage and dreams
Have come and gone so quickly—
And change looms.
We are grown.

Thirteen years ago we met and now we go our separate ways.
Thirteen years ago—and here we are, adults.
We grew together, thirteen years—and it is over now.
We are grown and we call goodbye.
We close the door and walk away—
We are grown—with our own lives to live.
Thirteen years are gone.

~Laura Williams

What's Next?

The future is called "perhaps," which is the only possible thing to call the future. And the only important thing is not to allow that to scare you.

~Tennessee Williams

I have a confession. I am absolutely addicted to reality TV. The drama, the unpredictability, the sheer unscripted freedom of it all just draws me in. Even so, I'd never really watched the reigning show of reality television: MTV's *The Hills*. But as a way to promote the series finale, the network ran every episode of all six seasons, counting down to the big event. It was during this marathon that I became a fan. I followed the stories of Lauren, Heidi, Stefanie, Lo, Kristen, Whitney, and Audrina from beginning to end at rapid fire pace. Naturally, I tuned into the grand finale. And I have another confession. I cried. But not just because "It's all over!" as other fans would moan. Because I related to those girls. Their lives were approaching a turning point, one that would affect their paths permanently. They had to decide what they wanted in life, where their careers were going, and who and what they were looking for. The season finale was when everything changed. Forever.

As I'm facing my senior year, I'm terrified. This is my last year in the town I've lived for the past eleven years. I'll no longer be near the schools that educated me, my first love, the friends who stuck with me or left me, and especially the theatre group that saved me, changed me, and helped me discover that the person I'd always wanted to be was who I really was all along. A year from now I'm leaving, and even if I come back, my home won't be the same. Someday it won't even be my home anymore.

Don't get me wrong; the future is going to be incredible. But right now, I'm terrified of it. I'm growing up. I have to decide what I want the rest of my life to be like, and how to achieve it.

I guess the big thing I'm really afraid of is the knowledge that one day, I'll have made it. I'll have an established career, whatever it may be, I'll have a husband, and someday I'll have kids. Then it will be their turn to be young, fall in love, then fall out of love again, make mistakes, and throw caution to the wind. I'll still have a life to live, but I'm so scared that I won't know what to do with it. I still want adventure and change and fear and to know that in any minute, my life could change forever. I want to be able to wonder, "What's next?"

But for now, all I can do is not take a day for granted, live every breath. The future is just that: the future. I can't live it yet. But I'm not going to sit around and wait. I'm going to... do things. Make things. Change things. I'm going to take that fear and use it to scare myself into being fearless. My present will sadly soon be my past. Because of that, I'm going to wring every last drop out of my last year so that 365 days from now I will stand with a smile on my face and tears in my eyes and look ahead and wonder, "What's next?"

~Lyssa Ray Hoganson

Just for
Teenagers

101 Stories of Inspiration
and Support for Teens

Meet Our Contributors
Meet Our Authors
Thank You
About Chicken Soup

Meet Our Contributors

Carmen Ang will be attending Simon Fraser University in the fall. She enjoys writing, reading and running. Carmen lives with her family and adorable puppy, Perry. One day she hopes to become a journalist.

Avery Atkins is a native Texan. She currently attends Colgate University where she is majoring in Molecular Biology and playing varsity soccer. Avery enjoys running, cooking, and watching college football with her family. Her ultimate desire is to glorify the Lord with her life.

Writing helps **Kelsey Bard**, one of our two M Magazine story-writing contest winners, control her emotions and figure out what she wants in life. She also enjoys singing, dancing, and traveling. Kelsey never imagined she'd be chosen to be in this book—all she can say is thank you.

Sara Bechtol is currently a junior in high school and is hoping to attend the University of Houston. She's had a passion for writing for as long as she can remember and even had her poetry published when she was fourteen. She is determined to become a bestselling author some day. E-mail her at bechtolsara@yahoo.com.

Alandra Blume is a West Virginian animal lover who adores reading, music, and rainstorms. She is a Christian, a freshman in college, and can be reached via e-mail at alblume@bluefield.edu. Bonnie is now a healthy ten-year-old and loves being with the family.

Lexi Bremer graduated high school in May 2011. Her college plans are to pursue a degree in elementary education. She enjoys playing sports, reading, spending time with family and friends, and any other fun activity. E-mail her at lexi_bremer2011@hotmail.com.

Angela Brewer will graduate from high school in June 2012. She has enjoyed writing all her life, and plans to expand her talents during college. She enjoys spending time with family and her close friends. This story was written in loving memory of Ryan A. Behrle. E-mail Angela at abrwrm@aol.com.

JoLyn Brown lives in Utah with her husband and son. She enjoys reading, writing, bike riding, working in her garden, and spending time with her family. She is writing her first young adult novel. E-mail her at brown.jolyn@yahoo.com.

Holly Brumm will be attending Eastern Michigan University in the fall to become a Pediatric Oncology nurse. She loves children and hopes to help them through the toughest time in their lives.

Jess Bunbury is a high school student. She enjoys writing, snow-boarding, drawing and horseback riding. She aspires to someday enter a pre-medical program at a local university. E-mail her at bunbury.jess@gmail.com.

Gabriella Carroll graduated, with honors, in June 2011, and is attending Saint Mary's College of California in the fall. She plans to study English, Communications, and Theology. Her interests include horses, youth ministry, and playing music. She aspires to be a writer or motivational speaker and musician for youth.

Christine Catlin is a teenager. Besides being a triplet, she has survived hypothermia, recovered from an eating disorder, and traveled to countries around the world. When not writing she plays sports, reads, and enjoys all life has to offer. E-mail her at thompson1news@yahoo.com.

Joseph Chan is a high school senior. He enjoys playing poker, trading stocks, and running long distances. He is also an avid environmentalist and the president of his school's environment club. He plans on attending the Wharton School of Business.

Tiffany Chan is a high school student. She loves writing, theatre, traveling, and Model United Nations. In the teen adolescence world that we all experience, Tiffany believes that there is much to be said; and words are there when all else fails.

Lucia Chen is a homework ninja (yes, that would be code for student). When she's not battling chemistry and calculus demons, she reads historical fiction, runs cross country, and watches soccer games. Along with bad poetry and funny memoirs, Lucia is writing her first novel, a time-travel romance with Napoleonic spies.

Eighteen-year-old, Southwest Florida resident **Korina Chilcoat** is a nationally published, award-winning writer whose work has been featured on the cover of *Teen Ink* magazine and in several national anthologies of writing. Check out her literary blog "Louder Than Words" at http://korinachilcoat.blogspot.com or, for inquiries, e-mail her at korinachilcoat@yahoo.com.

Madeline Clapps lives in Brooklyn, NY, and is a writer, editor, and proofreader for Chicken Soup for the Soul. She has worked on many books, but most recently she was an editor for *Chicken Soup for the Soul: Just for Preteens*, and this book, *Chicken Soup for the Soul: Just for Teenagers*. Madeline also designs *The Inner Circle*, the Chicken Soup for the Soul communiqué for contributors. She graduated from NYU in 2010 with a double major in Vocal Performance and Journalism, and is now pursuing a career as an actor and singer. She is a founding member of Libra Theater Company, where she also serves as Communications Director. Madeline spends her free time exploring Brooklyn, playing Scrabble, exercising, and eating good food. She loves being a part of the Chicken Soup for the Soul family! E-mail her at madelineclapps@gmail.com or check out www.maddyclapps.com.

Claudia Connors' mind is usually wandering into unknown and whimsical places. Even so, she manages to maintain her place on the honor roll, soccer team, and dearest friends and family members' hearts. She dreams of becoming a famous author. E-mail her at halogirl96@yahoo.com.

Kaity D. is currently studying dramatic arts and hopes to pursue a career in journalism or acting. Kaity is an avid traveler and plans to visit each continent. She has a passion for dance, music, and literature. As a member of Me to We youth Mobilizers, Kaity is an active volunteer devoted to bettering her global and local community.

Kaylee Davis graduated with honors from Hampton University in 2011 with a B.A. in Journalism. She will attend law school at George Washington University in the fall. Kaylee enjoys spending time with friends and family, the beach, and writing. She plans on practicing law and hopes to publish a children's storybook. E-mail her at kaylee_elise@yahoo.com.

Morgan Deich has always loved to write. She knows that Alzheimer's is a growing problem but she feels this story will send words of encouragement or help to others dealing with it. Morgan thanks her family for all their support and would like to dedicate this story to her grandpa.

Ashley Démoré is currently attending high school. She enjoys playing soccer, the piano and watching movies.

Jonathan Diamond is sixteen years old. He loves writing and is honored to have his story published in the *Chicken Soup for the Soul* series. In his spare time he enjoys reading, spending time with his family, traveling, and writing fiction. Jonathan hopes to have more of his writing published in the future.

Christine Dixon is a freelance writer, and is currently studying book publishing at Ryerson University. She currently writes a food and drink column for *Cottage Magazine* in Canada. E-mail her at vangoach@bmts.com.

Holland Driscoll is fourteen years old and lives with her family. She has a lot of pets, and spends a ton of time swimming and running. Holland would like to thank her extremely supportive and loving family, teachers, and friends for always being there for her.

Kalie Eaton is a junior high honors student. She enjoys poetry, songwriting, and photography. She lives with her mother and dog. Kalie was inspired to write by her English teacher, Pat Pelham, and her brother, Jerod.

Erin Eggleston is a high school student. She enjoys fencing and writing. She plans to be a writer when she is an adult and would love feedback. E-mail her at nttratswen@gmail.com.

Ryan Eng is currently a high school junior keeping up his studies to maintain his high grade standards. His free time is mostly spent with his favorite hobby, tennis. In the future he plans to major in Chemistry. E-mail him at rye@q.com.

Janell Evans is an honors high school graduate and is currently attending Schoolcraft College, later transferring to the University of Michigan Ann Arbor. Highlights of her life are graduating high school a year early, being crowned Miss Westland 2010, and competing in Irish dance around the country. E-mail her at janellevans22@yahoo.com.

Steven Farmer was born and raised in Clarksdale, MS. He's currently attending college in pursuit of a degree in nursing. Steven enjoys hunting, fishing, kayaking and photography. He plans to become a Nurse Anesthetist one day. E-mail him at deltahuntersteven@yahoo.com.

Amy Green is a Professional Writing major at Taylor University. When she's not writing or daydreaming, you can find her reading, singing in Gospel Choir, and playing board games. Her dream job would be writing chapter books for children or working as an editor at a publishing company.

Crystal Haigh, one of our two M Magazine story-writing contest winners, is currently a high school student. Her ambition is to be an English teacher. Crystal enjoys singing, dancing, swimming and reading. E-mail her at chcatgirl@comcast.net.

Melissa Harding grew up in Arizona, studied in New Zealand, served as a missionary in Costa Rica, and now lives with her husband and children in Colorado. She speaks at women's events and conferences, helping women discover intimacy with God. E-mail her at mel.d.harding@gmail.com or hear her speak at www.comebreathedeep.wordpress.com.

Jennie Hartstein has a very optimistic attitude toward life! Though she has struggled with eating disorders for a number of years, Jennie has used the experiences to shape who she is, and tries to spread the message of acceptance through poetry and her story of recovery.

Phillip Hernandez received his B.A. from James Madison University in May 2011. Phillip enjoys cooking, collecting music and vinyl records, playing guitar and piano, wandering in big cities, traveling outside the U.S., and visiting beaches. He plans to continue to have his writing published. E-mail him at philliphernandez89@gmail.com.

Lyssa Ray Hoganson plans to attend Georgia College and State

University to major in theatre. She enjoys acting, reading, writing, watching old movies, pampering her cats, and hanging out with her family and friends. Lyssa Ray previously contributed to *Chicken Soup for the Teenage Soul: The Real Deal Challenges*. E-mail her at lyssa.ray93@yahoo.com.

Latrice Holmes is a student at Chemeketa Community College. She plans to become a Juvenile Probation Officer and Counselor. Latrice loves basketball and her family.

Ainsley Holyfield was raised on the bayous of Monroe, LA. She loves spending time with her family and friends. She enjoys finding ways to help others and her community. She attends the University of Georgia and plans to attend law school.

Kimberly M. Hutmacher is the author of eighteen books. She enjoys sharing her knowledge and love of writing with people of all ages. Visit her website www.kimberlyhutmacher.com to learn more about Kimberly, her books, and her workshop offerings.

Linda Jackson is the author of the middle grade novels *The Lie That Binds* and *When Lambs Cry*. She also writes for educational publishers, developing stories for reading assessment testing. Please visit her website at www.jacksonbooks.com.

Irene Jiang is a junior in high school. She loves to swim, play soccer, hang out with friends, and sleep. Reading has always been one of her favorite pastimes. In the future, she hopes to study science and continue writing, as well (if only for fun).

Ron Kaiser lives in New Hampshire and is far, far, luckier than any man who has ever lived on earth, because he is married to a woman so strikingly beautiful that she makes Helen of Troy look like an alpaca in comparison. Ron teaches English, loves his little boy William, and writes in hope of publishing novels and short story collections. E-mail him at kilgore.trout1922@gmail.com.

Fallon Kane is a senior in high school. She has the most amazing family in the world and wants to thank her mother, brother, Kyle, Meredith, and Lucille for all of their amazing support over the years.

R. Kooyman is a high school student who loves volleyball and writing. She is a Christian and has a great family of five (including herself) and a puppy. She is the oldest and the only girl. This is her first published work.

Erika LaPlante graduated from high school in 2010. She currently attends Northeastern University, majoring in International Business. She would like to thank Don Corsetti for encouraging her to submit her story to the *Chicken Soup for the Soul* series.

Mary Elizabeth Laufer has a degree in English Education from SUNY Albany. As a Navy wife and mother of two, she moved around the country for twenty years, and now works as a substitute teacher in Oregon. Her stories and essays have been published in several anthologies.

Lauren Lesser is a high school senior with a love for writing, softball, and making others smile. She plans to continue chasing her dream of becoming an author and is thrilled to have her poem published by Chicken Soup for the Soul.

Adina Lichtman has been admitted to NYU and intends to pursue a career in social work. Adina hopes that everyone who reads her story will be inspired to never judge a book by its cover. E-mail her at Adinalich@gmail.com.

Victoria Linhares is a seventeen-year-old high school student and aspiring writer. She enjoys traveling, art, and literature. Her favourite book is *Extremely Loud and Incredibly Close* by Jonathan Safran Foer. E-mail her at victorialinhares@ymail.com.

Audrey Mangone received her B.A. in English with honors from the University of Massachusetts, Lowell. She went on to get her Master's Degree in English as a Second Language Education. She is currently an English teacher. When not teaching, she's busy publishing articles in local magazines and newspapers. E-mail her at audreymangone@gmail.com.

Melanie Marks has had over fifty stories in magazines such as *Highlights*, *Woman's World* and *Teen Magazine*. She's had four children's books published, and numerous teen novels including: *The Dating Deal*, *A Demon's Kiss*, *Paranormal Punch*, and *The Stranger Inside*. Visit her at www.byMelanieMarks.com or e-mail her at melanie@byMelanieMarks.com.

Lisa Meadows received her B.A. from Waynesburg University and Masters of Social Work from Marywood University. She is a social worker and a dog trainer in Pittsburgh, PA. She enjoys laughing at bad jokes, walking her dogs, and being outdoors.

Keri Metcalf is currently a high school student. "A Closed Door" is her first published story. She enjoys singing, writing, reading, traveling, and much more.

Erin Miller is a sophomore in high school. She continues to strive for academic excellence. Erin enjoys playing the violin and singing. She cherishes her family and friends. Erin's mom, Marie-Therese Miller, is an author of non-fiction books for teens and children. Please visit her website at www.marie-theresemiller.com.

Laura Miller lives in Michigan with her husband and children. She graduated with a degree in English from WMU and likes to spend her free time reading, writing and exploring the great outdoors. She has had several short stories and poems published, and is currently working on a novel. E-mail her at lauramllr09@gmail.com.

Morgan Miller is studying journalism and writing at Grand Valley State University and plans to graduate in 2012. Born and raised in Medina, OH, she enjoys writing and playing music. After college, she hopes to pursue her dream of becoming a bestselling writer.

Brianne Monett-Curran is currently pursuing a Bachelor of Science degree, in Seattle, WA, where she lives with her husband. She enjoys camping, traveling and a good cup of coffee.

Chido Muchemwa is currently a student at the University of North Texas. She hopes to graduate in a couple of years with a Bachelor of Science in Economics and go on to graduate school. She loves to write short stories in her spare time.

Ben Mueller is a teacher, elite triathlete, speaker, and author residing in Sycamore, IL. He teaches math and health classes at Hinckley-Big Rock High School. He enjoys speaking to audiences about the principles to success. To set up a speaking event, e-mail him at theTigerRunner@ aol.com or visit his website at www.theTigerRunner.com.

At fourteen, **Chelsea Murphy** won an award for a personal narrative she wrote and at sixteen she entered a provincial contest for Teens Against Drinking and Driving which donated one thousand dollars to her high school's TADD group. Chelsea plans to become an English teacher/writer. E-mail her at chelseamurphy-xo@hotmail.com.

L.S. Murphy is a young-adult writer whose short stories have been published in *Orion's Child* and *Luna Station Quarterly*. She is currently at work on her first novel. Learn more at LSMurphy.com.

D.D. Myrick graduated from Fairleigh Dickinson University with a B.A. in communications. She is currently working on her first novel and is continuously at work on her blog dialogwithdd.blogspot.com, in which she chronicles her life living with mild cerebral palsy. She also tours as a God inspired inspirational speaker.

Brittany Neverett is just a small town girl who wanted one of her true-life stories published by the time she graduated high school. She loves writing fiction and non-fiction stories and poems and enjoys spending time with her family and friends.

Suzanne Nicastro is a former middle and high school principal. She received her Bachelor of Arts degree in English from the University of California, Santa Barbara, and a Master of Education, with honors, from Chapman University. Suzanne is an author and consultant. Please visit her website at www.suzannenicastro.com.

Faith Northmen received her Bachelor of Arts, with honors, concentration in Medieval Literature, and Master's degree from the University of California, Irvine. Faith teaches high school English and actively studies history and science-fiction/fantasy. E-mail her at englishgoverness@yahoo.com.

Marady Owens has won several short-story writing competitions, writes several blogs, and hopes to achieve her dream of being a novelist, songwriter and activist. When she isn't reading or writing, she enjoys music, film, scrapbooking, and spending time with her twelve pets. E-mail her at maradyowens@ymail.com.

J.D. Palmer is a sophomore in high school. He is currently a member of both the New Trier Swim Team and Water Polo Team. When he is not in the pool, he enjoys listening to music and playing guitar.

Heidi Patton is an aspiring journalist. She writes for her school newspaper and plans to continue writing at the University of San Francisco. She loves traveling, running, volunteering, and the

Oregon coast. She once won a contest for the best fifty-five-word short story. E-mail at heidipatton6@hotmail.com.

Lia Peros received her Bachelor of Music with high honors from New York University in 2010. She is currently pursuing a career in acting and singing in NYC. In her free time, Lia enjoys cooking, tap dancing, and the magic that is Netflix. E-mail her at liaperos@gmail.com.

Marsha Porter has written numerous short stories and articles. She co-authored a movie guide that reviewed over 20,000 films. She perfected the 500-word essay in grade school where it was the punishment du jour. Currently, she teaches high school English.

Lilly Putsche is in ninth grade. She enjoys singing, dancing, writing and animals.

Cari Resnick received her B.A. in communications with a minor in English from Curry College in 2004. She loves being a stay-at-home wife and mom with two boys and one on the way. Cari enjoys running, reading, and Bible studies. She hopes to be a published children/young-adult author someday. E-mail her at Cari.Resnick07@gmail.com.

Kim Rogers earned a degree in Journalism from the University of Central Oklahoma. Her articles have been published in *Highlights for Children*, *Chicken Soup for the Soul* books, and many other publications. She loves to travel and spent four years in Germany and one year in South Korea where she taught English. Kim lives in Oklahoma with her husband and two children.

Teresa Silva started writing in her junior year of high school. It was writing that helped her express herself and her life experiences during adolescence. She attends junior college and plans to attend culinary school to carry out her dream of being a chef. Teresa enjoys dancing, movies and shopping.

Samaira Sirajee will be attending University of Pennsylvania in the fall. Samaira enjoys singing, baking, playing tennis, and volunteering. She plans to major in Business Management and hopes to work for a nonprofit charity organization. She currently lives in Temecula, CA.

Sami Smith will be attending Drake University in the fall and intends to major in writing. She enjoys music, traveling, and spending time with her amazing family and friends. She hopes to turn her passion of writing into a career she loves.

Diane Stark is a former teacher turned stay-at-home mom and freelance writer. She is a frequent contributor to the *Chicken Soup for the Soul* series, and she loves to write about the important things in life: her family and her faith. E-mail her at DianeStark19@yahoo.com.

Alexis Streb was born in 1997 and has always been a Navy brat. She has been all over the world, from Guam, to D.C. and back again. Alexis is a homeschooled vegetarian who reads and plays soccer all the time. E-mail her at alexis.streb@hotmail.com.

Ari Susu-Mago has been an avid reader and writer since the age of five and hopes to remain so until her dying day (other passions include paleontology, singing, French, and tea). She currently attends Yale University and plans to write speculative fiction for teenagers someday. E-mail her at ari.susumago@gmail.com.

Annmarie B. Tait resides in Conshohocken, PA, with her husband Joe Beck and dog Sammy. In addition to writing, Annmarie also enjoys cooking and singing Irish and American Folk Music. Annmarie has stories published in several *Chicken Soup for the Soul* volumes as well as the *Patchwork Path* series. E-mail her at irishbloom@aol.com.

Hinako Takeuchi is a high school student. Hinako likes hanging out with friends, reading, and writing. Hinako's dream is to make a bridge between Hungary, America, and Japan. Email her at hinako.takeuchi@gmail.com.

Adriana Tapia-Bernal is a high school student. She enjoys reading and writing, going to concerts, and traveling. Adriana plans to major in Psychology, however, she is also interested in teaching English for high school students.

Anna Thielen is in the ninth grade. Her interests include horseback riding, music, art, and writing. Anna plays the violin and she loves to travel around the world. One of Anna's favorite trips was the visit to Thailand, the trip featured in the story.

Rebecca Thomas is a senior in high school. In her free time, she loves to read, write, and watch her local hockey team play. She plans to go to college for physical therapy.

Megan Thurlow studies at Kansas State University, and is a member of the Pi Beta Phi fraternity for women. She enjoys reading, singing, acting and playing sports in her free time. Megan's future plans are undecided. E-mail her at mthurlow@k-state.edu.

Vickie Vainionpaa is a Fine Arts student from U Waterloo. She enjoys writing in her spare time, along with painting, drawing, and running. She plans to be a high school art teacher after she finishes University. E-mail her at vickiev92@gmail.com.

Tracie Weaver is nineteen years old and was born and raised in Atlanta, GA. She enjoys traveling, going to school, singing, and writing. Tracie plans to write books for children, and maybe become an inspirational speaker one day.

Monica C. Webster graduated from the University of Toronto with a Bachelor of Arts and a minor in English, and has recently returned to school in order to receive her Bachelor of Education. Among her many interests, Monica enjoys reading, writing, art and nature. E-mail her at monica@websterartgallery.com.

After studying English and Theatre, **Trudy Weiss** chose acting as her career. She lived an idyllic life in a thatched cottage in Devon, UK, before returning to Toronto with her son. He is now a fabulous teenager, experiencing the tumultuous joy and angst fondly remembered and ruthlessly exploited in her poemericks. E-mail her at tweiss@sympatico.ca.

Haley Whiteway lives in Toronto, and has graduated from Wexford Collegiate. She would like to thank "the girl behind her" for inspiring this story, and her English teacher, Ms. McGinn, for the four years of English that encouraged her to write in the first place.

Laura Williams graduated with a Bachelor of Arts in English and hopes to one day publish more poetry, as well as a few of the ideas swirling around wildly in her brain. She wrote "Thirteen Years" in her last days as a high school senior.

Juliette Rose Wunrow is currently a high school student. Prior to moving to the United States she and her family lived in the Fiji Islands and New Zealand. After high school, she plans to attend college in the New England area. Her interests include writing, art, French, and running.

Amanda Yancey graduated high school in 2010, with honors, after enduring two major spinal surgeries. She is currently attending Chemeketa Community College and plans to transfer to Portland State University. Amanda enjoys traveling, riding horses, painting, writing stories, and spending time with her family. She is currently working on a young-adult novel.

D. B. Zane is a middle school teacher and mother of three teenagers and an aspiring writer. In her free time, she enjoys reading and taking walks with her dog. E-mail her at dbzanewriter@gmail.com.

Meet Our Authors

Jack Canfield is the co-creator of the *Chicken Soup for the Soul* series, which *Time* magazine has called "the publishing phenomenon of the decade." Jack is also the co-author of many other bestselling books.

Jack is the CEO of the Canfield Training Group in Santa Barbara, California, and founder of the Foundation for Self-Esteem in Culver City, California. He has conducted intensive personal and professional development seminars on the principles of success for more than a million people in twenty-three countries, has spoken to hundreds of thousands of people at more than 1,000 corporations, universities, professional conferences and conventions, and has been seen by millions more on national television shows.

Jack has received many awards and honors, including three honorary doctorates and a Guinness World Records Certificate for having seven books from the *Chicken Soup for the Soul* series appearing on the New York Times bestseller list on May 24, 1998.

You can reach Jack at www.jackcanfield.com.

Mark Victor Hansen is the co-founder of Chicken Soup for the Soul, along with Jack Canfield. He is a sought-after keynote speaker, bestselling author, and marketing maven. Mark's powerful messages of possibility, opportunity, and action have created powerful change in thousands of organizations and millions of individuals worldwide.

Mark is a prolific writer with many bestselling books in addition to the *Chicken Soup for the Soul* series. Mark has had a profound influence in the field of human potential through his library of audios, videos, and articles in the areas of big thinking, sales achievement, wealth building, publishing success, and personal and professional development. He is also the founder of the MEGA Seminar Series.

Mark has received numerous awards that honor his entrepreneurial spirit, philanthropic heart, and business acumen. He is a lifetime member of the Horatio Alger Association of Distinguished Americans.

You can reach Mark at www.markvictorhansen.com.

Amy Newmark is Chicken Soup for the Soul's publisher and editor-in-chief, after a thirty-year career as a writer, speaker, financial analyst, and business executive in the worlds of finance and telecommunications. Amy is a *magna cum laude* graduate of Harvard College, where she majored in Portuguese, minored in French, and traveled extensively. She and her husband have four grown children.

After a long career writing books on telecommunications, voluminous financial reports, business plans, and corporate press releases, Chicken Soup for the Soul is a breath of fresh air for Amy. She has fallen in love with Chicken Soup for the Soul and its life-changing books, and really enjoys putting these books together for Chicken Soup's wonderful readers. She has co-authored more than three dozen *Chicken Soup for the Soul* books and has edited another three dozen.

You can reach Amy through the webmaster@chickensoupforthesoul.com.

Thank You

We owe huge thanks to all of our contributors. We know that you poured your hearts and souls into the thousands of stories and poems that you shared with us, and ultimately with each other. We appreciate your willingness to open up your lives to other Chicken Soup for the Soul readers and share your own experiences as teens, which we know was both an exciting and a challenging time in your life. We loved your stories and they brought back our own memories of those years.

We could only publish a small percentage of the stories that were submitted, but we read every single one and even the ones that do not appear in the book had an influence on us and on the final manuscript. Our editor Madeline Clapps, who was a teen herself just a few years ago, read every submission to this book and put together the manuscript with great care and a real understanding of the kinds of stories that would be most helpful, and also entertaining, for our readers. Our summer intern Jacqueline Palma, who is a fabulous writer herself and a published Chicken Soup for the Soul contributor, read and graded thousands of stories that were submitted for this book. Our assistant publisher, D'ette Corona, worked with all the contributors and their parents as kindly and competently as always, obtaining their approvals for our edits and the quotations we carefully chose to begin each story. Senior editor Barbara LoMonaco and editor Kristiana Glavin performed their normal masterful proofreading and made sure the book went to the printer on time.

We also owe a very special thanks to our creative director and book producer, Brian Taylor at Pneuma Books, for his brilliant vision for our covers and interiors. Finally, none of this would be possible without the business and creative leadership of our CEO, Bill Rouhana, and our president, Bob Jacobs.

Improving
Your Life
Every Day

Real people sharing real stories—for seventeen years. Now, Chicken Soup for the Soul has gone beyond the bookstore to become a world leader in life improvement. Through books, movies, DVDs, online resources and other partnerships, we bring hope, courage, inspiration and love to hundreds of millions of people around the world. Chicken Soup for the Soul's writers and readers belong to a one-of-a-kind global community, sharing advice, support, guidance, comfort, and knowledge.

Chicken Soup for the Soul stories have been translated into more than forty languages and can be found in more than one hundred countries. Every day, millions of people experience a Chicken Soup for the Soul story in a book, magazine, newspaper or online. As we share our life experiences through these stories, we offer hope, comfort and inspiration to one another. The stories travel from person to person, and from country to country, helping to improve lives everywhere.

Share with Us

We all have had Chicken Soup for the Soul moments in our lives. If you would like to share your story or poem with millions of people around the world, go to chickensoup.com and click on "Submit Your Story." You may be able to help another reader, and become a published author at the same time. Some of our past contributors have launched writing and speaking careers from the publication of their stories in our books!

Our submission volume has been increasing steadily—the quality and quantity of your submissions has been fabulous. We only accept story submissions via our website. They are no longer accepted via mail or fax.

To contact us regarding other matters, please send us an e-mail through webmaster@chickensoupforthesoul.com, or fax or write us at:

Chicken Soup for the Soul
P.O. Box 700
Cos Cob, CT 06807-0700
Fax: 203-861-7194

One more note from your friends at Chicken Soup for the Soul: Occasionally, we receive an unsolicited book manuscript from one of our readers, and we would like to respectfully inform you that we do not accept unsolicited manuscripts and we must discard the ones that appear.

Special bonus!
2 extra stories...
from Chicken Soup for the Soul
Teens Talk High School

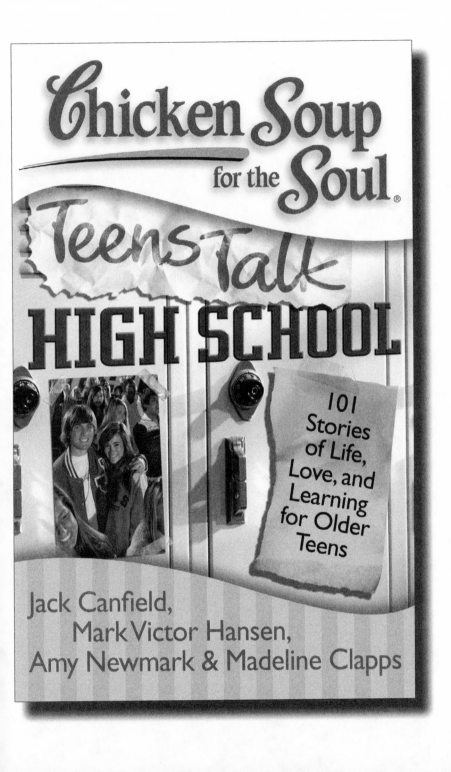

Chicken Soup for the Soul®

Teens Talk

HIGH SCHOOL

101
Stories
of Life,
Love, and
Learning
for Older
Teens

Jack Canfield,
Mark Victor Hansen,
Amy Newmark & Madeline Clapps

Teens Talk

HIGH
SCHOOL

That Was Embarrassing

Comedy is tragedy plus time.

~Carol Burnett

The Test

I think the next best thing to solving a problem
is finding some humor in it.
~Frank A. Clark

This was it. The moment of truth. It was right there and then that the rest of my life was going to be determined. This over-the-top, life changing experience was my driver's test.

If you ask adults about their driver's test, they'll say something along the lines of, "Oh, it's no big deal!" or "There's always next time." Well, not for me. I don't fail—whether it's a final exam or a quiz in class. For me there was only one chance. There was only one try.

There I was, in my grandmother's Pontiac Grand-Am, alone. I watched my mother walk into the building and I began to worry. As I look back on it now, I am—well—embarrassed. I sat there, hands tightly grasping the steering wheel, knuckles white, with beads of sweat dripping down my cheeks. My left leg was shaking, not one of those fun, overly-excited shakes. No, it was a shake brought on by the complete and utter fear of failure. I checked everything. "Lights, check. Mirrors, check. Seat belt, check." I was ready. As I looked around for a final time, I noticed that my lip gloss had faded. Instinctively I reapplied my gloss and, while I was at it, my blush. Hey, a girl always has to look good. For all I knew, my instructor could have been a gorgeous twenty-year-old.

"Tap, tap," he knocked on my passenger window, gently. It was time. I turned to my right and there he was. He was tall... and scary.

I unlocked the door and he let himself in. "Hello," he said. I had no idea what to say. A mellow "Hi" would be too casual. Of course at the same time a stern "Hello" would have seemed too forceful and possibly angered him. I sat there. After a few moments that felt like minutes, I replied with an "Um, hey." After the typical exchange of "how are you" he asked me the big question: "Are you ready to get this show on the road?" Hmm, well let's think about this—NO! How could anyone be ready for this test? I know I sure wasn't.

Deep breath. Okay, I was ready. I can remember it so vividly. As I went to put the car in drive, I accidentally hit the windshield wiper fluid bar. I quickly fixed it and put the car into gear. I turned to over to Mr. Lewis and, to put it simply, he did not look happy. I began to move forward. As we came up to the first stop sign, I stopped. I began to talk to myself, "very good." As I did this, Mr. Lewis turned to me. He gave me one of those quizzical looks. How rude! So what—I was talking to myself, just giving myself a little encouragement. He had no right to make me nervously rethink what I just did! Oh well. I moved on.

We turned the corner and I saw it—the flags arranged in a square. I knew what that meant: parallel parking. Parallel parking is, as someone wise once put it, stupid. How often will a driver need to parallel park? I surely knew that I would never have to. Needless to say, I hate parallel parking. Once I pulled up next to the flags, I stopped.

Mr. Lewis looked at me: "Come on now, get to parking." I looked at him. Knowing I could not ignore the inevitable, I began to park. I unbuckled my seatbelt and began to turn my right arm behind the passenger seat next to me. As I reached for the headrest behind Mr. Lewis, "SMACK!" I hit him in the head. I hit him in the head. I HIT him in the head.

Oh my gosh. I quickly pulled both of my hands to my mouth, partly in shock and partly to cover my giggling smile. He turned toward me. "I am so sorry. I had no idea. I am so, so sorry. Can I start over?" I can't believe I hit him in the head. Not only did I hit him, but I also had the nerve to ask if I could try it again. "Let's just keep going," he said. I put the car in drive.

I hit him. This thought kept on running through my mind. But I had to stay focused. I had to pass this test. Deep breath. The next few minutes went well. I did not run over anyone, or hit them for that matter. I stopped at all the right times. I watched my speed and did not forget to use my turn signal. I kept on repeating one simple phrase in my head for moral support: "Go me." Then as we approached what I thought was our last turn, I saw them again—the dreaded flags. They were a bright, fluorescent orange, a color one usually only sees on Halloween. It is a cringe-worthy orange that upsets the stomach. These flags were my enemy. While I was evaluating these repulsive flags, Mr. Lewis spoke for the first time since our little incident, "Ninety degree back-in up ahead."

There we were again, parking. At least this time I could understand the purpose of ninety degree parking. It could come in handy in many different situations, like loading a boat onto a trailer or going into a driveway. Despite the many uses of this method, I still decided I was never going to do it once I had my license.

I pulled up next to the flags. Here we go again. As I turned my head a few times, I was mindful of where my arm was. I didn't hit him this time. Right as I began to think I could actually successfully finish this task, it happened again. This time, I hit the flag instead of the instructor. As my eyes began to tear up, Mr. Lewis spoke: "We're done." After my twenty minutes with this man I had concluded two things. First was that he was a man of few words. Second was that he had an unusually hard head.

I choked back my tears and began to drive forward. "Screeeeeech." My car was making a noise. I turned to Mr. Lewis, "Did I break it?" I asked. "No, you're dragging the flag under your rear bumper," he replied. Before I could yet again apologize, he stepped out of the car and went to fix the flag. After a few minutes of Mr. Lewis weaving the flag out from under my car, he sat back down in his seat and I drove back to the parking lot—without any accidents.

Before he exited the car, I turned to Mr. Lewis and began to cry. I thought that maybe I could play the sympathy card. It did not work. He said, and I quote, "Maybe next time kiddo." Maybe next time?

There was no next time! This was it! After I was sure the door was closed, I broke down in tears.

Once my mom came to the car and sat down, I told her about the whole ordeal. Contrary to what I had expected, she laughed. No, she didn't just laugh. She had a laughing attack. Somehow, through my tears, I began to laugh also. Now as I look back, I realize how funny the whole thing actually was. So what? I didn't pass. Oh well.

I did eventually go back and take the test again. I passed—and I didn't even hit anyone.

~Julie Pierce

Girl Most Likely to...

A laugh is a smile that bursts.
~Mary H. Waldrip

Do people really die of embarrassment? I've heard that expression often. But do you think actual death certificates say that? I've always wondered, because mine almost read:

Age of death: 16.
Cause of death: Embarrassment.

"What a pity!" teary-eyed mourners would have whimpered. "What a senseless loss!"

It was the summer before my junior year. Several friends and I decided that it would be fun to enroll in an eight-week drama class that would culminate in a full-scale theatrical production. Some of us acted (marvelously, I might add!), some constructed amazing scenery, some handled a gazillion props, others made magic with their make-up, costuming, or audiovisual skills.

I barely recall the play's title or any of my lines, but the memory forever branded on my brain, fresh as if it happened last week, is one particular day... I mean, one particular scorching hot day. Eight of us were gathered together on our hour-long lunch break, sitting around, commenting on the sweltering heat—fantasizing about how refreshing an ice cream cone would be. Kathy gleefully announced that she had her parents' car that day and could drive us to the nearby ice cream shop, ensuring that we would return before rehearsals resumed. Everyone loved the idea, so Kathy told the drama teacher that we were racing to the store. Mr. G said okay, but that only one person could accompany her. I volunteered, so we wrote down everyone's "orders" and collected their money. Kathy made a beeline for a shiny blue car, opened the doors, and slid in. "Hurry," she said, patting the passenger seat.

"Wow!" I exclaimed, whiffing that brand-new-car smell as the A/C fought with the stifling heat. "I can't believe your parents let you drive this!"

"It's my reward for getting good grades," Kathy purred. "Pretty cool, huh?"

"Cool reward, indeed! And thank God for these cloth-covered seats. Can you imagine what the sun would have done to leather seats? Ouch!"

We arrived at the ice cream shop within minutes. "Rats," I gasped, springing from the car. "I should have peed before we left school."

"We'll be fast," Kathy promised.

Lesson #1: Never believe promises about anything over which the person making the promise does not have complete control.

(I always make "mental notes" of life's important lessons.)

Apparently, everyone in the whole neighborhood had decided to cool off with ice cream. The line was a mile long. Okay, I'm exaggerating. But when you've gotta go real bad, it just seems like a mile. "Listen," I whispered. "You wait in line while I go pee."

I approached the cashier, saying quietly, "Excuse me, ma'am. May I please use your restroom?"

"It's for employees only," she grunted.

"I've really gotta go," I softly begged. "Would you please make an exception?"

"I SAID the BATHROOM is for employees ONLY!" the woman snapped. Several nearby customers snickered.

So much for asking discreetly. I slunk back into line with Kathy, but the wait seemed endless. We decided to abandon our mission so we wouldn't return to school late, thereby holding up the whole rehearsal. Our friends would understand. Just as we started leaving, the line miraculously sped up. The clock was ticking, but Kathy hurriedly ordered a variety of eight double-scoop cones while I politely paid the cranky cashier. Smiling, she responded, "Sorry about the bathroom. It's a strict company policy."

Lesson #2: Don't shoot the messenger.

(Maybe Miss Sourpuss was cranky because someone else had already shot her.)

One-by-one, the ice cream scooper-outer man carefully placed each colorful order into the plastic cone holder on the counter. Kathy and I thanked him, grabbed two cones in each hand and sprinted back to the car. Needing to retrieve the keys from her purse, she asked me to take the cones from her right hand. I somehow managed to do so, precariously juggling six cones. She opened her car door, then mine. Holding three cones in each hand, I obviously couldn't close my door after getting in. "Help!" I called after her. Kathy raced back. We looked at each other and started giggling like crazy. Kathy attached my seatbelt for me, and closed my door. She bounced into the driver's seat, reached over, closed her door with her right hand (given that she was still holding two cones in her left one), and single-handedly attached her seatbelt. If I hadn't already been strapped in, I would have been rolling on the floor. Kathy thought that she was being so careful, but she got ice cream everywhere.

My sticky friend pretended to glare at me, but cracked up. "How am I going to drive? This is a stick shift! For two people on the honor roll, we're not very bright, are we?" We laughed harder than ever before we caught a glimpse of the dashboard clock. We had seven minutes to drive back, distribute the cones to our sweltering classmates, and hop on the stage. And I still had to pee—bad!

Kathy thrust some "chocolate mint" and "peppermint surprise" at me. "Here! You've gotta take these!"

"How?" I howled, tears streaming down my face. "I can barely balance three in each hand."

Assessing the situation, Kathy took charge. "Just hold them here." She reached over and wedged her two cones between my wobbly, bony knees.

The tires and I squealed in unison, but my shrieks were in response to the rapidly melting ice cream that was dripping all over my hands and lap. By now, my ribs ached. Unfortunately, this unique situation reminded Kathy of a joke... which she decided to recite. In retrospect, this was more poor judgment because we were already in hysterics. When she said the punch line, I completely lost it. Literally. I lost all the pee that I'd been holding in for the past forty-five minutes.

The next few minutes are a blur. I vaguely recall that Kathy screamed, but I don't know if it's because we were almost in an accident from her splitting a gut or because she was horrified to suddenly realize that she'd have to tell her parents why the passenger seat was so soggy and sticky. At that moment she probably didn't care that I would certainly die from embarrassment when we had to get out of the car at school. In fact, this scenario was pretty much a given. I mean, I had light colored shorts on, and there was no way I could hide what had just occurred.

When we pulled into the school lot, I could see our friends eagerly awaiting their specially ordered cones. They started walking over to the car after spotting us. Little did they know that their double-scoop ice cream was half melted all over my lap. Little did they know that their sixteen-year-old friend (moi) — who was holding their cones — had just wet her pants. Something told me that they wouldn't want their treats anymore.

Worse than that, as nice as my friends were, I knew that "the word" would spread rapidly and I'd be the laughing stock of the school for weeks or months or even years ahead. Kathy's parents would probably warn other parents at upcoming PTA meetings to never let me in their cars. They would probably put notices in the school newspaper and on bulletin boards.

I had obviously stopped laughing by then, and was fighting back tears. My heart started pounding so fast that I thought it would burst. Hmmm, I concluded. That's probably how people die of embarrassment. The stress just makes them have a stroke or heart attack. Well, rats. I sure had a lot more to do in life, but at least my inevitable end would be quick.

I looked over at Kathy and mumbled, "I'm soooo sorry! Will your parents freak out?"

She smiled at me sweetly and said firmly. "I have a strange feeling that they'll believe this was an accident. And you've gotta admit—this will make a great story! You will survive this and even laugh about it one day. So ya know what? You might as well start laughing now!"

What kind of line was that?!

I scanned my storage of the "mental notes" I keep, and something sprang to mind:

You teach people how to treat you.

Kathy was right. I turned to her and grinned. "Open my door, undo my seatbelt, and get those damn cones out from between my knees." She did so, and I fumbled out of the car, my hands and lap completely covered in melted ice cream, a very obvious localized "wet" spot on my shorts. Our six friends burst into laughter, and so did I.

Kathy said, "Apparently, you can't take her anywhere!"

"You can if I'm wearing a diaper!" I replied indignantly. "Ice cream, anyone?"

Woohoo! I will certainly make the school yearbook as "the girl most likely to wet her pants...."

Lesson #3: I'd be so ashamed to die of embarrassment... I'd MUCH rather die laughing!

~Karen Waldman

www.chickensoup.com